Making Policy Happen

Public policy processes are more complex, uncertain and contested than ever before. They are also more open: those involved in policy work may be managers or professionals, in or out of government – and not necessarily at senior levels. The readings in this book introduce those aspiring to senior positions to the debates, concepts, approaches and perspectives that they need to master if they are to navigate the white water of contemporary policymaking.

This collection draws on all the key disciplines – economics, social policy, political science, public administration and management, international relations, leadership studies – and includes contributions from North America and Europe.

The editors are all members of the Centre for Public Leadership and Social Enterprise at the Open University Business School. **Dr Leslie Budd** is an economist by training who has published widely in the field of the relationship between international financial markets and regional and urban economic development, and has undertaken teaching and research in universities in the UK, France and Germany, as well as consultancy for governmental bodies on competitiveness, entrepreneurship and social enterprise. **Dr Julie Charlesworth** has held research and teaching posts in management, social policy, and geography and her interdisciplinary research focuses on the management of inter-organizational working in public services. **Professor Rob Paton** helped pioneer the use of what is now known as 'blended learning' for management and professional development. He has undertaken research and consultancy in a wide range of public and nonprofit settings, with particular interests in the uses and abuses of measurement, leadership in value-based organizations, and learning processes.

The Open University Business School

The Open University Business School offers a three-tier ladder of opportunity for managers at different stages of their careers: the Professional Certificate in Management; the Professional Diploma in Management; and the Masters Programme.

This Reader is the prescribed Course Reader for the Shaping Public Policy: Contexts and Processes Module (B856) which is part of the Masters in Public Administration at the Open University Business School. Opinions expressed in this Reader are not necessarily those of the Course Team or of the Open University.

Further information on Open University Business School courses and qualifications may be obtained from The Open University Business School, PO Box 197, Walton Hall, Milton Keynes, MK7 6BJ, United Kingdom; tel OU Business School Information Line: +44 (0) 8700 100311.

Alternatively, much useful course information can be obtained from the Open University Business School's website at http://www.oubs. open.ac.uk.

Making Policy Happen

Edited by

Leslie Budd, Julie Charlesworth and Rob Paton

Routledge
Taylor & Francis Group

LONDON AND NEW YORK

OU Business School

First published 2006
by Routledge
2 Park Square, Milton Park, Abingdon, Oxon OX14 4RN

Simultaneously published in the USA and Canada
by Routledge
270 Madison Ave, New York, NY 10016

Routledge is an imprint of the Taylor & Francis Group, an informa business

© 2006 Compilation, original and editorial material, The Open University

Typeset in Perpetua and Bell Gothic by
Newgen Imaging Systems (P) Ltd, Chennai, India
Printed and bound in Great Britain by
TJ International Ltd, Padstow, Cornwall

British Library Cataloguing in Publication Data
A catalogue record for this book is available from the British Library

Library of Congress Cataloging in Publication Data
A catalog record for this book has been requested

ISBN10: 0–415–39767–7 (hbk)
ISBN10: 0–415–39768–5 (pbk)

ISBN13: 978–0–415–39767–4 (hbk)
ISBN13: 978–0–415–39768–1 (pbk)

Contents

Strategy in public organizations

Service redesign

Ethics in public administration

Acknowledgements

Lots of people have helped in this project – whether they realize it or not. We gathered many ideas from discussions over the years with John Benington and Jean Hartley at Warwick. Colin Talbot now of Manchester University has been another leader in the renewal of programmes for public managers, and a source of much good advice in developing the course of which this reader is a part. Colleagues in the Faculty of Social Sciences within the OU have been very supportive.

We are also indebted to our administrative, course management and secretarial colleagues – Gill Gowans, Glenna White, Pat McCarthy, Val O'Connor and Jean Rowe – who were both patient and tireless when it came to organizing the final manuscript.

Most of all, we are grateful to the authors for permission to use their work in this form. As there were so many key readings we wished to include, we have ruthlessly edited their work – deleting sections, as well as footnotes and references. If anyone imagines these pieces are not adequately supported in the literature, then we are to blame – as consulting the originals will immediately make clear. And in the case of the books we have presumptuously cannibalised, we hope the extracts here encourage many readers to obtain the full texts – in each case, they are richly rewarding.

The publishers would like to thank the following for permission to reprint material.

John, P. (2003) 'Is there life after policy streams, advocacy coalitions, and punctuations: using evolutionary theory to explain policy change?', *The Policy Studies Journal*, 31:4, 481–498. Reprinted by permission of Blackwell Publishing.

Barrett, S. (2004) 'Implementation studies: time for a revival? Personal reflections on 20 years of implementation studies', *Public Administration*, 82:2, 249–262. Reprinted by permission of Blackwell Publishing.

Klijn, E-H. and Koppenjan, J. F. M. (2000) 'Public Management and policy networks: foundations of a network approach to governance', *Public Management*, 2:2, 135–158. Reprinted by permission of Taylor & Francis Journals. www.tandf.co.uk

Heclo, H. and Wildavsky, A. (1974) *The Private Government of Public Money: Community and Policy inside British Politics*, Macmillan. Reprinted by permission of Palgrave Macmillan.

Rose, R. (1990) 'Inheritance before choice in public policy', *Journal of Theoretical Politics*, 2:3, 263–291, © 1990 Sage Publications. Reprinted by permission of Sage Publications Ltd.

Drache, D. (2001) 'The return of the public domain', *The Market or the Public Domain, Global Governance and the Asymmetry of Power*, Routledge. Reprinted by permission of Taylor & Francis Books.

Pierre, J. and Peters, B. G. (2000) 'Governance at three levels', *Governance, Politics and the State*, Macmillan. Reprinted by permission of Palgrave Macmillan.

Crouch, C. (2004) 'The state and innovations in economic governance', *The Political Quarterly*, 75:1, 100–116. Reprinted by permission of Blackwell Publishing.

Keohane, R. S. and Nye, J. S. Jr (2000) 'Globalization: What's new? What's not? (And so what?)' in D. Held and A. McGrew (eds) *The Global Transformation Reader*, Polity Press. Reprinted by permission of the authors.

Ruggie, J. G. (2003) 'Taking embedded liberalism global: the corporate connection' in D. Held and M. Koenig (eds) *Taming Globalization: Frontiers of Governance*. Reprinted by permission of the Polity Press Ltd.

Pierre, J. and Peters, B. G. (2000) 'Communitarianism, deliberation, direct democracy and governance', *Governance, Politics and the State*, Macmillan. Reprinted by permission of Palgrave Macmillan.

Beresford, P. (2004) 'Service users, social policy and the future of welfare', *Critical Social Theory*, 21:4, 494–512, © 2004 Sage Publications. Reprinted by permission of Sage Publications Ltd.

Baldwin, R. and Cave, M. (1999) *Understanding Regulation. Theory, Strategy and Practice*. Reprinted by permission of Oxford University Press.

Pollitt, C. (2000) 'Is the emperor in his underwear? An analysis of the impacts of public management reform', *Public Management*, 2:2, 181–199. Reprinted by permission of Taylor & Francis Journals. www.tandf.co.uk

Kernaghan, K. (2000) 'The post-bureaucratic organization and public service values', *International Review of Administrative Sciences*, 66, 91–104, © 2000 Sage Publications. Reprinted by permission of Sage Publications Ltd.

Newman, J. (2001) 'Joined-up government: the politics of partnership', *Modernising Governance. New Labour, Policy and Society*, Chapter 6, © 2001 Sage Publications. Reprinted by permission of Sage Publications Ltd.

Broadbent, J. and Laughlin, R. (2003) 'Public private partnerships: an introduction', *Accounting, Auditing and Accountability Journal*, 16:3, 332–341. Reprinted by permission of Emerald Group Publishing Ltd.

Clarke, J. (2003) 'Scrutiny through inspection and audit: policies, structures and processes' in T. Bovaird and E. Loffler (eds) *Public Management and Governance*, Routledge. Reprinted by permission of Taylor & Francis Books.

Paton, R. (2003) 'Taking measures – lessons from the literature', *Managing and Measuring Social Enterprises*, Chapter 3, © 2003 Sage Publications. Reprinted by permission of Sage Publications Ltd.

Heifetz, R. A. (1944) 'Leadership as adaptive work', *Leadership Without Easy Answers*, Belknap Press. Reprinted by permission of Harvard University Press.

Moore, M. H. (1995) 'Organizational strategy in the public sector', edited from *Creating Public Value*, Harvard University Press, copyright © 1995 by the President and Fellows of Harvard College. Reprinted by permission of the publisher.

Seddon, J. (2003) 'Beyond command and control', extracted from *Freedom From Command and Control. A Better Way to Make the Work Work*, Vanguard Publishing. Copyright © 2005 by Productivity Press, a division of Kraus Productivity Organization Ltd. www.productivitypress.com

Moore, M. H. (1995) 'Acting for a divided, uncertain society', edited from *Creating Public Value*, Harvard University Press, copyright © 1995 by the President and Fellows of Harvard College. Reprinted by permission of the publisher.

Every effort has been made to contact copyright holders for their permission to reprint selections in this book. The publishers would be grateful to hear from any copyright holder who is not here acknowledged and will undertake to rectify any errors or omissions in future editions of this book.

Introduction to Book

THIS COLLECTION IS FOR people who are charged with *making policy happen* – that is, people who are professionally involved in devising, advocating, drafting, negotiating, interpreting, enacting, monitoring or reviewing public policy. 'Making policy happen' can mean two things. It may refer to bringing a policymaking process to fruition – so that a (more or less) agreed policy can be *announced*, providing thereafter a justification and direction for various specific initiatives. Or it may refer to policy *implementation* – the design and development of programmes, regulations, codes, new agencies or services through which policy directly or indirectly affects the lives of citizens. These two senses correspond to what can be seen as the two halves of the policy game (and many would say it is the second half, when who has won and who has lost and by how much is actually determined, that really matters). But being wary of distinctions between policy and implementation, we intend both meanings – which is to say, we are interested in the whole, never-ending game.

We refer to all the activities involved as 'policy work'. Such policy work is a broad concept and its central characteristic is that it is a higher-order activity. Its impacts are indirect: it produces frameworks (of direction, authorisation, restriction, principles, resources, etc.) within which a wide range of governmental and non-governmental actors must operate. As such, policy work is abstract and immaterial. Its primary medium is the *document* – it consumes, generates and produces papers of all sorts. It is about the facts concerning what are taken to be societal issues (affecting whom, why, how often, where, at what costs? . . . but also, always: says who and on what basis?). But equally it is about the values (the mix of aspirations, principles and commitments that matter for particular communities) from which those societal concerns spring. So policy work involves politics: it is about conflict management and the integration of divergent societal interests as much as technocratic problem-solving; and policy formulations have to be expressive as well as instrumental. Hence, too, policymaking is often an arena for battles of ideas; it is as much about narratives and making sense of the past (why is this happening to us?) as it is about improving the future.

Who does policy work? Once, the answer was easy: top civil servants and a restricted number of analysts and advisors associated with political parties, industrial associations and trade unions. Whether this was ever a *good* answer is another matter, but irrelevant. For all sorts of reasons – including many set out within this collection – it is now clear that in an open society, public managers of any seniority, and many in or aspiring to senior positions in civil society, third sector and consulting organizations, will have to undertake some sort of policy work, and probably sooner rather than later.

Initially, the idea of policy work can seem both glamorous and important, because it is potentially far-reaching in its consequences. But it will also, frequently, seem frustrating, a sink for time and effort offering little in tangible results, and, indeed, often irrational to the point of absurdity. Because of this, the primary purpose of this volume is to offer theories relevant to policy work that will enable those involved to engage positively and intelligently in processes that are necessarily challenging and uncertain.

The arrangement into four sections reflects this central purpose. Part 1, *Understanding policy processes*, offers theories of policymaking that go deeper than, for example, conventional notions of a policy cycle, or the assumptions of instrumental rationality. Part 2 explores the settings within which policy work takes place, that is, the *Governance contexts*. Understanding these settings and how they are evolving is essential: they largely determine who the players will be, and the rules of the game. The readings in Part 3, *Instruments and discourses*, explore the sorts of material out of which particular policies are fashioned, the technical and rhetorical means at the disposal of policymakers when they attempt to address public concerns. Finally, the readings in Part 4 examine different dimensions of the *leadership* involved in doing policy work to good effect.

The readings chosen are all, and without apology, theoretical: that is, they present generic concepts, explanations and proposals, applicable across the full range of public action and services. They provide core material highlighting pervasive issues and common trends manifest in different ways across different fields of public service and in many countries (as the inclusion of contributions from scholars based in continental Europe and North America shows). As such, they offer, from various vantage points, a series of reports and sketch-maps of what is a vast and shifting landscape. But they do not and cannot provide a consistent atlas. Rather, they are resources for readers to elaborate and extend their own 'big pictures' of the runaway world in which policy work takes place and to which policymakers must respond.

The theories presented are not just about understanding in some abstracted and detached way. They have 'bite'. This is because many of the ideas discussed, for better and for worse, are *influential*: they inform, shape and underpin policy: they are adopted by policy analysts and advocates to provide justifications and narratives for policy proposals, as part of the constant inter-change between policy theory and policy practice. Indeed, one can hardly do policy work without learning the language of policy – with both the insights it offers and the inevitable slipperiness, misuses and obfuscations. Just as policy work is inherently abstract, theories of policy work can seem even more elusive, not least because they draw on so many different academic disciplines (economics, political science, international relations, organisational behaviour, psychology are all represented in this collection). What matters is to become familiar enough with the terms, and how and why they are used, so one can appreciate what it is they do provide *without* either being overawed or simply dismissive of 'theory and jargon'.

Moreover, many of the ideas presented here are actually very practical – they can help one step back, clarify what is going on, and offer new orientations. However, to be used this way, it is important that (as in our own programme) the breadth of these readings is complemented by depth provided in other ways. In particular, reports, 'grey literature' and resources drawn from the areas – say, health care, the criminal justice system, local government – in which those professionally interested in these issues are working, are vital. Such contextualizing resources show how the broad trends discussed in this volume are being enacted, and how general concepts can be usefully put to work, in particular settings.

'Application' in this sense does not, of course, mean following rules and recipes (though deliberately taking one-step-at-a-time is generally the way to start learning and internalizing new concepts). It means being able to relate the concepts meaningfully to one's own setting; it means being able to draw on them in the face of challenging circumstances – in order to make better sense of what is confusing, to find a different way forward, or simply to ask better questions. To be able to do this one must be familiar with the ideas, and have them at the back of one's mind and thus readily available in reflective moments. Such practical understanding only develops by working with the ideas in relation to real situations – reading in the hope of remembering is never anything like enough.

PART ONE

Understanding policy processes

INTRODUCTION

IF ONE ASKED SENIOR officials in central or local government how policy is made, the strong likelihood is that their answer would include reference to a series of stages or phases. This might end in 'implementation' – or it might involve a cycle, in which implementation is followed by 'evaluation and review' leading back to (say) 'agenda setting'. Such an answer would almost certainly be predicated on the decisions of some authoritative, deliberative body; and it would assume a choice process oriented to the achievement of particular policy goals. Of course, such senior officials know perfectly well that things rarely happen quite like this; the processes are much more confused, uncertain and contested than such models imply. Nevertheless, they would find it hard to describe in any succinct and convincing fashion how policy really does emerge.

One way of thinking about the readings in this section is that they all challenge central elements in the conventional, rationalistic accounts of policymaking; and they introduce additional elements, or develop broader theories, concerning how policies actually happen.

In Reading 1, Peter John reviews the extensive literature on public policy theory. Relative newcomers to the social sciences may initially find the cascade of different concepts and perspectives daunting. But it provides a lucid introduction to the diverse range of theories that can be and are used to reconstruct what is happening in policy processes – many of which are referred to again in later readings. His purpose as a distinguished researcher is to prepare the ground for developing better (more comprehensive) theories – and he ends suggesting some ways in which an evolutionary theory might be formulated to explain the ways in which public policies change and develop over time. Of course, in the context of this volume, most readers will be more interested in whether they provide usable models and frameworks that can illuminate particular events and situations in their own experience. In this respect it may help to realize that most of the theories he mentions are variants, but on a larger canvas, of ideas that may already be familiar in an organizational context. He alludes to this in his discussion of institutions; and, likewise, the theory of policy streams and windows that he mentions was derived quite directly from James March's celebrated 'garbage-can' theory of decision-making in organizations (it focused on the way 'problems' become attached to 'solutions' in contexts where decisions are possible – with results that may be unexpected but are not therefore random or irrational).

Reading 2, by Susan Barrett, also provides a lucid review of a large body of literature. She reflects on three decades of theory development in implementation studies. This gives a valuable historical perspective on the way the field of policy studies has developed – partly under its own dynamic and partly in relation to developments in governance. Thus the 1970s were a time of innovation in policy studies, introducing more strategic approaches and a focus on the reasons for policy failure – with implementation regarded as essentially a top-down process. Attention increasingly turned to the role of 'bottom-up' approaches during the 1980s and a greater understanding of interaction and iteration between the different stages. But then implementation studies were increasingly influenced by the 'new public management' in the 1990s and the focus shifted towards issues such as strategic management and change. With the complexity of partnership arrangements and an increasing number of agencies from different sectors involved in policymaking and implementation, Barrett suggests the time is ripe for a revival of interest in implementation – to incorporate concepts of change, networks and partnership.

Reading 3, on policy networks, departs even more radically from conventional notions of policymaking. The authors are leading proponents of a theory that claims, essentially, that policymaking makes more sense if it is seen, not as located in and around governments, but as being undertaken by and through policy networks and policy communities. In this reading, the authors succinctly set out the core concepts of policy network theory. It has its origins in 'bottom-up' implementation studies, but has gained greater prominence in recent years as part of the debates on governance. They explore the components of policy networks as a series of interactions through 'games' with sets of rules – a recurring motif in a number of theories.

Readings 4 and 5 focus on the importance of budgeting within the policy process. Without a budget there is no policy; indeed, one might even say that budgeting is where policy really happens. Reading 4 is extracted from a chapter in Hugh Heclo and Aaron Wildavsky's classic study of relations between the UK Treasury and other government departments. They examine the private face of public life, the hidden, informal workings of government. Particular arrangements and terminology will be different, of course, but what they describe is likely to resonate with anyone who has worked in large organizations. It focuses on the necessary role of political bargaining in relation to rational plans, and the need to contain the tensions involved in inherently conflictual relationships. The parallels between this discussion, and that of Klijn and Koppenjan's account of policy games, are obvious.

Richard Rose (Reading 5) discusses the importance of 'inheritance' in the policy process, in other words the commitments and public expenditure plans developed by, and inherited from, previous governments. This, too, is derived from a classic study, one that posed important questions in a particularly ingenious way, making it possible to examine them empirically using data covering government actions over an extended period of time. The empirical data on which his argument is founded is now dated (as it focused on the period up to the mid-1980s) and this aspect has been substantially edited from this reading. However, the main conclusions about the nature and importance of inheritance in public policy are still highly relevant and provide a sobering reminder to managers and politicians about the scope for change in the exercise of their roles. But this is not to argue that policymakers are powerless and nothing makes a difference. Because he takes the long view, Rose also highlights the impact that even modest new programmes or adjustments to programmes can and do have over the long term.

Perhaps the most important thing about all these theories is that they offer some 'distance' and perspective on the vicissitudes of particular policy processes, a vantage point from which it is possible to see the shape of the woods even as one is struggling among particular trees.

Peter John

EXPLAINING POLICY CHANGE

From: John, P. (2003) 'Is there life after policy streams, advocacy coalitions, and punctuations: using evolutionary theory to explain policy change?', *The Policy Studies Journal*, 31:4, 481–498

Objectivity cannot be equated with mental blankness; rather, objectivity resides in recognizing your preferences and then subjecting them to especially harsh scrutiny – and also in a willingness to revise or abandon your theories when the tests fail (as they usually do).

(Stephen Jay Gould, *The lying stones of Marrakech: Penultimate reflections in natural history*, pp. 104–105)

TEN YEARS HAS ELAPSED since the last major advance in public policy theory. For it was in 1993 that two key books were published: Baumgartner and Jones' *Agendas and Instability in American Politics* and Sabatier and Jenkins-Smith's *Policy Change and Learning*. [. . .] Both attracted a great deal of attention; they were complementary, and they set off research programs in the forms of detailed empirical research, edited collections of studies (e.g., Baumgartner & Jones, 2002), and extensive commentary in the rest of political science. Important work has emerged since, such as Jones's *Politics and the Architecture of Choice* (2001) and the collection of essays in Sabatier (1999), but nothing has changed the direction of thinking in the same way that the cluster of books and articles at the beginning of the 1990s did.

[. . .]

Theorizing about public policy

When considering about how to theorize about public policy, there are two things to bear in mind. One is the nature of theory in the social sciences; the other is the character of public policy. For empirical researchers, theory is a body or system of propositions about the causal relations that link together elements of the social, economic, and political worlds. These relations are regularized, having applicability over a range of cases, both in space and time. Theory in social science is usually based on claims about the nature of human action and power relationships, and seeks to provide a coherent and consistent account of reality. [. . .] Theories differ, of course, in their applicability; but they are linked by the aim to generalize, and in themselves they do not yield hypotheses. What theories do is to generate models, which are more restricted assumptions about social and political relationships from which hypotheses can then be derived and tested.

Researchers in the field of public policy want to understand why public decisions and their outcomes change, stay stable, vary from sector to sector, and differ in their consequences for the publics that consume and appraise them. It is a distinctive and problematic area of study, far more inclusive than others. [. . .] Public policy tends to include in its baseline all political activity and institutions – from voting, political cultures, parties, legislatures, bureaucracies, international agencies, local governments, and back again, to the citizens who implement and evaluate public policies. In addition, decision making varies vastly from sector to sector, a claim that is the core contribution of public policy studies to political science knowledge, but which complicates the task at hand. The problem is compounded by the absence of a clear chain of causation from public opinion to parties and bureaucracies and back again. As many writers on public policy have lamented (cf. Sabatier, 1999), there can be no "stages" model of the political process to provide a simple map because of the multiple sources of causation, feedback, and the sheer complexity of what is going on. [. . .] Coming up with theory that creates some simplicity or parsimony and that takes account of complexity is quite a challenge. The move to simplicity may simply impose a tautology or overextend a set of plausible and partial models of political action to the whole of the policy process. [. . .]

Importing theory from mainstream political science

One answer to the search for theory is to take ready-made ones already in use in political science, as they often have a policy dimension. The problem is that such theory may not be well adapted to the many faceted character of the policy process; moreover, many of these theories have difficulties of their own.

Institutionalism: old and "new"

The best candidate for such an approach is institutionalism. This is the idea that formal structures and embedded norms have an effect on human action. [. . .]

In part, institutions are formal arrangements, such as electoral systems, the division of powers, and the salience of the higher courts; but there are also the practices embedded in formal organizational arrangements, which are sometimes called standard operating procedures. The former sense is better for empirical testing, and comes out with the hardly startling finding that institutions matter for policy outputs and outcomes (Lane & Ersson, 1999). Unless institutions are entirely circumvented by networks and power relations, they generally affect how policy is made as they influence the speed at which political systems attend to public problems, the efficiency with which they aggregate public preferences, and the way in which policies attract rent seekers and principals seek to control their agents (Strom, Muller, & Bergman, 2003). Given that institutions constrain public action and affect the costs and benefits of political participation, such an effect is to be expected. But does institutionalism explain policy change? In part, it does, but institutionalists find it harder to explain bursts of change, such as improvements in policy performance or the imminence of policy disasters, which are some of the crucial issues. Institutions can account for change when they adapt, especially in relation to one set of interests and policy concerns. [. . .] Institutional reform can also promote change, say, between levels of government. Moreover, it is possible that institutions themselves adapt. They may evolve according to their own rules, and so affect the choices of policymakers. In spite of these nuances, it is not certain that institutional approaches offer an all-encompassing theory of policy change, mainly because institutions are better at explaining the dampening rather than the amplifying of political processes. They are generally stable, which means they set out routines and constrain human action.

Socioeconomic change

Socioeconomic changes must play their role in explaining policy change in the form of shocks and influences on the political system. A lot of academic energy was spent on the socioeconomic causes of policy change before the 1980s, but then doubts about macro schemes of politics set in and systems theorists of all sorts fell out of fashion. It is possibly the case that the intellectual reaction against systems theory and functionalism has gone too far, and social science should start examining complex systems again, perhaps through the idea of coevolving social processes. But social scientists do not now accept the basic assumption that there is a transmission belt from society and the economy to the political system and its institutions, as the latter influences the former, and both are highly variegated. [. . .]

Rational choice theory

Rational choice theory examines policy change, variation, and stability by examining the strategies of actors located within political institutions and in society at large. Outcomes are the effects of these choices, which may not reflect the aggregation of preferences of decision makers but rise from strategic interaction imposed by the structure of the choices, such as from the size of the payoffs. Collective action may fail in many contexts, but it is possible to overcome this dilemma through the evolution of cooperation, the operation of smart institutions, the presence of selective incentives, and the actions of entrepreneurs. Thus environmental policy or urban development policy may result from the degree of collective action possible, which may lead to policy change or stability.

[. . .]

But rational choice does not offer solutions for all cases and contexts. It is better at explaining outcomes when preferences are settled; it finds it harder to explain where those preferences come from and why they should change. Thus it becomes part of the analysis of public policy without being all encompassing: an essential part of the toolkit of political scientists, ready to apply to certain contexts, such as coalition building, for example, which provide testable hypotheses.

Adapting theory from mainstream political science

When taken as a set of hypotheses and claims, few researchers would want to work without a theory of choice, an account of socioeconomic change and an understanding of the influence of institutions, but these approaches do not work as well as all-encompassing theories of public policy. So do models developed by public policy researchers fare better?

The best candidate is group or network theory, which has emerged through the subgovernment literature and from organizational sociology. This theory claims that the structure of the coalitions across the complex policy sectors determines policy outputs. The long-term relationships between interest groups and executive agencies evolved into more complex networks between public and private organizations as the number of institutions and participants in the policy process grew after the 1960s, when public problems became more intractable and policy sectors less distinct from each other. [. . .] In part, such explanations could be seen as a subtle from of institutionalism – the influence of regularized constraints on public action, which operate outside and across the formal institutions. But these accounts suffer from some of the same problems as institutionalism because networks are static in character. They may not even be much of a constraint, being epiphenomenal to the social and political systems they occupy. Thus social or organizational change usually affects networks, which occurs at the same time. When power relations are at stake, the existence of a network among organizations does not seem to be a particularly strong influence or constraint on human action. In the brutal world of politics, loyalty is a luxury that few can afford. [. . .]

Ideas

Ideas were the hot public policy topic of the 1990s. Public policy scholars became interested in the effects of knowledge on public policy. To what extent do thoughts or ideations about an issue such as poverty or deprivation act independently of the interests that advocate them? Knowledge in the policymaking world consists of claims about the origins and solutions to public problems, which link to normative claims and may either be accepted or debated by the participants in the policy-making process. Even though most knowledge is social in its construction, the argument is that the process of collecting evidence, the creativity in generating the ideas, and the skills at deploying them give ideas independence.

[. . .]

As with the other approaches in public policy, the application of ideas to public policy is not a theory but the identification of a set of causal processes that link to others. These are contingent on each other, and one is neither logically nor empirically prior. It might seem bland to say that institutions, socioeconomic processes, networks, choices, and ideas interact with each other, but it is a truer statement than saying that one of these processes drives the others. [. . .]

"Synthetic" accounts of the policy process

In the 1990s, more complex accounts of policy streams, advocacy coalitions, and punctuations emerged. What these theories or frameworks offer is a conceptualization of the relationship between the five core causal processes. These frameworks may be called synthetic, largely because they bring together much of the research on institutions, networks, socioeconomic process, choices, and ideas (John, 1998).

Policy streams and windows

The first is Kingdon's (1984, 1995) account. He found that policymakers often do not always know where policies come from, particularly when they are asked to explain how it was that a proposal emerged rather than another. Kingdon argues that there is an element of chance or a stochastic element, which explains the fluidity and rapid change of the policymaking process. He does not say that randomness dominates or provides the sole explanation, as there is an interaction between randomness and the more recognizable processes of problems, policies, and politics. [. . .]

Kingdon's account is close to an evolutionary model of public policy. He writes that policymaking is a "complex adaptive system" (1995, p. 224) in which agents react to changing environments and there is "continual Darwinian selection." [. . .]

Kingdon uses evolutionary ideas to highlight the dynamic and contingent aspects of his account. It is a useful component of his account of policy change, without being an evolutionary model. There are, however, some useful clues as to how one could emerge. Kingdon argues that possibilities and limits of combinations create unique outcomes because "[e]verything cannot interact with everything else" (1995, p. 207). In other words, there are certain combinations of ideas and proposals that have the potential to evolve, but not others.

[. . .]

The policy advocacy coalition framework

Sabatier and Jenkins-Smith's (1993) policy advocacy coalition framework is different than discussed above. The key idea of the framework is that there exist sets of core ideas about causation and value in public policy. These coalitions form because certain interests link to them. There are several such ideas, which create about two to four coalitions, and it is possible to map these networks of actors within a policy sector. Change comes from the ability of these ideas to adapt – in their noncore aspect – ranging around a whole series of operational questions and "what works" in any one time or place. Partly in response to wider social and economic changes or from political events and also from policy learning, the balance of power in these networks changes and the structure and memberships of the coalitions alter.

The cogency of this approach is threefold. First, it leaves behind the idea that policy sectors are composed of integrated networks; instead, they are a political terrain through which different collations fight it out, which is far closer to contemporary reality. Second, the ideational approach to policymaking is fully integrated into the way in which the coalitions operate, so it provides a grounded way of understanding the importance of discourse in the political process. Third, the advocates have developed an effective research program to map the development of advocacy coalitions, through the coding of representation to legislative committees.

The approach has a neat account of policy change, which occurs through the interaction between wide external changes or shocks to the political system and the success of the ideas in the coalitions, which may cause actors in the advocacy coalitions to shift coalitions, even just for tactical reasons. [. . .]

An evolutionary theory of public policy

[. . .] There are a number of ways of applying evolutionary ideas in the social science, but some are not particularly relevant for public policy. Part of the problem is that the debate about evolution is not clear, with many terms being used vaguely or rhetorically. Evolution in biology refers to a change in the gene pool of a population over time. [. . .]

The other set of writings about policy and social theory uses the evolutionary label to examine patterns of rapid policy change or system change and to study where cultures and policy ideas seem to evolve in stages. The evolutionary take on social history offered by Runciman (1989) resembles this pattern, whereby cultures evolve. [. . .]

The most powerful application of evolution to the social science is evolutionary psychology, but it does not make sense to use this in general public policy theory, though it is useful as a guide to decision-making. [. . .] But again, such processes and outcomes do not add up to an evolutionary model of public policy; they are about the impact of biological evolution on public policy.

Rational choice and memetic models

Rational choice theory and memetic models, or a combination between the two, can offer an account of the causal process at work. The advantage of the rational choice approach, particularly evolutionary game theory, is that it can provide a rigorous account of change over time. The cost is the need to adhere to the assumptions behind the game; but if they hold, even partially, there is a form of evolutionary selection, especially as it is possible to relax some of the more problematic assumptions and assume some bounded rationality.

An example of what is possible is Ward's game theoretic accounts of state change (1998, 2003). He sets out a coordination game to explain why the state may adopt certain policies to regulate business. There is a population of firms and a population of governments. He examines the phenomenon of coevolution, whereby new styles of economic and political governance evolve together. The evolutionary take on this is how mutants or alternative strategies affect the game. [. . .] From the policy point of view, there would need to be a number of policymakers, say branches of the state or state and local governments, and a range of other actors, and what matters is whether the subset can get selective benefits from innovation and can support each other.

[. . .]

Proponents of such accounts of evolution need to think carefully about what is being selected. To answer this question, social scientists have debated the existence of memes. As invented by Dawkins (1976), a meme is an information pattern, held in an individual's memory, which is capable of being copied to another. Memes transmit over time, influence behavior, and become successful. They are different to genes in that they are more mutable, but for the evolution idea to work, there must be some stickiness or permanence to them and a sense that the ideas exist apart from each other. So although an environmentalist and an economic development advocate may share some ideas, it is clear what distinguishes them. Thus it makes sense to examine the success and failure of environmentalist ideas, for example.

The unit of selection is the idea or practice, which needs expression by a human agent, who has an interest in the idea's survival. The human agent is defined by the interest but needs the idea to provide direction and identity. Ideas need to have concrete expression in human agency – they need a carrier. Ideas are made of different elements, which may correspond to the genes in the mimetic account. Mutation occurs through random processes of trial and error of these elements, either through errors or through what biologists call recombination – when elements recombine to make new genes. Stronger forms of evolution occur when new species are created – speciation.

[. . .] In terms of policy, the key people are Kingdon's policy entrepreneurs, who are activists with a particular interest in the success of the policy, though in a less acute sense everyone is an entrepreneur who has a stake in the policy outputs and outcomes: the citizens who vote for policies, politicians who seek to maximize votes and capitalize on policy opportunities, and bureaucrats who have a stake in the implementation of particular policy choices. [. . .] What happens is that the idea not only takes hold in people's heads, but it become institutional-ized in practices and routines, such as by governments as in Ward's game, which then continue over time. Similar to the punctuated equilibrium model, the evolutionary equilibrium is hard to dislodge.

Empirical investigations

Evolution does not disrupt the claims of the policy streams accounts; what it claims to offer is a better account of the causal processes at work in policy change. In that sense, evolution is not a new paradigm; it is just an extension of the public policy theory of the 1990s.

[. . .]

Unfortunately, detailed studies are rare, possibly because selection is a messy business and it is hard to identify memetic processes. [. . .] Another familiar criti-cism is that it is possible to say that much of what happens in politics is not the result of imitation but of power. Even Runciman (1999) recognizes this: "And what about cultural behaviour which is the result not of imitation or learning but of enforced obedience to instructions from lawgivers and other people in positions not merely of influence but of power?" (page 2112) There are also problems with memes, as they lack the clarity of genes and seem to be an amalgam of thought processes and practices. [. . .] Even if memes exist, they are anything but standard.

Researchers on evolution need to address the problems of transferring models from the natural to the social world, mainly because the causes are dif-ferent. As it is not possible to identify mechanisms in the same way, it may be the case that evolutionary theory becomes just another way of representing social and political facts, not adding very much to conventional narratives and models. [. . .] The conscious choices that political actors make are made not only to advance their interests but are about what kind of world they prefer. Evolutionary approaches based on the automatic adjustment of fitness for pur-pose will never work smoothly and probably serve as the background for the emergence of new political ideas rather than their sole determinant.

Conclusion

This journey through the policy theory literature does not reveal an imminent change to the central debates in public policy theory. [. . .] This review seeks to show that it is a further possibility for advance, largely within the same mode but with more attention to the core causal processes than before. With more fine-grained tools of analysis, writers in public policy can proceed with less fear that they are applying social science labels that describe rather than explain the policy process. Evolutionary theory is one possible line of advance, which might be able to uncover processes not normally observed by political scientists. Although much is uncovered by institutional processes, long-term social and economic ideas, networks, strategic interaction, and the conscious adoption of ideas, the claim is that random processes, competition, and selection exert a background influence, which can drive the policymaking and implementation processes.

[. . .]

References

Baumgartner, F., & Jones, B. (Eds.) (2002). *Policy dynamics*. Chicago: University of Chicago Press.

Dawkins, R. (1976). *The Selfish Gene*. Oxford: Oxford University Press.

de Greene, K. (1994). The challenge to policy-making of large-scale systems. *Journal of Theoretical Politics, 62*, 161–188.

John, P. (1998). *Analysing public policy*. London: Cassell.

John, P. (1999). Ideas and interests; agendas and implementation: An evolutionary explanation of policy change in British local government finance. *British Journal of Politics and International Relations, 11*, 39–62.

John, P. (2000). The uses and abuse of evolutionary theory in political science: A reply to Alan McConnell and Keith Dowding. *British Journal of Politics and International Relations, 11*, 89–94.

Jones, B. (1994). *Reconceiving decision-making in democratic politics: Attention, choice, and public policy*. Chicago: University of Chicago Press.

Jones. B. (2001). *Politics and the architecture of choice*. Chicago: University of Chicago Press.

Kingdon, J. (1984). *Agendas, alternatives, and public policies*. Boston: Little, Brown.

Kingdon, J. (1995). *Agendas, alternatives, and public policies* (2d ed.). Boston: Little, Brown.

Lane, J., & Ersson, S. (1999). *The new institutional politics*. London: Taylor and Francis.

Runciman, W. (1989). *A treatise on social theory* (vol. 2). Cambridge, United Kingdom: Cambridge University Press.

Runciman, W. (1999). Darwinian soup. *London Review of Books, 21*, p. 2112.

Sabatier, P. (1999). The need for better theories. In P. Sabatier (Ed.), *Theories of the policy process* (pp. 1–17). Boulder, CO: Westview.

Sabatier. P., & Jenkins-Smith, H. (1993). *Policy change and learning: An advocacy coalition approach*. Boulder, CO: Westview.

Sabatier, P., & Jenkins-Smith, H. (1999). The advocacy coalition framework: An assessment. In P. Sabatier (Ed.), *Theories of the policy process* (pp. 117–166). Boulder, CO: Westview.

Strom, K., Muller, W., & Bergman, T. (2003). *Delegation and accountability in parliamentary democracies*. Oxford, United Kingdom: Oxford University Press.

True, J. (2000). Avalanches and incrementalism – making policy and budgets in the United States. *American Review of Public Administration, 30*, 3–18.

True, J., Jones, B., & Baumgartner, F. (1999). Punctuated-equilibrium theory: Explaining stability and change in American policymaking. In P. Sabatier (Ed.), *Theories of the policy process* (pp. 97–115). Boulder, CO: Westview.

Ward, H. (1998, March). "Bandwagons roll" – or not: The co-evolution of modes of regulation and patterns of rule. Paper Presented at ECPR Joint Sessions, University of Warwick.

Ward, H. (2003). The co-evolution of regimes of accumulation and patterns of rule: State autonomy and the possibility of functional response to crisis. *New Political Economy, 8*, 179–202.

Susan M. Barrett

IMPLEMENTATION STUDIES: TIME FOR A REVIVAL?

From: Barrett, S. (2004) 'Implementation studies: time for a revival? Personal reflections on 20 years of implementation studies', *Public Administration*, 82:2, 249–262

[...]

Impetus and motivation for implementation studies

THE LATE 1960s AND early 1970s could be described as a period of growing concern about the effectiveness of public policy and governance. This concern was addressed by a range of initiatives to enhance the policy content of government decision making, to improve public decision-making processes and the co-ordination of policy (joined-up thinking) and to streamline management structures and service delivery. These days, the 1970s tend to have a bad press, but it was a period of important innovation in the field of policy studies. For example the mid-1960s saw a shift from two-dimensional land use plans to the concept of a strategic plan as a statement of reasoned policy, and similar policy plans were subsequently promulgated for social services, housing and transport (DHSS 1972). Policy capacity was enhanced in local government by the employment of research staff to review and evaluate policy effectiveness and to formulate alternative courses of action, and in central government by the creation of departmental Policy Units, the Central Policy Review Staff (CPRS) within the Cabinet Office, and the development of Programme Analysis Review (PAR) in the early 1970s. Ideas and techniques for linking policy objectives and resource allocation derived from the American Planning Programming and Budgeting System (PPBS) spawned the development of corporate planning philosophy, aimed at improving the connectedness of government policy and co-ordination of service delivery.

Similar concerns were reflected in the concurrent development of academic policy studies as a multi-disciplinary and applied subject of research (Heclo 1972) focused around three main areas:

1   Policy analysis: concerned with understanding and explaining the substance of policy content and processes of decision making;
2   Evaluative studies: concerned with understanding and assessing policy outcomes as a basis for evaluating effectiveness;
3   Organizational studies: concerned with understanding the operation of political and administrative organizations as behavioural systems, and prescriptions for improving performance.

[...]

It was also the time of the introduction of the new concept of strategic policy plans, influenced by systems thinking to emphasize planning and policy development as a process of response to changes in the environment characterized by ongoing monitoring and review of policy performance. [...] The emphasis on monitoring policy effectiveness spawned a wide range of evaluative studies here and in the US. Such studies tended to show that in spite of the plethora of policies and plans, 'performance' more often than not still seemed to fall short of policy expectations. Concern shifted from the 'what' of policy outcomes to the 'why' of perceived policy failure, and to focus on the actual process of translating policy into action – the process of implementation – as exemplified by Pressman and Wildavsky's classic implementation study subtitled 'How Great Expectations in Washington are Dashed in Oakland; or Why it's Amazing that Federal Programs Work at All. . . .'(1984).

[...]

Approach to understanding the policy–action relationship

Much of the existing policy studies literature at the time tended to focus on the politics of policy making, assuming implementation as an essentially topdown administrative and hierarchical follow on process. Policy, once formulated and legitimated at the 'top' or centre, is handed in to the administrative system for execution, and successively refined and translated into operating instructions as it moves down the hierarchy to operatives at the 'bottom' of the pyramid. With increasing attention paid to policy *effectiveness*, evaluative studies were starting to highlight the problematic of implementation, and identify key factors deemed to contribute to what was perceived as 'implementation failure'. These [. . .] include:

1   Lack of clear policy objectives; leaving room for differential interpretation and discretion in action;
2   Multiplicity of actors and agencies involved in implementation; problems of communication and co-ordination between the 'links in the chain';
3   Inter- and intra-organizational value and interest differences between actors and agencies; problems of differing perspectives and priorities affecting policy interpretations and motivation for implementation;
4   Relative autonomies among implementing agencies; limits of administrative control.

The core argument of Policy and Action [Barrett and Fudge 1981] was to challenge the traditional policy-centred view of the implementation process, and *a priori* assumptions about the existence of hierarchical relations between policy making and implementation. It was suggested that implementation should be regarded as an integral and continuing part of the political policy process rather than an administrative follow-on, and seen as a policy-action dialectic involving negotiation and bargaining between those seeking to put policy into effect and those upon whom action depends. The political processes by which policy is mediated, negotiated and modified during its formulation continue in the behaviour of those involved in its implementation acting to protect or pursue their own values and interests. Policy may thus be regarded as both a statement of intent by those seeking to change or control behaviour, and a negotiated output emerging from the implementation process.

This negotiative perspective shifts analytical attention away from a focus on formal organizational hierarchies, communication and control mechanisms, to give more emphasis to the power-interest structures and relationships between participating actors and agencies, and the nature of interactions taking place in the process, as key factors shaping the policy/implementation outcomes.

This conceptualization of implementation as 'negotiated order', involving bargaining and negotiation between semi-autonomous actors pursuing or protecting their interests, was further developed [. . .] by a number of key ideas emerging in the organizational field. These included, notably, resource-dependency/exchange theory models of inter-organizational power relations [. . .]. Perhaps of key significance was Strauss's work [1978] conceptualizing all social order – including organizations – as the product of negotiation rather than coercion; his research in psychiatric units pointed to the existence of discretionary power to bargain even in the most rule-bound of environments. This, together with the growing literature on so-called 'street-level bureaucrats' (see, for example, Lipsky 1980; Prottas 1979), explored the existence and nature of discretionary power – or scope for action – in organizational settings. Also explored were the ways that such discretion was being used by front-line operatives either to develop 'coping mechanisms' in the absence of clear policy rules or to negotiate policy modification in action.

[. . .]

Implementation agencies are likely at any point in time to be responding to a wide variety of policy initiatives or environmental pressures from a range of sources. Rather than asking whether and how a particular policy has been implemented, or comparing outcomes against original policy objectives, which assumes *a priori* a causal link between the policy and outcomes observed, implementation studies needed to start with what was actually happening at delivery/recipient level (the 'bottom') and explore why from the 'bottom up'. In order to identify the factors influencing action and behaviour – including the role (if any) played by policy in shaping behaviour and outcomes – Elmore (1980) coined the term 'backward mapping'. He regarded this as an analytical approach for improving the 'implementability' of policy design. He also saw it as a methodology for conducting implementation and evaluation studies. [. . .] Hjern and Porter (1981) talked similarly about building, bottom-up, a picture of the particular 'implementation structure', the network structure of actors and parts of organizations as well as their relationships and interactions in influencing outcomes.

Issues in theory development

In the early 1980s academic debate was polarized around the apparently competing claims of so-called 'top-down' and 'bottom-up' approaches to conceptualization of the implementation process. In some respects the polarization of debate was associated with differing value and disciplinary perspectives on the role of policy in governance. The top-down model was reflected in traditional structures of governance and public sector organization, emphasizing the separation of politics and administration, and co-ordination and control through authority and hierarchy. Those espousing or defending the top-down model saw it as a normative ideal for putting policy into effect. Policy should be made 'at the top', and executed by 'agents' in compliance with policy objectives. The role of implementation studies was to identify the causes of implementation problems or failure, and suggest ways of enhancing the likelihood of obtaining compliance with policy objectives, generally focused on strategies for improved communication of intentions, co-ordination of the 'links in the chain', management of resources and control of implementing agents.

The 'bottom-up' categorization was a somewhat misleading label, including both alternative approaches which regarded implementation as part of a policy-making continuum in which policy evolved or was modified in the process of translating intentions into action, and new methodologies for implementation/evaluation studies. The bottom-up 'camp' (Berman 1978; Hjern, Hanf and Porter 1978) was associated with those espousing a micropolitical view of intra- and inter-organizational behaviour, and included a range of models, some emphasizing consensus building, influence and exchange processes (persuasion, positive-sum negotiation and learning), and others emphasizing conflict and the exercise of power (zero-sum negotiations and power bargaining) in the policy-action relationship.

Although somewhat protracted and confusing, the top-down/bottom-up debate did raise a number of important questions and issues concerning the purpose of implementation analysis, and indeed the meaning of implementation. First was the question of what implementation studies are trying to do. Are they about prescription or description? Is the purpose to design better policy, achieve greater control over policy outcomes, and/or to seek understanding and explanations of what happens in practice? Top-down approaches could be regarded as essentially prescriptive – what ought to happen, but were seen by critics as failing to provide adequate description or understanding of the complexity of interactions taking place in implementation processes. Bottom-up approaches tended to focus on understanding and explanation on the basis that it is not possible to prescribe without understanding. From a top-down perspective, bottom-up approaches to conceptualization were criticized for failing to offer any prescriptions for practice, or for offering prescriptions tantamount to accepting that policy as executed would be subverted or modified to reflect the interests of the most powerful upon whom action depended, and could potentially be seen as subverting the proper role of governance.

Linked to the debate on prescription versus description is the question of what is meant by implementation. Is implementation about achieving conformance or performance (Barrett 1981)? Policy-centred approaches to analysis of necessity involve comparing outcomes against *a priori* statements of intent or targets. Performance is thus judged in terms of achieving conformance with policy targets and standards. In practice, so-called performance criteria tend to operate more as conformance criteria; often the minimum level or standard deemed to constitute satisfactory performance.

For some types of regulatory policy (for example, health and safety), conformance or compliance may be an essential objective. But much public policy is couched in more permissive and discretionary terms; the objective being to permit and encourage innovative courses of action within a framework of procedural rules. Here, output targets or performance criteria are harder to specify in advance, and, as pointed out by Williams (1971), the demands of public accountability are likely to mean that *performance* in the sense of potentially risky innovation, will be tempered by tight administrative and procedural controls, that is, conformance which becomes an end in itself for judging performance.

Interactive and negotiative models of implementation tend to see performance as the achievement of what is possible within a particular policy implementation environment (that is, the array of actors and interests, their relative bargaining power, degree of change or value conflict involved, and so on). From this perspective, judging performance is a matter of more pluralistic and bottom-up evaluation to assess outcomes in terms of who has gained or lost what and how has this been affected or influenced by policy.

Crucial to this view of performance is a positive attitude to discretion. A key contemporaneous debate centred on attitudes to discretion (Bacharach and Lawlor 1980; Lipsky 1980; Prottas 1979). Social and welfare policy analysts, with a tradition of emphasis on issues of equity and common standards in service delivery, tended to view discretion as something to be limited as being potentially discriminatory. For example, research on street level bureaucrats raised questions about whose policy was actually being implemented. Thus, Lipsky's thesis gave rise to considerable debate regarding whether discretion was desirable and necessary or whether it was anti-democratic and reflected inadequate top-down control and so acted to subvert policy (Linder and Peters 1987). On the other hand, those in disciplines or professions where negotiated and contractual relations with clients and consumers were the norm, tended to see discretion as both positive and necessary, as the space within which negotiation and bargaining of positive sum outcomes can take place.

[. . .]

During the 1980s a so-called third generation of implementation models emerged, which either focused on the refinement of negotiative and learning conceptualizations within different policy environments, or sought to synthesize elements of the top-down and bottom-up approaches or focus on the dialectics of the policy-action relationship (Sabatier 1988; Goggin *et al*. 1990; Palumbo and Calista 1990). [. . .] This has offered a new way of looking at concepts of power and negotiation in implementation as the dialectic between structure and agency, which reinforces a view of performance, or what happens in practice, as a function of the scope or limitations of scope for action (rules and roles), and the use made of that scope (values and interests).

The 1990s: implementation studies out of fashion?

In parallel with this interest in implementation, during the late 1970s to the early 1980s, there was an additional agenda in the public policy literature concerning financial stringency and economic efficiency. Then, gradually, the political analysts joined the economists in elucidating a thesis of the New Right during the late 1980s. The beginning of the 1990s heralded the synthesis of previous work and gave attention to the managerial impact of the New Right in terms of the New Public Management and the operationalization of Williamson's transaction cost thesis into a more fully developed expression of quasi markets. The literature at the end of the 1990s was influenced by a condition to the quasi market thesis, this condition being 'the new economic sociology' and the idea of relational markets. An interesting nomenclature had developed as a shorthand to describe the numerous changes which occurred in public sector welfare since 1979, namely, 'reformist', 'rolling back the state' and 'reinventing government'.

[. . .]

In the world of policy studies, business management language and ideas replaced the discourse of public administration. Planning and policy-making became imbued with concepts of strategic management, and concerns about the process of implementation were superseded by emphasis on change management and performance targets. The shift in ideological priorities was reflected in the structure of public research funding and in research funding opportunities. To a certain extent it can be argued that the apparent demise of implementation studies represented no more than academic opportunism; using different language and labels for the same issues.

At the same time, public service agencies and managers had little choice but to embrace the radical shifts that had occurred in policy direction. The shake up of public service organizations involving the introduction of quasi-market competition, contracting out of professional services and performance orientation in performance-related pay and short term contracts generated the search for new models of public management seeking to reconcile concepts of public service with private business principles. The combination of increased policy centralization and agency decentralization and contracting out reinforced the separation and distance between politics and administration. This in turn served to reassert the dominance of normative, top-down, coercive process models of policy implementation or performance, and of 'performance' as conformance with policy targets.

In this new policy construction there was perhaps less perceived need for studies of implementation since there was a belief that the 'reforms' in the public services associated with the New Public Management had addressed the key problems of 'implementation failure' which include a lack of clear unambiguous policy objectives, resource availability and control over implementing agencies.

For example, in respect of clear and unambiguous policy objectives, there was now an increased emphasis on specific performance targets and standards. Formal contracts for service provision appeared to leave no doubt about what was expected to be achieved and what would be regarded as satisfactory performance. In respect of resource availability, privatization, marketization and public/private partnership initiatives were aimed at both reducing the public cost of service provision and injecting new resources from the private sector. Finally, as far as increased control over the discretionary power of implementing agencies was concerned, measures included: the curtailing of professional autonomies by bringing professionals into line-management accountability structures with managerial accountability for performance, replacing inter-agency power bargaining with market-based competition, and contracting out.

Managers were now responsible for putting policy into effect and also to blame if things went wrong. Success or failure was judged on the basis of meeting pre-set targets for ensuring delivery on policy targets. From this perspective there was little sympathy or concern for reaching agreements or making compromises between competing or autonomous interests, or indeed in research aimed at understanding what was going on in the process.

The all-pervasiveness and cultural hegemony attained by new managerialism has also resulted in the suppression of dissent and policy challenge. It is difficult to challenge without appearing to be 'against' improving performance and effectiveness. More insidious than the explicit 'gagging' clauses introduced into contracts of employment have been the self-censorship effects of this cultural hegemony: compliance, caution and risk avoidance in the interests of survival. [. . .]

It could be argued that the ideological and service reforms that have occurred in the public services over the past three decades have taught those who study the public policy process a number of lessons that in turn can be both seen through the lens of implementation studies and at the same time cause that lens to refract in different ways. An important lesson has been the conceptualization of a new role for the state as a consequence of contemporary changes in the public sector.

These vary from the 'managerial' state, or 'neo-Tayloristic' state (Pollitt *et al.* 1990); the 'contract' state (Stewart 1993); and 'entrepreneurial' government (Osborne and Gaebler 1992), but perhaps the most graphic descriptions came from Hood (1995) and his 'Headless Chicken State' or 'Gridlocked Contract State'.

In short, it became possible to see the state as an enabler rather than a provider, government has been depoliticized and re-cast as business and neo-management. Equally importantly, was the lesson of public organizations becoming 'de-coupled' from the relationship between service delivery and political control, well exemplified by the proliferation of 'agencies' as one of the structures through which to deliver public services.

All of these descriptions of a new role for the state have considerable implications for the implementation of policy. The 'Headless Chicken' state is one wherein there are 'no clear rules of the road' or demarcation of responsibilities (Hood 1995, p. 112). Similarly, a disaggregated or de-coupled state meant that the important collaborative and network links needed for implementation was threatened. Agency proliferation without the cohesion and co-ordination of hierarchy resulted in fragmentation and the loss of important implementation feedback loops in both the vertical and horizontal (Holmes 1992).

The very processes of policy implementation are themselves deeply politically dependent, having both a macro and micro political context. Given the argument that there has been a changing role for the state, then the importance of context in policy implementation becomes even more important. It is in this context that the globalization and potential transnational character of future public services could have a great impact upon implementation. Hood (1995) points out that the global paradigm of the New Public Management ignored the very different and typically 'path dependent' local political agendas of public management (p. 106).

Time for a revival?

[...] Yet there are growing concerns, emerging from audit and evaluation processes, about the unintended consequences of the dirigiste model of policy implementation embedded within current practices. Amongst these unintended consequences are a top-down coercive pressure to meet prescribed targets that has led to the skewing of service priorities, for example, hospital waiting lists, and even the manipulation of figures for fear of the consequences of failure (performance becomes conformance). There is then the lack of recognition of the complexity, time and resources involved in achieving the organizational capacity to achieve effective change (implementation as the enculturation of change). Finally, we are also able to identify, a continuing tension, between the normative expectations of managerial control of the policy implementation process and the experienced reality of inter- and intra-organizational micro-politics in the policy-action relationship (characterized by multiple negotiations between semi-autonomous agents with often-competing interests and divergent values).

There is a certain sense of *déjà vu* in these issues relating to the efficacy of the top-down managerial model for implementing policy innovation and organizational change. Managerialism sought to address the perceived problems of administrative bureaucracy, but over-emphasis on coercion and conformance has resulted in a lack of attention to the dynamics of organizational process and the dialectic between structure and agency in the process of change.

I would thus argue the *need* for a revival of interest in implementation studies. First, there is more than ever a need to invest in studies of implementation and change processes, both conceptual and empirical; studies aimed at both understanding and explaining the dynamics of the policy-action relationship, and seeking to develop more appropriate prescriptions than currently demonstrated by the experience of managerialism for the negotiation of change. There is still a lack of attention to process in governance theory and practice, in particular explicit attention to the appropriateness of differing conceptualizations of the policy-action relationship to desired outcomes (means and ends). What are the relative benefits and feasibility of negotiation/learning strategies versus more coercive strategies in differing policy environments? The understanding of process is also an essential part of capacity building, addressing questions such as: Is this doable? How might it work? What would it take?

Second, there is a need for renewed emphasis on multidisciplinary working in policy studies. No one discipline can claim to be the exclusive home for policy studies, and there are substantial benefits for theory development in synthesizing ideas from a plurality of disciplines addressing similar issues from different perspectives. [. . .]

Third is the renewed need to address the central paradox of control and autonomy in achieving desired performance/outcomes. How to balance the requirement for public accountability with consumer responsiveness, respect for difference and local autonomies, creativity, and so on? How to avoid performance becoming conformance with targets at the expense of broader goals?

Last but not least I would argue the need for a new emphasis in research and practice on the relationship between ethics, social responsibility, public accountability and control in implementation. Increased attention to ethics and social responsibility in the policy process is overdue, and would bring into the implementation debate issues such as the value conflict between professional principles and codes of ethical practice versus the management performance imperatives. [. . .]

References

Bacharach, S. and F. Lawlor. 1980. *Power and Politics in Organisations*. San Francisco, CA: Jossey Bass.

Barrett, S. 1981. 'Local Authorities and the Community Land Scheme', in S. Barrett and C. Fudge (eds), *Policy and Action*. London: Methuen.

Barrett, S. and C. Fudge (eds). 1981. *Policy and Action*. London: Methuen.

Barrett, S. and M. Hill. 1984. 'Policy, Bargaining and Structure in Implementation Theory: Towards an Integrated Perspective', *Policy and Politics*, 12, 3, 219–40.

Berman, P. 1978. 'The Study of Macro and Micro Implementation', *Public Policy*, 27, 157–84.

DHSS. 1972. Town and Country Planning Act, circular 35/72.

Elmore, R. 1980. 'Backward Mapping: Implementation Research and Policy Decisions', in W. Williams *et al.* (eds), *Studying Implementation*. New York: Chatham House.

Goggin, M. L., A. O'M. Bowman, J. P. Lester and L. J. O'Toole. 1990. *Implementation Theory and Practice: Towards a Third Generation*. Upper Saddle River, NJ: Scott Foresman.

Heclo, H. 1972. 'Review Article: Policy Analysis', *British Journal of Political Science*, 2, 1 (January 1972).

Hjern, B. and D. O. Porter. 1981. 'Implementation Structures: a New Unit of Administrative Analysis', *Organisation Studies*, 2, 211–27.

Hjern, B., K. Hanf and D. Porter. 1978. 'Local Networks of Manpower Training in the Federal Republics of Germany and Sweden', in K. Hanf and F.W. Scharpf (eds), *Interorganisational Policy Making*. London: Sage.

Holmes, M. 1992. 'Public Sector Management Reforms: Convergence or Divergence?', *Governance*, 5, 4, 472–83.

Hood, C. 1991. 'A Public Management for All Seasons', *Public Administration*, 69, 1 (Spring), 3–19.

Hood, C. 1995. 'Contemporary Public Management: a New Global Paradigm?', *Public Policy and Administration*, 10, 2 (Summer), 104–17.

Linder, S. H. and B. Guy Peters. 1987. 'Relativism, Contingency, and the Definition of Success in Implementation Research', *Policy Studies Review*, 7, 1, 16–27.

Lipsky, M. 1980. *Street Level Bureaucracy*. New York: Russell Sage.

Osborne, D. and T. Gaebler. 1992. *Reinventing Government*. Reading, MA: Addison-Wesley.

Palumbo, D. J. and D. J. Calista (eds). 1990. *Implementation and the Policy Process*. Policy Studies Association/Greenwood Press.

Pollitt, C., S. Harrison, D. J. Hunter and G. Marnoch. 1990. 'No Hiding Place: On the Discomforts of Researching the Contemporary Policy Process', *Journal of Social Policy*, 19, 2, 169–90.

Pressman, J. and A. Wildavsky. 1984. *Implementation*, 3rd edn, Berkeley, CA: University of California Press.

Prottas, J. 1979. *People Processing*. Boston, MA: D. C. Heath.

Sabatier, P. 1988. 'An Advocacy Coalition Framework of Policy Change and the Role of Policy-oriented Learning Therein', *Policy Sciences*, 2, 1, 129–68.

Stewart, J. 1993. 'Rational Choice Theory, Public Policy and the Liberal State', *Policy Sciences*, 26, 4, 317–30.

Strauss, A. 1978. *Negotiations: Varieties, Contexts, Processes and Social Order*. San Francisco, CA: Jossey Bass.

Williams, W. 1971. *Social Policy Research and Analysis*. New York: Elsevier.

Erik-Hans Klijn and Joop F. M. Koppenjan

PUBLIC MANAGEMENT AND POLICY NETWORKS: FOUNDATIONS OF A NETWORK APPROACH TO GOVERNANCE

From: Klijn, E-H. and Koppenjan, J. F. M. (2000) 'Public management and policy networks: foundations of a network approach to governance', *Public Management*, 2:2, 135–158

Introduction: networks and the governance debate

THE APPARENTLY BROAD CONSENSUS that has developed around the idea that government is actually not the cockpit from which society is governed and that policy making processes rather are generally an interplay among various actors has led to a full-scale search for new governing methods and a discussion on governance and public management (Kooiman 1993; Rhodes 1996). This has fused with discussions in public administration on managerial reform and the adoption of business management techniques under the heading of new public management (NPM), a framework for implementing these reforms.

Governance, public management and network management

Governance can roughly be described as the 'directed influence of societal processes'. Many kinds of mechanisms, some of them quite complex, are involved and these do not only originate from public actors (Kooiman 1993; Kickert *et al.* 1997). Thus it is no surprise that the word 'governance' has become a catchword in the last few years and that it has been used in many different contexts. [. . .] These seem to fall largely into two groups of definitions. In one case, governance pertains to notions of reducing the state and distinguishing between government and governance. Government should be reduced or more done with less (Osborne and Gaebler 1992), mainly by employing new public management techniques. In the other case, the term governance is reserved for theories and cases that take into account the interdependencies of public, private and semi-private actors. In this definition governance refers to self-organizing networks. Ideas on network management [. . .] fit in this category. The two conceptualizations of governance have totally different perspectives on public management and the role of government in society, and they draw their theoretical inspiration from very different sources.

While 'new public management' represents an attempt to translate managerial ideas from the private sector to public organizations, such as contracting out, client orientation and the introduction of market mechanisms 'network management' focuses more on mediating and co-ordinating interorganizational policy making. The theoretical basis for this alternative view is found in the network approach to policy.

[. . .]

The aim of this article is to critically evaluate both the network approach and the criticism it has encountered in order to clarify existing misunderstandings and to improve network theory as a framework for the explanation, evaluation and improvement of public policy and public management.

[. . .]

The theoretical foundation of the network approach

The theoretical roots of the policy network approach

The use of the network concept in policy science dates back to the early 1970s. In implementation studies, especially in what has become known as the 'bottom-up approach', as well as in intergovernmental relations literature, the concept has been used to map relation patterns between organizations and to assess the influence of these patterns for policy processes.

[. . .]

The policy network approach builds on this process model since it also focuses attention on the interaction processes between interdependent actors and the complexity of objectives and strategies as a consequence of that interaction. An important difference with the process model is that in the network approach, more attention is given to the institutional context in which complex interactions take place. In an attempt to elaborate the institutional context of complex interaction processes, network theoreticians are inspired by interorganizational theory.

The central starting point of the interorganizational approach is that the environment of organizations consists of other organizations. In order to survive, an organization requires resources from other organizations. These organizations engage in exchange relations with each other and a network of mutually dependent actors emerges. There is substantial attention in interorganizational theory for the links between organizations and the strategies used by organizations to influence the exchange processes [. . .].

[. . .] The network approach assumes that policy is made in complex interaction processes between a large number of actors which takes place within networks of interdependent actors. These actors are mutually dependent so policy can only be realized on the basis of co-operation. This co-operation, however, is by no means simple or spontaneous, and it requires types of game management and network constitution.

Clarification of central concepts: policy networks as a context of interactions

[. . .]

Within networks, series of interactions occur around policy and other issues. These series of interactions can be called games (Crozier and Friedberg 1980; Rhodes 1981; Scharpf 1997). Their positions in the network and the strategic action in the game determine the positions of the players. During the game, actors operate within the established resource distribution and set of rules, which are to a large extent framed by the network. In addition, they have to operate strategically in order to handle the given dependencies in the game so that they can achieve their own objectives.

Policy processes can thus be seen as a collection of games between actors. In these games, each of the various actors has its own perceptions of the nature of the problem, the desired solutions and of the other actors in the network. On the basis of these perceptions, actors select strategies. The outcomes of the game are a consequence of the interactions of strategies of different players in the game. These strategies are however influenced by the perceptions of the actors, the power and resource divisions in the network and the rules of the network.

Concerted action and network management

A central question within the network approach is how concerted action is established around a concrete issue. Actors need to co-operate in order to achieve satisfying outcomes. This is not always easy, despite durable dependencies, since major conflict may arise at the process level about, for instance, the distribution of costs and benefits of a solution. Policy is made and policy processes occur in the tension between dependency and the diversity of goals and interests. And while this tension can be more or less regulated by the rules and resource distribution in the network, the tension will exist and needs to be solved in any policy game.

Since co-operation and collaboration of goals and interests does not happen of its own accord, steering of complex games in networks is necessary. These steering strategies, i.e. network management, are primarily focused on the improvement of co-operation between involved actors (O'Toole 1988). The sometimes implicit assumption is that satisfying outcomes for actors are not possible without network management. Network management is thus an independent variable in the development of policy processes.

[. . .]

The network approach as an explanatory model

The network concept is said to be merely a metaphor, and that because of this the network approach lacks real explanatory power. The question is: to what extent can structural approaches to networks explain policy outcomes and processes? How do these network features relate to actor behaviour and their interactions? [. . .]

We suggest that the issue of co-operation is central to the policy network approach. Given the dependency of actors on each other's resources, policies can only be developed when actors make their resources available. Therefore, in the network approach, explanations for the success or failure of policy processes are based on the extent to which co-operation has been achieved. Co-operation cannot be achieved when interactions between actors stagnate, are blocked or have led to undesired or unforeseen consequences, or because interactions are influenced by institutional characteristics. Explanations that fall into this latter category are based on the premise that rules limit the behaviour of actors even when the actors themselves may have violated these rules consciously or unconsciously.

Thus, explanations for the development of interaction processes in networks are found both in institutional characteristics – the resources and the rules – and in the characteristics of the interaction situation – the players, their stakes and their strategies. [. . .]

Process variables as factors for success and failure

The network approach assumes that policy outcomes are the result of interaction of strategies of various actors. The involvement of these actors is a consequence of the fact that they possess resources that require their involvement in the handling and solution of a particular problem. They can block interaction processes by withdrawing their resources: they have veto power. Replacement of these resources is not always possible and when it is, it might be costly and time consuming. The same can be said for attempts to coerce co-operation, for instance by ordering a municipality to change its zoning plan if it does not do so of its own accord.

An important explanation for failing to realize concerted policy outcomes is the fact that actors are insufficiently aware of their external dependencies. In this case they assume that they can solve the problem alone or that they can impose their solution on other actors. But even when actors are aware of their external dependencies, it is often quite an undertaking to bring the various goals and interests together. Differences and disagreements in perceptions between actors may cause conflicts and block the interaction. Only when actors are able to bring their perceptions together and formulate common goals and interests will policy games lead to satisfactory outcomes. Learning processes are thus very important in policy games and process management seeks to stimulate these. Preferences of actors are not fixed (Weick 1979; March 1988). [. . .]

On the other hand, actors may lose interest in policy games so that stagnation occurs. These can be the consequence of the low priority that a policy problem has in the perception of one or more actors. Stagnation and blockades may also be a consequence of an undesirable balance between interaction costs and expected outcomes of policy games or of risks related to policy games as a consequence of unexpected strategies of others. Thus there is a risk that as soon as they have profited in the interaction process, actors exit or threaten to exit, which leaves other actors empty-handed. This problem typically exists when parties commit to transaction-specific investments that cannot, or not easily, be used for other transactions (Williamson 1979; Barney and Hesterly 1996). And then there is always the danger that outsiders may profit from the mutual efforts of a particular group without having made any contribution to the endeavour (free-rider problem). In this case, network management should focus on the organization of interactions and protection of interests of the actors involved (De Bruijn *et al.* 1998).

[. . .] Lack of awareness of mutual dependencies, conflicts of interests, interaction costs and risks are important explanations for the failure of concerted policy. Conversely, the emergence of concerted action is explained through the acknowledgement of mutual dependencies, converging perceptions, the existence of incentives which improve co-operation and the limitation of interaction risks through the application of types of game management.

The structure of the network as explanation

As argued, explanations for the success or failure of policy processes are divided into process variables and factors connected to the structure of the network. Concerted solutions have to be established in games. When network level factors for the explanation of success and/or failure of policy and policy processes are included, game and network are linked; after all, it concerns the question of how characteristics at the network level influence the development of the game.

Intensive interaction between actors creates a specific resource distribution that influences the functioning of the network. Actors recognize/acknowledge that certain resources are relevant or even necessary to the realization of policy outcomes. These resources provide actors with veto power. The resources enable them to veto interaction processes and they thus acquire a privileged position in the network and in the games within that network. The greater the veto power of an actor, the more indispensable the actor is to the policy games. The success of policy games is thus partially determined by the degree to which indispensable resources, and the actors who own them, are involved (Scharpf 1997). Changes in the resource distribution in the networks are, therefore, reflected in the policy games. [. . .]

[. . .] Interactions between actors from various networks may be difficult because they do not interact otherwise or have few rules to regulate their interactions. In other words, automatic co-ordination mechanisms and a degree of trust are lacking, and this results in higher interaction costs.

Rules play an important role in the development of policy processes. Rules enable actors to depart from minimal institutional agreements in their interaction. This reduces transaction costs and simplifies collaboration (Scharpf 1997; Hindmoor 1998). Initially, without knowledge of the network, it is difficult to arrive at general statements about the influence of rules on policy networks. Rules are social constructions of actors in a network, and they differ from network to network. Research has shown, however, that rules of conflict management and mediation, as well as rules to protect autonomy and position, are important for determining the possibility of co-operation (Klijn 1996a; Scharpf 1997). The stronger the territorial demarcations in a network and the weaker the rules for conflict management and mediation, the more difficult decision making will be. The lack of trust and useful sanctions makes it difficult to prevent exploitative behaviour on the part of actors.

These examples illustrate the structuring nature of rules in networks. They can improve or limit certain styles of interaction. Thus the lack of conflict regulating mechanisms and trust will more quickly lead to non-co-operative outcomes of 'mixed-motive' policy games which usually result in less for the actor than more co-operative strategies. There are no mechanisms to prevent or decrease incidences of opportunistic behaviour (Scharpf 1997). The central characteristic by which these outcomes are produced is trust. [. . .] Rules are one of the most important pillars of trust, but herein lies a problem. Actors can violate rules, whether formal or informal, because the result might be attractive to the actor. In this sense, rules do regulate but not determine and they can be changed. Each analysis of decision making in networks must take this into account. Particular attention should be focused on the process of reformulation and reinterpretation of rules as a consequence of circumstances external to the network and the strategic choices of actors. [. . .]

The role of power and conflict in networks

Within the network approach literature, works that emphasize network management are critiqued for elevating co-operation to a norm and for insufficiently considering the role of conflict and differences in power. Indeed, co-operation is an important element of network theory, both with respect to the explanations of success and failure and the development of prescriptions. But power and conflict are not excluded from consideration.

Power, conflict and durable relations

Without co-operation, actors who find themselves in situations of mutual dependencies cannot realize their objectives. This does not mean that co-operation is established without conflict. Nor does it mean that actors will manage to co-operate. Durable dependency relations do not necessarily mean that no conflict will emerge over the distribution of costs and benefits in concrete policy processes. [. . .]

The lack of a dominant actor does not imply that resources are equally distributed among actors (Knight 1992). Also, rules may operate to the advantage of some, and to the disadvantage of other actors. This is implied by the fact that rules have been formed during earlier interactions. The inequalities resulting from earlier interactions are incorporated into the existing rules. A change of rules is thus also (but not exclusively) a battle for power between actors (Burns and Flam 1987). In this sense the network approach is quite attentive to 'invisible' forms of power, traditionally known as 'the mobilisation of bias' (Bachrach and Baratz 1962) such as rules which shape the problem definitions and entrees of the actors in games and networks.

[. . .]

Veto power, network management and less privileged interests

Nevertheless, less powerful actors may influence decision making. They can use their veto power and their ability to use resources for blocking decision making and thus create stagnation or blockade. Since stagnation and blockade result in extra costs – at the very least – more powerful actors need to consider their less powerful colleagues. In order to encourage actors not to use their veto power, some degree of convergence of perceptions must be achieved. This is also a demonstration of the importance and the need for process management. [. . .] The starting point of process management is to enhance the learning capability of policy processes by including information and interests of various actors so that more complete policy initiatives can be developed. From a network approach, the involvement of actors is not only recommended for normative reasons, but also for reasons of effectiveness and efficiency. Expertise and knowledge for handling policy as well as other sorts of problems is not available in one place only and thus a confrontation of policy initiatives with information and interests of other actors is necessary. Power differences influence the way in which this process evolves. As long as actors hold veto power, they have influence.

A more serious problem occurs when actors have no veto power and/or are excluded from interaction by other parties. This can happen when interaction patterns between actors result in a certain degree of network insularity (Laumann and Knoke 1987; Rhodes 1988). Outsiders can only access the network if they familiarize themselves with the rules of behaviour and the language of the network (Klijn 1996a).

[. . .]

Public actors and policy networks

In the network approach, public actors do not play the dominant role they often are ascribed in other public administration perspectives. This has evoked criticism. The network approach is accused of considering government merely as 'an actor among actors', which can lead to problems of democratic legitimacy or accountability (Hirst 1994; Rhodes 1997). Sometimes critics describe networks as closed subsystems dominated by established interest groups, which impede innovation and maximize their private interests at the cost of others. As a result the common interest is neglected and the primacy of politics is eroded (Ripley and Franklin 1987; Marsh and Rhodes 1992; De Bruijn and Ringeling 1997). From this point of view it is inconceivable to present a network approach as a normative theory. Yet this is what we do when we derive evaluation criteria and prescriptions from network theory.

[. . .]

The special position of government

Network theory by no means presumes that governments are like other actors. Governments have unique resources at their disposal and work to achieve unique goals. They occupy a special position, which in most cases cannot be filled by others. Resources that determine this special position include: sizeable budgets and personnel, special powers, access to mass media, a monopoly on the use of force and democratic legitimization. Access to these resources provides governments with considerable power. However, they also encounter certain limitations as a function of their uniqueness (Kickert *et al.* 1997):

- The tasks of government define to a great extent its interdependence and often condemn it to interactions with particular social and administrative partners that it cannot freely choose.
- In performing its duties, government is frequently not allowed to 'goal bargain'. In this respect, it often does not have the option of carrying out tasks through negotiation.
- Governments are bound to the norms and rules they wish to impose on others: principles of good government, consideration for minorities and

adversaries, guidelines of democratic regulations, et cetera. Where other actors operate with strategic ingenuity, governments are expected to show exemplary behaviour.

- Because of its public nature and democratic monitoring, more demands are made on government's strategic interactions. These actions are scrutinized by the watchful eye of the media.
- Government is not only expected to operate effectively and efficiently, its actions must also be legitimate: they must be 'backed' by politicians and political parties, but there must also be social acceptance of public policy.

So, while their unique position means governments have access to special resources; it also limits their possibilities to use them in order to attain their goals in network situations.

But the objective statement of these conditions may not be getting at the real core of the debate about the role of governments in networks. The debate is mainly about the normative implications of becoming engaged in networks: public actors represent the common interest and that is why they should not enter into interactions and partnerships with other parties in society. One counter argument that makes such a normative position problematic is that since governments are indeed dependent, this way of thinking simply does not help when they have to deal with the genuine complexities of their tasks and environment. But we may also go more deeply into the question regarding why the representation of the common interest is at odds with engaging in network processes. What does representation of the common interest mean? Does it imply that the objectives of governmental organizations are superior to those of other actors, because they are mandated by elections (i.e. the will of the people)?

[. . .]

If common interest has any meaning at all, it is because it refers to the importance of criteria such as proportional representation, openness, equity, fairness, reliability, et cetera. Note that these are all criteria that concern the quality of the interaction process rather than the content of policies or decisions. And that it is precisely network management that has been developed as an instrument to ensure that interaction processes have these qualities. Network management is the means by which the quality and openness of processes can be achieved. If the representation of the common interest is defined in this way, there is no reason to persist in the claim that entering into network-oriented processes is contrary to the representation of the common interest. Quite the contrary: because it is the task of governmental organizations to uphold and further the common interest, they should, rather than refraining from network games, actively seek to organize and manage them.

However, there remains the criticism that the position of representative bodies will be eroded by engaging in negotiation processes with private and semi-private partners (Rhodes 1997). Because of the non-transparent and uncontrolled processes in networks, the primacy of politics will be threatened. But then again, the position can be taken that by responsible and prudent engagement in networks, government can help prevent processes from succumbing to these shortcomings. [. . .]

Public management in networks: roles for governmental organizations

When confronted with a network-like situation, governments may choose among the following options.

First, they may choose not to join in network games. This means that they will try instead to unilaterally impose their ideas and goals on other social actors. This will require a huge investment in decision-making and implementation activities since there are existing dependencies that will need to be dealt with and the power of the opposition will need to be broken. The risks are high: is there sufficient and stable political support for such a strategy? How sure can we be that goal attainment means effectiveness and efficiency, given that policy development is based on imperfect information and that the strategic behaviour of target groups must be taken into account? And what does this mean for relations with parties on whom governments remain dependent both in the future and in parallel situations?

Second, governments may decide to carry out their tasks in co-operation with other public, semi-public and private actors. Often, entering into dialogue with non-governmental organizations is considered quite legitimate and a standard operating procedure. We explicitly mention co-operation with other public actors because it is entirely possible that various governmental organizations, in performing their tasks, discover that they are dependent upon each other. But not every form of co-operation is acceptable or manageable. For instance, hierarchical supervisory relations between public actors may limit the possibilities of horizontal co-operation.

Third, government can take up the role of process manager and try to facilitate interaction processes aimed at the resolution of certain problems or the realization of projects. The fact that government is supposed to protect the common interest, safeguard democratic values and be publicly accountable for its actions frequently makes it acceptable to others as a process manager. However, it is not always possible or sensible for governmental organizations to accept such a role. [. . .]

Fourth, governments may choose to take up the role of network builder. Given the special resources of governments and their role as representative of the common interest, governments seem to be eminently suited for this role. But at the same time, strategies aimed at changing network features have themselves to be handled in game situations and need to be negotiated with other involved parties in order to result in stable network changes. These changes cannot be achieved instantaneously. This means that network constitution is not instrumental to the realization of substantive government goals in concrete game situations. A serious danger in operating within games for governments is that these four roles get confused. This may occur for strategic reasons, or if government is inexperienced with a new role and, in the middle of a difficult situation, reverts to old routines. [...] Clearly confusion of roles can lead to misunderstandings and conflict among actors and can prove to be costly in terms of effectiveness and efficiency, but especially with regard to the reliability and legitimacy of government.

Conclusion

In this article, we have argued that the policy network approach has developed into a relatively elaborate, empirically grounded and recognizable theoretical framework. With the help of this framework, policy processes can be analysed, explained and evaluated. And it offers clues on which prescriptions regarding strategies, game management and network structuring can be based.

Despite this scholarly and substantial work, the network approach can hardly be considered to be widely accepted as a theory on which practitioners in the public sector base their actions. It is therefore not surprising that the descriptive and explanatory aspects of the theory until now have received more attention than its prescriptions. However, we believe that network theory will prove to be an important source of inspiration for the development of public management. The nature of tasks that governments in contemporary complex societies are confronted with will not allow for command and control reactions. Because of the ambiguity and complexity of these tasks, governments will have to learn to enter into partnerships with other parties. Network management strategies will have to become part of their standard operating procedures.

In The Netherlands, for instance, this view is widely recognized and experiments have even been started to develop public policies in co-operation with politicians, civil servants, private companies, pressure groups and citizens. But at the same time there is a hesitation and resistance to abandoning existing routines and to giving up the power to determine the content of policies unilaterally. As a result these experiments often remain marginal and half-hearted.

[...]

References

Bachrach, P. and Baratz, M. S. (1962) 'Two Faces of Power', *American Political Science Review*, 56:4 pp. 947–52.

Barney, J. B. and Hesterly, W. (1996) 'Organisational Economics: Understanding the Relationship Between Organisations and Economic Analysis' in S. R. Clegg, C. Hardy and W. R. Nord (eds) *Handbook of Organisation Studies*, London: Sage.

Benson, J. K. (1982) 'A Framework for Policy Analysis' in D. L. Rogers and D. A. Whetten (eds) *Interorganisational Co-ordination: Theory, Research, and Implementation*, Ames: Iowa State University Press.

Burns, T. R. and Flam, H. (1987) *The Shaping of Social Organisation: Social Rule System Theory with Application*, London: Sage.

Crozier, M. and Friedberg, E. (1980) *Actors and Systems: The Politics of Collective Action*, Chicago, IL/London: University of Chicago Press.

De Bruijn, J. A. and Ringeling, A. B. (1997) 'Normative Notes Perspectives on Networks' in W. J. M. Kickert, E. H. Klijn and J. F. M. Koppenjan (eds) *Managing Complex Networks*, London: Sage.

De Bruijn, J. A., Ten Heuvelhof, E. F. and In't Veld, R. J. (1998) *Procesmanagement. Over Procesontwerp en Besluitvorming*, Schoonhovcn: Academic Services.

Hindmoor, A. (1998) 'The Importance of Being Trusted: Transaction Costs and Policy Network Theory', *Public Administration*, 76:spring pp. 25–43.

Hirst, P. (1994) *Associative Democracy: New Forms of Economic and Social Governance*, Cambridge: Polity Press.

Kickert, W. J. M. ed. (1997) *Public Management and Administrative Reform in Western Europe*, Cheltenham: Edward Elgar Publishing.

Kickert, W. J. M., Klijn, E. H. and Koppenjan, J. F. M. eds (1997) *Managing Complex Networks*, London: Sage.

Klijn, E. H. (1996a) *Regels en Sturing in Netwerken. De Invloed van Neswerkregels op de Herstructuring van Naoorlogse Wijken*, Delft: Eburon.

—— (1996b) 'Analysing and Managing Policy Processes in Complex Networks: A Theoretical Examination of the Concept Policy Network and its Problems', *Administration and Society*, 28:1 pp. 90–119.

Knight, J. (1992) *Institutions and Social Conflict*, Cambridge: Cambridge University Press.

Kooiman, J. ed. (1993) *Modern Governance: New Government–Society Interactions*, London: Sage.

Laumann, E. O. and Knoke, D. (1987) *The Organisational State: Social Choice in National Policy Domains*, Wisconsin, WI: University of Wisconsin Press.

March, G. (1988) 'The Technology of Foolishness' in J. G. March (ed.) *Decisions and Organisations*, Oxford: Basil Blackwell.

Marsh, D. and Rhodes, R. A. W. (1992) *Policy Networks in British Government*, Oxford: Clarendon Press.

Osborne, D. and Gaebler, T. (1992) *Reinventing Government: How the Entrepreneurial Spirit is Transforming the Public Sector*, Reading, MA: Addison-Wesley.

Ostrom, E. (1986) 'A Method of Institutional Analysis' in F.-X. Kaufman, G. Majone, V. Ostrom (eds) *Guidance and Control in the Public Sector: The Bielefeld Interdisciplinary Project*, Berlin: De Gruyter.

Ostrom, E., Gardner, R. and Walker, J. (1994) *Rules, Games and Common Pool Resources*, Ann Arbor, MI: University of Michigan Press.

O'Toole, L. J. (1988) 'Strategies for Intergovernmental Management: Implementing Programs in Interorganisational Networks', *Journal of Public Administration*, 25:1 pp. 43–57.

Rhodes, R. A. W. (1981) *Control and Power in Central–Local Government Relations*, Farnborough: Gower.

—— (1988) *Beyond Westminster and Whitehall: The Subsectoral Governments of Britain*, London: Unwin Hyman.

—— (1996) 'The New Governance: Governing without Government', *Political Studies*, 44:4 pp. 652–67.

—— (1997) *Understanding Government*, Buckingham: Open University Press.

Ripley, R. B. and Franklin, G. (1987) *Congress, the Bureaucracy and Public Policy*, Homewood, IL: Dorsey (first published 1976).

Scharpf, F. W. (1978) 'Interorganizational Policy Studies: Issues, Concepts and Perspectives' in K. Hanf and F. W. Scharpf (eds) *Interorganisational Policy Making*, London: Sage.

—— (1997) *Games Real Actors Play: Actor Centred Institutionalism in Policy Research*, Boulder, CO: Westview Press.

Weick, K. E. (1979) *The Social Psychology of Organising* (2nd edn), New York: Random House.

Williamson, O. E. (1979) 'Transaction Costs Economics: The Governance of Contractual Relations', *Journal of Law and Economics*, XXII:2 pp. 233–61.

Hugh Heclo and Aaron Wildavsky

VILLAGE LIFE IN CIVIL SERVICE SOCIETY: DEPARTMENT–TREASURY BARGAINING

From: Heclo, H. and Wildavsky, A. (1974) *The Private Government of Public Money: Community and Policy inside British Politics*, Chapter 3, Macmillan

[...]

THE TREASURY IS RESPONSIBLE for managing the economy, departments for managing their subject matter. Since the Second World War, this theoretical distinction has been increasingly accepted by both sides and it has contributed much to the improved spirit of co-operation between Treasury and spending departments. Yet relationships between the two also constitute a mixed-motive game. Each can both help and harm the other immeasurably. They need each other but they also need to get around one another. Their conflicts are rooted in the institutional differences that separate those whose criteria for success depend on spending (and hopefully accomplishing) more, and those whose first obligation is to keep spending (and hence taxes) within acceptable limits. Their co-operation works through membership in a common society where some perform the substantive operations and others authorize the necessary funds.

Departmental views of the Treasury are suffused with ambivalence. They admire but fear it. The more droll are likely to refer half-seriously to the Treasury as 'a necessary evil – necessary and evil'. They know someone has to guard the purse and manage the economy but wish they did not have to suffer for it. They hope the Treasury will avoid concentrating on minute details, but they are not happy when it delves into major policies. All the Treasury people care about is totals, departmental people will complain, in the same breath muttering that the Treasury men think they know the department's business better than those who are entrusted with it. Department people like to feel protected in general but free in particulars. They want Treasury men to understand them but not at the price of interference. They want the Treasury to be powerful except where they differ, cynical except where they need trust, and benevolent except when other departments are depriving them of a fair share of funds.

The Treasury and its minister, the Chancellor of the Exchequer, are responsible both for raising taxes and for managing the economy. Historically the theory of the British constitution has been that the Chancellor, with the Treasury behind him, supports the interest in maintaining or reducing taxes against claims of the spending ministers who gain by doing more. The Chancellor is blamed for increasing taxes; other Cabinet members are praised for spending more than their predecessors. [. . .]

There is, then, no chance that Treasury behaviour will be right for everybody. It is not in the nature of things for Treasury and departments to chime together in perfect harmony. Yet it would be entirely misleading to begin by describing the inevitable conflicts. To talk with officials in the Treasury and spending departments is to enter a fundamentally cohesive world of insiders. Their conflicts are comprehensible only against the broader background of their co-operation. Treasury and departments live off and through each other. And they know it.

The ambience of collaboration

[. . .]

Ministerial conflict on expenditures is like the collision of mammoth icebergs; before the tips impinge, the grinding and crunching has already been well under way below the surface. The battle begins with whomever in the department finance division is at that time dealing with his Treasury counterpart. [. . .] There is only so much friction that anyone can cause without deeply antagonising Treasury officials and thus harming the departmental case on many issues. Clearly it is better to agree with the Treasury than to disagree, if not on each and every case, at least on the range of issues.

Co-operation is facilitated by the fact that, despite department allegiances, all officials are part of a greater civil service society. Among those at the top of the service, the bond may be particularly close. By the time they have arrived their official career paths are likely to have criss-crossed many times. Those further down may not know each other but still they know enough about each other to understand that they are dealing with 'a member of one's own group'. The statement of one Treasury assistant secretary can stand for the feeling expressed to us by most officials. 'It's difficult for an outsider to appreciate how chummy things are in the Civil Service. You've probably known each other for fifteen years – lots of informal contacts and socialising. You ring each other up and gossip about things. Not everyone agrees with this style of doing things, but most do. Formal discussion follows after informal chats.'

[. . .]

The terms 'Treasury' and 'spending department' are collective nouns suggesting discrete chunks of organisation. In terms of people, however, they are a vast flux of inter-changing personnel within the one civil service society. Discussion of civil service cohesion, usually in terms of 'elitism', has typically concentrated on the sociologists' favoured themes – socio-economic background and conditions of entry to the service. We contend that a more immediate and important form of socialisation occurs by virtue of officials' post-entry movement within the government community. 'Transfer between Departments,' wrote a permanent secretary of the Treasury, is one of the most vital sources for the service's 'bond of unity'.

[. . .]

The circulation pump of career mobility in the civil service, flowing into every corner of Whitehall and back again, establishes the preconditions for co-operation between Treasury and departments. If the Treasury recruited only or mainly from its own ranks, its members would lack contact with department officials who, in the event, could hardly have found room for prior service in [the Treasury]. [. . .] The flow of careers appears complex precisely because the Treasury wishes both to preserve and to pass on, to colonise others and to conserve its own values.

[. . .]

None of this is to suggest that Treasury men acquire in a few years some manner of institutional-financial ideology which they then carry with them the rest of their working lives. One thing they learn is that each organisation has interests it will be in their duty (and to their advantage) to protect. Work contact does not mean that the Treasury's view will always be uppermost in their bargaining, but it does help Treasury and department officials to know how to get along and what to expect from each other. [. . .]

Co-operation in the common society of officialdom is enhanced not only by civil servants' movements but also by their working arrangements. The shadowy personal networks merge into more formal but still blurry structures. Whitehall and its vast departmental fortresses are honeycombed with joint groups, working parties, and interdepartmental committees of officials – some *ad hoc* and some formal, some meeting only once or twice and others working for several years. Treasury men are likely to be found involved in almost any major departmental or interdepartmental committee, sometimes as full members, sometimes as occasional visitors, and many times merely watching and listening from a polite distance. An organisation chartist's nightmare perhaps, but this flux of working arrangements does allow officials to meet when, where, and in the manner they deem necessary, usually with a minimum of formality.

[. . .]

The greater the interchange of personnel and interdepartmental collaboration between the departments and Treasury, the better the chance that they will
be able to accommodate their differing perspectives. But it would be vain to
believe that they will ever reach complete understanding. Departmental needs
for spending conflict with the needs of the Treasury for control. Their need for
predictability in spending plans confronts the Treasury's desire for adaptability in
managing the economy. Even the same need may carry a variety of meanings to
different institutions. To the Treasury, security denotes being protected against
surprise by sudden expenditures. To the spending departments, being secure
means they can go ahead with large, long-term schemes, confident that the
money will not suddenly be yanked away. There are real conflicts here and not
just failures of mutual understanding. Between the Treasury's abstract claims as
manager of the economy and the department's abstract claims as manager of the
subject matter, there must be a concrete resolution.

Important issues are at stake. Money and subject matter merge into public
policy as claims are made for limited financial resources. There is no limit to possible improvements in the quality and almost none in the quantity of government
activities, especially since the demands for public goods and services are likely to
grow with increased supply. Moreover, political administrators are paid to recognise not only unsatisfied demands but also areas of unmet need that may lack
clearly articulated demands. Practical answers to the question of when (timing),
how (standards), and what (priority) demands and needs can be addressed are
usually interwoven with winning the expenditure resources to act. A motorway,
prison-building programme or change in the school-leaving age may be accelerated or delayed for years. Policy makers have no standards for calculating the
ultimate utility of their programmes but can and do bargain over how far
improvements will be made in the performance measures of government itself:
numbers of nursery school places, miles of motorway, geriatric beds per 1,000
of elderly. [. . .]

Strategies and deals

Departmental participants in the expenditure process refer to it as one of
'constant haggling' and 'argy bargy'. Bargaining is incessant, and the Treasury
likes it that way. The Treasury does not and, as we have seen, knows it could not,
exercise control by giving flat 'no's' to the departments' proposals. If it did,
Cabinet meetings would bog down as departments bypassed the Treasury and,
worse yet, the Treasury would alienate its life-sustaining sources of trust and
information in the spending departments. Even when it is clear to Treasury
officials that general expenditure cuts are eventually going to be necessary, they
would rather begin by bargaining to find out where the 'give' is in the
departments' cases.

[. . .]

What do departments fight about with the Treasury? Almost everything at
the beginning. 'There is,' as a top Treasury official said, 'a necessary ritual dance.

He inflates to enable you to cut and you bargain him down to show you can cut.' Why do you need this much? This forecast is inflated; the time schedule is over-optimistic; that section is inconsistent; another item contradicts experience. Very often the margin of accuracy being argued back and forth between Treasury and department is narrower than that on which a small business would operate. Experienced bargainers know that despite any new sophisticated expenditure techniques what often matters is not the issue but the bargaining itself.

[. . .]

Strategies are what we call the department's efforts to increase or maintain its satisfaction. Both sides know, for instance, that efforts to secure stable increases can often be begun by commissions of inquiry made up of specialists in a particular field who naturally believe that their vocation should be supported at the public's expense. All such committees recommend increased spending. The process of inquiry itself generates articles in the press and papers in the more influential periodicals. Commissions make good forums for launching publicity campaigns. Though the Treasury may clamp down on a department which uses public funds to plead for more of the same, it is not difficult to find interested groups who will carry the burden in public. [. . .]

Departments make every effort to seize upon a cause that is popular in its day. Technical and vocational education expanded, explained one departmental strategist, because it could be tied to the popular economic growth argument. A single programme can serve diverse purposes. The truth may be bent, though not necessarily broken, by finding that one rationale, among others, that will meet the public mood of the moment. [. . .]

A favourite department strategy is targetry: to get a target established, by indirection if not by explicit ministerial statement, and seek to drive expenditures up to that higher level. The target may range from wishful thinking about how much money the department can spend to specific physical goals – so many houses, hospitals or miles of motorway by a certain date. Establishing goals for a lower pupil–teacher ratio, or a high standard of amenity in school design and construction, may be worth a great deal in the long run. [. . .]

Much bargaining is sufficiently stereotyped to have earned its own sobriquet. Departments propose offsetting savings which they know must be put back. Some officials call this 'the sore thumb' or 'beggar's sores' technique (you don't want to hit or touch it). The skilled practitioner agrees to offer compensatory savings but chooses items which are sure to reawaken painful memories of the political consequences that allegedly occurred the last time a cut was applied or proposed in this area.

[. . .]

Departments occasionally turn their acceptance of cuts into a strategic move. By sacrificing early rather than waiting 'you can cite your record of giving your ewe lamb for the general welfare'. But this is a temporary stance and generally department officials doubt that there is much goodwill to be gained by continuously accepting cuts without a fuss. 'If you're going to be helpful,' according to one experienced department negotiator, 'do it quickly and make a meal of it all at once.'

The following summary list of suggested practices for getting along with the Treasury, provided by several officials, would be accepted by most of their breed:

1   Consult early and thoroughly. Do not give the Treasury a proposal at the last minute and say that it has no consequences if it does.
2   Rather than trying to hide it, give the costs (in a sufficient depth of years) to show if there really is going to be a large charge.
3   Clear the line beforehand with other departments and show your awareness of the sideways effect of the proposal (e.g. if more staffing is required you'll look good to the Treasury if you show them you have cleared it with the Civil Service Department).
4   Send extensive information to the Treasury.
5   In trying to get more, preserve your credibility by dealing in reasonable negotiating margins.

What is at stake is not merely courtesy and bureaucratic decorum. Experienced members in the tightly-knit community value such rules of the game, for they are rules which help them contain very real conflicts and a game about deadly serious questions of public policy. Depending as they do on mutual confidence, political administrators are not likely to take advantage of the game, only play it. Caring as they usually do about the substantive issues, they will play it to the hilt.

One might think the most frequent Treasury move to counter departmental strategies is to have its minister, the Chancellor of the Exchequer, refuse requests for increased spending and carry his Cabinet colleagues with him. Treasury officials will settle for that if they must, but reliance on such overt force is not wise policy. A direct strategy bespeaks too much risk and exertion. Ideally the Treasury would prefer to circumvent all difficulties by having sufficiently inculcated norms of self-restraint in departments so as to mute the initial expenditure proposal.

[. . .]

Not all bargaining is incessant 'argy-bargy'. An occasional but important strategic move is, in effect, to declare a moratorium on strategic moves and to make a deal. By making a deal, the department can achieve a higher rate of growth than it might have had to settle for, together with the assurance that the new funds will not suddenly disappear during an economy drive. The Treasury guards itself against the possibility that a new programme or an expanding old one, if approved against its recommendations, will lack safeguards limiting its future growth. Each participant seeks stability in different directions. Each may be willing to take less than it might have done as the price of doing better and with greater assurance than could otherwise have been the case. The stage is set for a mutually advantageous arrangement.

[. . .]

The anatomy of a deal is worked out by parties that have a stake in reaching agreement. Suppose that the Treasury knows full well that a certain type of programme has been starved of funds and is likely to shoot up in the near future. The department hopes that it will but, having suffered unpredictable and erratic cuts in the past, would like to safeguard itself. Experienced department officials believe that, while their case is powerful, there is no limit on the improvement theoretically possible and, as they say, 'it is no good asking for the moon. Since everything cannot be done at once it must be done gradually.'

[. . .]

Underspending, transfers and delegation

[. . .]

The expenditure process contains built-in opportunities for Treasury intervention. These occur when a department spends less or more than the amount allotted to it, when it tries to transfer funds from one category to another, and when it seeks authority to make expenditure within certain limits without formal Treasury review. Though underspending, transfers and delegations appear to be technical financial topics, suitable only for desiccated accountants, these concepts involve institutional relationships that may well turn out to be decisive in determining a particular level of policy. The question of who has the right to spend may answer the question of what the money is spent on. Even if no policy differences result, the treatment of underspending, transfers and delegation tells us much about how the Treasury and departments keep conflict within bounds.

From the Treasury viewpoint, it is foolish to insist on maintaining every possibility for intervention. [. . .] The modern Treasury not only feels more confident of its collaborative closeness to departments, but also believes that cost consciousness can be best instilled by making departments more responsible for worrying about their own cost controls. By no means do all of the 'old sweats' accept this new orthodoxy, but most see the merits of the more subtle approach to getting your own way. Thus the Treasury tries to maintain rules that allot greater responsibility to departments while at the same time allowing its own men to move in when necessary.

The spending departments, for their part, always have an interest in seeking to increase their financial flexibility so long as doing so does not put them at a disadvantage. Departments like some margin over their actual spending expectations in order to protect themselves against overspending, even if this margin does eventually manifest itself in underspending. They find it convenient to transfer money around from one programme to another, making up underspending on one item with overspending on another; by so doing, they can lessen the requirements imposed on them for precision within each category and enhance their opportunities for adapting to new circumstances. [. . .]

Underspending

In a strictly impartial world, underspending and overspending would be but two equal faces on the same coin of uncertainty; unexpected extra expenses would always tend to cancel out unexpected savings. In the world as it is, this is by no means true. [. . .]

Underspending is always a subject of some amazement (if not amusement) to outsiders because they assume that departments have an interest in spending right up to the last pound. And so they do – to a point. One thing that frustrates this desire is the uncertainty of the real world. Money may become available too late in the year to set up the apparatus necessary to process and spend it. Men required to operate the programmes may be difficult to hire and appear too late to receive the portion allotted to their salaries. The material required may be unobtainable or have to be procured from abroad, subject to well-known delays. Should construction be involved there may be no end of difficulties in getting started and completing the work. [. . .]

These uncertainties are greatly multiplied when expenditure decisions are being assessed, not simply for the next year, but up to five years ahead. [. . .]

Underspending is not simply a function of uncertainty but also of the administrative practices of expenditure control. It is becoming more common largely because of incentives created by the emerging system of control – the control of overspending. To be sure, department officials do not like to underspend because 'You are in the dog house with the Treasury.' More important, according to a finance officer, is 'the danger that the Treasury will not be willing to give so much money the next time around'.

[. . .]

Overspending is strongly suppressed; underspending incurs mild rebuke.

One conceivable consequence of these differential incentives is that departments might 'water' their expenditure plans to leave a safety margin against overspending. [. . .] Treasury officials, who believe in 'tight estimating' as a creed, are confident of their ability to squeeze any such water out of the figures. 'That is known to [the departments] as well as it is to us.'

[. . .]

Transfers

Department officials are well aware that 'there is always a tendency to be optimistic about how quickly you will be able to spend your money'. Knowing that they have never yet managed consistently to come out just right, finance officers will try to get agreement with the Treasury that, if they overspend on some items and underspend on others, they can make transfers.

[. . .]

With some programmes, over or underspending can be accommodated without transfers by adjustments for subsequent years. In road building, for example, the Treasury recognises contracts as an appropriate balancing device, awarding more or less contracts the second year to balance under or overspending in the previous year. But most current expenditure programmes are not so conveniently governable and the Treasury official is left with his usual devices, among them trust, political sensitivity, and consistent argument.

Broadly speaking, the permissible scope of transfers will depend on the quality of the department's own controls and the nature of the expenditure. The former is a variation on the theme of trust; the discretion allowed in transfers will tend to vary with the Treasury's confidence in the internal controls of the department. With a poor departmental record of control, the Treasury will be, as one of its undersecretaries said, 'awkward and suspicious'.

The nature of expenditures involved in a transfer covers a variety of criteria. The Treasury watches hawklike for politically sensitive transfers. On the whole it is likely to accept the department's assessment of the substantive merits of the expenditures, but will object if 'for political or other reasons, the proposed savings transferred are likely to get put back when the yells and screams start'. Again, the Treasury disapproves of precedent creating transfers. Proposals which involve a once-and-for-all expenditure are likely to be allowed transfers. Other proposals (such as a switch from current to capital expenditure and thus eventually more current expenditure) allowing the department later to claim that something is 'established policy' are coolly received.

[. . .]

When is underspending (inability to programme money) really a saving (carrying out an activity at lower cost)? When is a transfer a blatant disregard of an agreement with Parliament and when is it a means of enhancing the public interest by spending where it will do the most good? The inability to answer these questions without long and acrimonious disputes, the suspicion on all sides that precious time is being wasted, the difficulty the Treasury experiences in rationalising its position, have all led to suggestions for delegating greater spending power to the departments. If they are responsible, why shouldn't they spend and be held accountable for the consequences? To answer that question, the Treasury must assert that it too has manifest needs – for money to save or re-allocate, for information by asking 'why', for power to make its preferences effective. Significantly, Treasury men have recognised that many of their interests are best served by increasing delegation.

[. . .]

Bargaining over delegated powers is important for department officials because it sets out the terms under which they will be able to make many future decisions. They seek delegated powers to help rather than hurt them. Only those in the Treasury who have been involved in the tough negotiations realise that public statements about the infinite desirability of delegation do not completely represent the position of all departments. After all, having lived with these regulations for years, there are bound to be people who have grown used to (and found ways around) them. They may be reluctant to change to the unknown. And, above all, the requirement of Treasury sanction is protective. When there is a chance that department officials will have to take more blame for restraint than they have done in the past, the abstract virtues of delegation pale.

[. . .]

Nowhere is the difference clearer between the public and private faces of expenditure community than in this question of delegation and Treasury sanction. One 'scores off others' (i.e. blames or otherwise uses fellow kinsmen and participants) on the inside, or at most at the fringes of the community, and not on the outside. The well-known doctrine of ministerial responsibility is only a special case of a much larger creed embedded throughout British government – the indivisibility of the Executive. In their public face, political administrators are thoroughly practised in making a splendid case for something they do not like. Among themselves, policy-makers find it easier to blame the Treasury, sometimes accurately but often to smooth the feathers of others inside the spending department.

[. . .]

Richard Rose

INHERITANCE BEFORE CHOICE
IN PUBLIC POLICY

From: Rose, R. (1990) 'Inheritance before choice in public policy', *Journal of Theoretical Politics*, 2:3, 263–291

POLICY-MAKERS ARE HEIRS BEFORE they are choosers. An individual must gain public office as a precondition of making public choices; only office-holders can make decisions that bind government. To enter office an individual must take an oath to uphold the laws of the land; these authorize public policies that are a legacy from decades or generations past. The content of the inheritance is not negotiable; it is a given, as durable as the statute books. A would-be office-holder may intend to introduce changes in this legacy, but a precondition of doing so is accepting, for the moment at least, the legacy of past administrations. The purpose of this paper is to explore the consequences that flow from this process of inheritance.

The outputs of government are not mere intentions, the preferences of temporary office-holders about what government ought to do. Outputs are what government does, that is, the *programmes* that constitute the goods and services of public agencies, such as paying social security benefits, building roads, or maintaining military defence. [. . .]

Programmes continue without regard to personalities or individual persons. By contrast, choices are discrete time-specific actions of individuals. However, individual choices take effect only in so far as they become institutionalized as commitments of public agencies. [. . .]

Much time of politicians is not spent in making choices, but in dealing with the consequences of inherited programmes that would not have been chosen by the current incumbents of office (Kaufman, 1981). In responding to these problems, policy-makers often endorse actions as 'lesser evils' forced upon them by commitments inherited from their predecessors.

Although inheritance comes before choice, it does not preclude choice. In the limited time the government of the day (or, in Washington terms, the Administration) is in office it can introduce some changes into the manifold of public programmes, and react to some novel situations without precedent or established commitments. Any measure that it introduces will continue having an impact after it has left office, becoming part of the legacy that its successors must accept. [. . .] Cumulatively, the limited choices that particular administrations make can produce big changes.

In order to think about the long-term course of public policy we must be aware of the importance of inheritance. Focusing upon the current choices of public officials, as in theories of public choice, confines attention to what is exceptional – the measures that immediately concern politicians who deal with matters of current controversy and the decisions that they can make. It neglects the many activities of government that continue by routine – and at any given time account for the overwhelming bulk of public expenditure.

[. . .]

The process of inheritance

Offices exist before individuals, and institutions give weight and authority to the actions of individual office-holders. Institutions do not change with the frequency of the government of the day. [. . .]

A social security clerk does not ask what the President or Prime Minister wants but whether applicants claiming cash benefits are entitled to receive the benefits that they claim. To determine this the clerk looks to rules and regulations, not election returns. The capacity of a government to run without any choices being made by elected politicians is routinely demonstrated in democracies with multi-party coalition governments. When a coalition collapses it may take a month for a new government to be formed; meanwhile, money is spent and taxes collected by the force of political inertia.

The legacy from the past

The legacy of a newly elected government consists of the accumulation of commitments made in previous decades, generations or centuries by *all* of its predecessors. Most public programmes continue indefinitely. Although the government of the day may repeal a few laws, most are left in place, and what were once new choices are added to an already substantial accumulation of previous commitments.

Britain is an extreme example of the inheritance of commitments from the distant past, given the uninterrupted exercise of parliamentary authority for many centuries. More than one-tenth of laws in effect at the beginning of the 1980s had been enacted *before* Queen Victoria ascended the throne in 1837, and more than one-third of contemporary legislation was on the statute book by the time her reign ended in 1901.

[...]

Programmes are carried forward by the force of political inertia. [...] Normally a new government enters office in the middle of a financial year; this delays the impact of its first full budget for up to 18 months. Time is needed to prepare new measures in a form that can be expressed in binding legislation and implemented by civil servants. A government with a stable parliamentary majority may have up to four years in office to add programmes to the legacy that it leaves. [...]

Most public expenditure today is devoted to programmes that are described in US budget documents as 'uncontrollable', because they are authorized by public laws and money must be appropriated to meet these continuing statutory commitments. Political inertia also raises the revenue to finance this expenditure, for most tax revenue is collected according to laws that long predate the government of the day. [...]

The legacy inherited by a newly installed government is non-negotiable. A new government must accept it, for the moment at least. [...]

Scope for choice

Once officials have understood the commitments that they have inherited, their next task is to identify the scope for choice in modifying its inheritance, changing the programmes that are directed toward established goals, or introducing new goals and programmes.

1   The inauguration of a new Administration creates expectations that a 'new' government will introduce new measures. Hence, a party that has prepared plans while in opposition can gain support for these new initiatives when its endorsement by the electorate is fresh in the minds of everyone. If it does not do so, then the longer it remains in office the more likely it is to be inhibited in making changes. [...]

2   The choice of personnel is a second way in which the government of the day can try to change established policies. Immediately after an election dozens of posts fall vacant at the top of government. There are many more opportunities to make appointments as retirement, death and resignation create vacancies. [...]

3   Budgets offer scope for choice at the margin. Given the scale of the budget in a mixed economy welfare state, a margin of a few percent amounts to tens of billions of dollars or billions of pounds, especially if a new government is in the fortunate position of inheriting a fiscal dividend of economic growth to use for increasing expenditure or tax cuts. Alternatively its legacy may be a growing deficit that forces an unwanted choice between raising taxes or cutting expenditure on popular programmes, or both.

4   Amending existing legislation by expanding the coverage of a programme or increasing the level of benefits assures that a choice is institutionalized, for the programme being amended is already in operation. The immediate effect of amendments to established legislation is usually small in relation to the totality of public policy. [. . .] However, an amendment can become a 'camel's nose', with its full-scale significance becoming gradually apparent. Indexing pensions was a decision which has added billions to the budget of successor governments, as pensions have automatically risen with inflation and economic growth (Weaver, 1988).

5   In the abstract, repealing legislation might appear a straightforward action but it is normally very difficult in practice because of the cluster of political interests and expectations that accumulate around established programmes. The government of the day accepts the great bulk of its inheritance of legislation, willingly or *faute de mieux*. Even when a British party votes against a bill in opposition, once in command of an absolute majority in Parliament it usually does not repeal laws that it had previously voted against. [. . .]

Every government introduces some new bills each year and novelty guarantees substantial political attention. In Washington, the President's lack of control of Congress means that an Act that a President signs may well be different from what the President would have chosen if he had been free to choose. In Britain the government of the day could use its parliamentary majority to push through controversial legislation of its choice; in fact, more than three-quarters of government measures are non-controversial Acts of Parliament. Non-controversial measures are less likely to be choices stamped with the values and preference of the government of the day; they tend to be the product of continuing negotiations between a Whitehall department and extra-governmental interests. They are measures for which the government of the day takes credit, even though it does not positively choose (that is, initiate) them (Van Mechelen and Rose, 1986; Jordan and Richardson, 1987).

Inherited programmes plus choices by the government of the day together constitute the Totality of Public Programmes (*TPP*). We can express this totality algebraically. At a given moment in time (*tn*), it is the sum of Inherited Policies (*InP*), from time past (*tn*−*x*), plus changes (*d*), in Inherited Policies introduced by the government of the day, plus New Policies (*NP*), introduced by the government of the day.

$$TPP_{tn} = InP_{tn-x} + d(InP) + NP \tag{1}$$

An advantage of thinking algebraically about the totality of public policies is that if budget expenditures are used to measure each type of programme one can identify with precision the relative weight of inherited programmes as against choices of the government of the day.

Leaving a legacy

Paradoxically, an administration has more time to exert influence after it has left office than while it is in office. A group of elected politicians have only a few years before they face re-election and possible defeat. Departure from office ends the opportunity to make fresh choices. But the influence of past administrations continues through what it contributes to the legacy left its successors. Just as a government entering office is highly constrained by its inheritance, so a government that has left office can determine in part what is done by its successors. [. . .]

Whereas the government of the day is on the receiving end of the process of inheritance, an administration no longer in office has given its successors a legacy that can endure. [. . .]

We can express the influence of a legacy algebraically by amending the first identity, so that time $n(tn)$ now represents the period when a specific Administration (As) was in office. In such circumstances public policy at a subsequent date ($tn + x$) is the sum of policies inherited by a given government, plus policy changes PC, introduced by the specific Administration and policy changes introduced by x successors ($As + x$).

$$TPP_{tn + x} = InP_{tn-1} + PC(As)_{tn} + PC(As + x)_{tn + x} \qquad (2)$$

When we view the totality of public policy dynamically, then we can identify both inheritance and choice; the distinction between the two depends upon the time-frame for analysis. A measure chosen by one administration becomes a part of the legacy of its successors. Every major programme is thus both a matter of choice *and* part of a legacy. An historian may regard the introduction of a novel social programme a half a century ago as an example of choice. But a contemporary policy-maker must treat it as an accomplished fact inherited from the past.

Testing the extent of inheritance

Given that the activities of every administration combine measures inherited from its predecessors and its own choices, the critical questions concern: To what extent are inherited programmes durable from one administration to another, and from one decade to another? To what extent can new programmes be introduced by the government of the day, and inherited programmes terminated? Since programmes differ greatly in their claims on public money, we must weigh as well as count them (Rose, 1988), asking also: Which type of programme – inherited or fresh choices – makes greater claims on the budget?

Hypothesis 1 (Fungibility). If inherited programmes are easily changed, then each government of the day should make substantial alterations in programmes and their appropriations.

Hypothesis 2 (Durability). If inherited programmes are durable, then the great bulk of programmes should continue through the years and account for the bulk of public expenditure.

In order to test these two competing hypotheses we need data about public expenditure at the programme level (Rose, 1985). Such data are rarely considered in studies of the growth of government. [. . .]

The routines of public expenditure provide the best source of data about programmes, for the sum of public expenditure is divided into hundreds of different allocations, each linked to a particular programme which is the responsibility of a particular department of government. Each budget line thus identifies a programme that receives public funding, has public officials to administer it, and laws that authorize it and state the conditions under which the programme can be operated and money spent. Each budget line is subject to the annual audit of sums spent, and a claim for the following year's expenditure is scrutinized within the agency responsible for the programme and by Treasury officials.

To test hypotheses about the duration of inherited programmes we need data for a much longer period of time than that reported in an annual expenditure review, a single Parliament or a single decade.

[...]

Durability of inherited programmes

Although we would expect the legacy of one government to survive more or less intact with its immediate successor, the greater the distance in time the less likely would inherited programmes be to survive, for the utility of a programme depends not only upon its intrinsic characteristics but also upon the larger environment of which it is a part. Thus, while the creators of a programme may be satisfied with its impact when it is initially implemented, changes in the world around it can stimulate re-evaluations, leading sooner or later to its abandonment. In other words, programmes that were good enough for the grandparents of the average Briton would not necessarily be suitable for the average person today.

When we examine government programmes in postwar Britain, programmes are remarkably durable, consistent with Hypothesis 2. Of the 118 different programmes that constituted the inheritance of the 1945 Labour government, more than five-sixths are still in effect more than four decades later; only nineteen had been terminated.

[...]

When we weigh programmes by their claims on public expenditure, durability is even more striking. Durable programmes accounted for £98.3bn in public spending in 1985. The average mean value of the nineteen terminated programmes was altogether £1.1bn, trivial by comparison with inherited programmes. In an average year the typical terminated programme accounted for little more than £50 m in current prices, and if all of them had remained in effect into the mid-1980s collectively they would have added only 1 percent to what is spent on programmes inherited from the distant past. Contrary to the rhetoric of fiscal conservatives, a government that inherits major spending commitments does not save a significant amount of money by scrapping programmes inherited from its predecessors.

Asymmetries of choice

A government that is free to choose can exercise choice in two contrasting ways: it can introduce new programmes and/or it can terminate programmes. In so far as the inheritance from the past is concerned, the government of the day terminates very few of these programmes. In so far as choice is symmetrical, then there would be little scope for the government of the day to introduce new programmes.

Theories of the growth of government assume the opposite: the choices of successive governments are expected to be asymmetrical, that is, far more new programmes are likely to be started than programmes inherited from the distant past are to be terminated. Inherited programmes are recognized as durable because they have significant support from those producing and benefiting from them; to attempt to repeal a programme would mobilize opposition from groups that expect it to continue. A government that introduces programmes that are high priorities of the majority party and its supporters can provide durable benefits, in so far as new programmes are routinely incorporated as part of the legacy of its successors.

The best grounds for a new programme to become durable are if it is chosen as a consequence of what Heclo (1974: 304ff.) calls social learning, that is, the accumulated experience of administrators and experts in a policy area. [. . .]

If each successive government can choose to add new programmes and rarely stop inherited programmes, then government can only grow. In so far as some programmes (and particularly new programmes) will not succeed, then each successive government will have to finance an increasing number of failures inherited from the past. Wildavsky (1979: Chapter 3) argues that past failures are not abandoned but serve as the excuse for introducing new programmes that are incorporated in the legacy of successive governments. He describes this as: 'policy as its own cause'. The cumulative result of such an asymmetry of choice would be an increasing amount of dead weight in public policy. As the dead weight increased it could threaten to crowd out the scope for new programmes to be introduced.

But if government makes choices under pressure, asymmetry could take an opposite form. In so far as new programmes of government are not the result of careful deliberation and the incubation of consensus but a response to immediate evidence of dissatisfaction, then they will be introduced as part of a process of trial and error. Simon's (1957) model of policy-makers as 'satisficers' can explain both the durability of inheritance and the fragility of new programmes. As long as there is not intense dissatisfaction with a problem that a programme addresses, it will persist. When unexpected and unwelcome events cause dissatisfaction, say, a big boost in unemployment or urban disorder, then policy-makers must search for new measures to dissipate dissatisfaction. Even if it does not know whether a measure will succeed, it must try to do something; actions are thus part of a more or less experimental trial-and-error process [. . .]. Another reason why new programmes may be likely to be terminated is if they are adopted as a response to crisis events (Polsby, 1984). A crisis programme may thus expire when the crisis passes.

In so far as choice occurs under pressure of dissatisfaction, then many new programmes would *not* be durable; they would be ad hoc responses, to be abandoned as and when it became evident that they were not dispelling dissatisfaction. Whereas Wildavsky's theory of policy as its own cause hypothesizes the irreversible expansion of public programmes, Simon's dissatisficing model of change by a process of trial-and-error predicts that the government of the day will be under pressure to introduce new programmes *and* to abandon those new programmes that fail to remove the dissatisfaction that prompted them.

[...]

The asymmetrical choices of British government show a trial-and-error pattern. New programmes are not continuously incorporated into the legacy of government; they are very fragile. [...] On average, for every three new programmes that the government of the day introduces it abandons two. Programmes inherited from before 1945 have been remarkably durable by comparison with those introduced in the postwar era; four times as many new programmes have been terminated as old line programmes.

[...]

The asymmetry of choice means that cumulatively the weight of inherited programmes is growing greater [...]. In 1945 a Labour government administered an inheritance of 118 peacetime programmes in its first full year of office. By 1979 the incoming Conservative government of Margaret Thatcher had inherited 227 programmes claiming £123bn. As the weight of the inheritance of the past increases, the relative significance of choice diminishes, for the new programmes that a government can introduce – and the extra money available to finance new programmes – is small by comparison with the legacy of past choices.

Conditions of choice and change

If political inertia explains the persistence of programmes from one administration to another, what explains such changes as the government of the day introduces to the legacy left its successors? Is it the nature of the party in office; the state of the economy; or differences between programmes dealing with life-long concerns as against changing market conditions?

Parties make no difference

The conventional logic of political choice in countries with popularly elected governments assumes that parties make a difference.

Hypothesis 3 (Parties matter). If a radical party is in office, it will choose to make more changes in public policy than a right-wing party.

Britain is unusual in that two parties have frequently alternated in office since 1945. It thus differs from countries where coalition government is more or less continuous, and those in which the same party almost invariably wins elections, such as Sweden or Japan. [...]

Yet the will of the party leadership is not the only influence upon public policies; there are some things stronger than parties (Rose, 1984: Chapter 8). A change in the governing party does not alter the effect of the international system upon the national economy. It only marginally alters the balance of pressure from groups whose co-operation is important to the success of many government programmes. In so far as the distribution of public opinion on an issue is unimodal, then an election result does not alter median preferences and values (Rose and McAllister, 1990). A change in the majority in the House of Commons is certain to change the names of Cabinet ministers, but it does not immediately alter the programmes for which they are responsible.

[...]

A change in party control of office can make some changes in the inheritance of public policy, but the extent of this change can easily be exaggerated. [...] Hypothesis 3 must be rejected. [...]

Inherited programmes grow faster when growth is anticipated

Changes in the condition of the economy ought to influence public policies by enlarging or contracting the fiscal scope for choice of the government of the day. If the economy is expected to grow, then the government of the day can introduce more programmes and increase expenditure more. When the economy is considered to be heading for difficulty, the government of the day may repeal more programmes and spending may increase more slowly or be cut.

Hypothesis 4 (Economic growth matters). The higher the expected rate of growth in the economy, the more programmes the government of the day will choose to introduce, and the more it will increase expenditure on inherited programmes.

Budgeting is prospective, involving choices in relation to expected future revenue; therefore, the expected rate of economic growth is particularly important for the choices of policy-makers. In a steady-state economy, future expectations will militate against fresh choices, but when the economy is buoyant this creates a climate in favour of introducing new programmes. Expectations of a recession create pressures for limiting new programmes and expenditure. The definition of the economic climate involves subjective judgments and forecasts formulated by policy-makers in anticipation of events, as well as objective statistics ascertained during and after a budget period (Mosley, 1984). It is a debatable question whether it is rational for politicians to expect growth, thus risking budgetary over-commitment, or not, thus risking unpopularity by squeezing resources for popular programmes and refusing to introduce new programmes.

[...]

Spending on inherited programmes would be expected to grow most rapidly when government anticipates growth, as policy-makers will want to claim political benefits from the anticipated fiscal dividend of a higher rate of economic growth.

[. . .]

Overall, the evidence supports Hypothesis 4, since the perceived economic climate influences the rate of increase in spending on inherited programmes. This does not mean the policy-makers can choose to expand spending whenever they like; they can only choose to do so if economic conditions appear favourable – and when they are not perceived as congenial, then this option is not possible. Furthermore, the great bulk of increased expenditure is devoted to programmes that the government of the day inherits from its predecessors.

Programmes matter

The government of the day inherits three different types of programmes: a limited number concerned with sine qua non activities that define the modern state, such as defence and the administration of justice and public order; economic programmes concerned with contingent and changing conditions in the market; and social programmes involving lifelong family concerns (Rose, 1976). In so far as programmes differ in durability, the likelihood of a programme remaining part of the ongoing legacy of government can be a function of attributes of programmes rather than a matter of choice.

Hypothesis 5 (Programmes matter).
(a) If programmes involve the sine qua non defining attributes of the modern state, they are likely to persist through inheritance.
(b) If programmes concern commitments integral to the life-cycle of citizens, they are likely to persist.
(c) If programmes concern changing market conditions, they are not likely to persist.

First in priority are programmes concerned with the *defining responsibilities* of the modern state, such as defence and law and order. Because these activities are of the essence of the modern state, we would expect little change in inherited programmes in this field – and this is the case. [. . .]

Social programmes make commitments throughout the life-cycle of individuals and families. Commitments to health care are life-time commitments; the median voter, age 40, expects to claim publicly financed care for upwards of 40 years, a period of ten or more general elections. The life-time of a person making social security payments extends for about 50 years from the first payments at age 16 to death. Education involves a child for a decade or longer, the duration of at least three Parliaments. A government that terminated programmes providing long-term or lifelong benefits for citizens would be disrupting plans that people have for their well-being throughout the life-cycle, such as their children's education, health care when needed and especially in old age, and income in retirement.

Social programmes are asymmetrical. Because they are part of the life-cycle (or even, life support) of ordinary people, they cannot be withdrawn but they can be expanded. [. . .]

The social programmes that claim the bulk of public expenditure today are inherited from past governments [. . .]. Hypothesis 5(b) is thus supported.

Although government has a continuing responsibility for the management of the economy, the logic of the *market* is very different from that of social programmes concerned with family and individual needs. The [. . .] extent of an economic cycle is only a few years, compared with 70 years in the life-cycle of an individual. Whereas needs for education, health care and income in old age are relatively predictable, the state of the economy a decade or more hence is not so predictable.

[. . .]

Whereas in social policy the government of the day inherits a legacy that it transmits virtually intact to its successors, public programmes concerned with the economy are contingent and fungible; hypothesis 5c is thus supported. When we view all the activities of government together, economic programmes appear deviant, for they often change, whereas the bulk of spending on public policy is devoted to programmes that the government of the day inherits from its predecessors and transmits intact in the legacy that it leaves to its successors.

Change without choice

Choice is purposeful: the model decision-maker makes choices in order to achieve an instrumental end. The object of choice is not activity for its own sake but the realization of an objective. We cannot understand choices without considering the intended end. By contrast, change may be unintended. Change can occur without decision-makers doing anything; it can occur because a programme is sensitive to alterations in the environment (for example, demographic demand for health care or fluctuations in foreign exchange markets) as well as to actions within government. The likelihood of unintended change increases the longer a programme persists through a process of inheritance, for the originator of a measure in 1910, 1930 or 1948 cannot anticipate the circumstances in which it will be in effect several generations later.

Ignoring long-term consequences

Policy-makers have many incentives to ignore long-term consequences. Harold Wilson was notorious for taking a media-oriented view of politics, concentrating upon what was immediately in the news, on the grounds: 'A week in politics is a long time'. White House media officials concentrate on tonight's TV bulletin, and let tomorrow take care of itself (Kernell, 1986). A politician who must run for re-election has limited incentive to worry about the problems that will face the next administration, if he or she is uncertain about being a member of it.

[. . .]

The behaviour of individual policy-makers is normally described as making incremental choices in a serial and disjointed fashion. Their choices are expected to have a short-term marginal effect upon a limited area of public policy, for example, increasing or decreasing spending on a given programme by a few percentage points in the year ahead (Braybrooke and Lindblom, 1963). The immediate consequences of a decision are important, for a policy-maker decides whether a measure is desirable after it is taken, not beforehand. If the immediate consequences are desirable, a decision can be maintained, and if not the course of action can be abandoned. The post hoc evaluation of consequences in the light of immediate feedback is an integral feature of incrementalism. Incrementalism also rejects the consideration of long-term consequences.

[. . .]

Yet choices taken without regard to their long-term consequences are not thereby made inconsequential; they can produce change without choice.

Change without choice occurs when the consequences of a series of actions lead to unexpected or unintended outcomes. [. . .] A historian interested in a long period of time, such as the Industrial Revolution or the Middle Ages, would think it meaningless to speak of a monarch or Pope collectively 'choosing' or 'deciding' feudalism or the Industrial Revolution. Changes occur as a cumulative consequence of many different activities. Even though some of these activities will reflect individual choice, the overall outcome will not be chosen by an individual or institution.

The longer the span of time and the more complex the network of cause and effect, the less probable it is to assume that the consequences of past choices have been anticipated. All the well-known arguments against rational synoptic decision-making are strengthened many times when the chain of causation extends over decades. [. . .]

Destabilization through inertia

Thinking of public programmes in terms of inheritance severely limits the scope for choice, but it does not rule out change, for inheritance is a dynamic process. [. . .] The possibility of making an impact 'downstream' in the river of time gives such choices as are made by the government of the day their long-term significance. Just as the mouth of the river collects many things that are not at its original source, so Total Public Policy in time *x* consists of far more than was intended by distant predecessors (see algebraic statement 2 above).

To understand how the inheritance of public policies leads to change without choice we can think of political inertia as an explanation of long term change in the collective actions of government. The theory of political inertia completes the logic of incrementalism, for while incremental theories of choice concentrate upon the immediate present, the timespan of concern to politicians, political inertia is about change through a substantial span of time. Viewing time as a lengthy and continuous process rather than as a series of ad hoc choices emphasizes the cumulative and unintended consequences of programmes that are inherited by one government of the day after another (Rose and Karran, 1987).

While a single decision by a particular policy-maker is an isolated event in time, its significance accumulates – going far beyond the control of the original proposer – when it is part of a continuing and cumulative process of government.

[. . .]

The choices of politicians introducing new programmes is not the primary cause of public expenditure quadrupling in real terms since 1946. New programmes account for less than one-third of the increase. Of the total increase of £100bn in public spending in the past four decades, two-thirds is accounted for by the growth in programmes inherited from before 1945. Since taxes are even more likely to persist through inheritance, this great increase in expenditure could be financed by the growth in revenue by taxes that had been inherited from an even earlier period (Rose and Karran, 1987: Table 5.1).

Whereas politicians can live from election to election, government is continuing. The inheritance of public policy is the cumulative sum of many actions taken by many governments, each carried forward by the force of political inertia. The greater the momentum behind a programme, the harder it is to slow down, redirect or stop it. [. . .]

References

Braybrooke, D. and Lindblom, C. E. (1963) *A Strategy of Decision*. New York: Free Press.

Heclo, Hugh (1974) *Modern Social Politics in Britain and Sweden*. New Haven: Yale University Press.

Jordan, A. G. and Richardson, J. J. (1987) *British Politics and the Policy Process*. London: George Allen & Unwin.

Kaufman, Herbert (1981) *The Administrative Behavior of Federal Bureau Chiefs*. Washington DC: Brookings Institution.

Kernell, Samuel (1986) *Going Public: New Strategies of Presidential Leadership*. Washington DC: CQ Press.

Mosley, Paul (1984) *The Making of Economic Policy*. Brighton: Wheatsheaf.

Polsby, Nelson (1984) *Policy Innovation in America*. New Haven: Yale University Press.

Rose, Richard (1976) 'On the Priorities of Government', *European Journal of Political Research* 4 (3): 247–89.

Rose, Richard (1984) *Do Parties Make a Difference?*, 2nd edn. London: Macmillan.

Rose, Richard (1985) 'The Programme Approach to the Growth of Government', *British Journal of Political Science* 15 (1): 1–28.

Rose, Richard (1988) 'The Growth of Government Organizations: Do We Count the Number or Weigh the Programmes?', in Colin Campbell and B. Guy Peters (eds)

Organizing Government, Governing Organizations, pp. 99–128. Pittsburgh: University of Pittsburgh Press.

Rose, Richard and Karran, Terence (1987) *Taxation by Political Inertia*. London: George Allen & Unwin.

Rose, Richard and McAllister, Ian (1990) *The Loyalties of Voters: A Lifetime Learning Model*. London: Sage Publications.

Simon, Herbert E. (1957) *Models of Man*. New York: John Wiley.

Van Mechelen, Denis and Rose, Richard (1986) *Patterns of Parliamentary Legislation*. Aldershot: Gower.

Weaver, Kent (1988) *Automatic Government: the Politics of Indexation*. Washington DC: Brookings Institution.

Wildavsky, Aaron (1979) *Speaking Truth to Power: the Art and Craft of Policy Analysis*. Boston: Little, Brown.

PART TWO

Governance contexts

INTRODUCTION

IN THE LAST DECADE, governance has become a pervasively important term in policymaking. In the most general terms, it refers to the overall direction, regulation and coordination of a system, and the structures and processes through which these are achieved. But this can mean very different things in the context of different academic disciplines. In management and organization studies, for example, 'governance' refers to the role and functioning of the board of directors or trustees whose responsibility is to oversee management and the audit and reporting that ensure continuing external legitimacy. By contrast, for sociologists the governance of societies is a far broader concept, generally achieved through some combination of hierarchies, markets and networks; and hence for them government, as we have come to understand it, is only one mode of governance.

In political science and policy studies the term has been embraced as part of the effort to comprehend what is happening to the roles and functions of government, and in particular the ways in which governments increasingly work with and through other agencies. The nature of these changes, and the reasons for them, are explored in the readings in this part. In general, they concern forces that cannot be easily contained within the jurisdictional limits of the nation-state. In the late 20th and early 21st century, one of the most important of these developments has been globalization. In the face of environmental degradation, disease pandemics, significant demographic change and immigration, greater political risk and conflict, the capacity of the state may be found wanting. Moreover, state institutions are seen as insufficiently accountable and responsive to greater public demands. These factors open up institutional gaps in government, which governance arrangements and practices are seen to fill in a number of public policy fields.

Globalization does not just influence economic and cultural factors. It also impacts governments very directly. Indeed, in public policy, globalization is both a variable and a parameter. That is, it is firstly a direct part of the process of policy formulation in addressing issues that originate outside and impact across national borders. Second, globalization places a constraint on national governments in the exercise of public policy. It is within this changed environment – where the legitimacy and capacity of public bodies has regularly been challenged – that Drache's *The Return of the Public Domain* makes a significant contribution. His starting point is that the ideological and policy dominance of the market as *the* organizing principle and mechanism is coming to an end. With hindsight, the high water mark of the neo-liberal political project was probably achieved in the 1990s, in the years of the 'Washington Consensus'. Since then its political and intellectual credibility has been tarnished by the consequences of the policies it inspired (such as the post-marketization economic meltdown in Russia, financial crises in the Far East, gathering resistance to the WTO agenda, Enron and other de-regulation fiascos). During this time too the problem of 'failed states' attracted greater attention, making it obvious that less government is not always better, and raising stark questions about the importance of institutional capacity and civil society. John Kay's (2003) *The Truth About Markets* provides an elegant, authoritative but devastating critique.

Nevertheless, discredited ideas tend to go on holding sway until something clear, credible and coherent is available to replace them. In that context, Drache is one of a number of writers trying to formulate a theory of the public domain, and a justification for public action, that is appropriate to the new global realities. Many of the issues he refers to are explored further in other readings.

Reading 7, *Governance at Three Levels*, reviews the challenges to traditional structures of government and, in particular, the displacement of state power and control upward, towards international actors and organisations; downward, towards regions, cities and communities; and outward, to institutions with autonomy from the state. By exploring the changes taking place at these different functional and spatial levels, the authors highlight the different conclusions that can be drawn about the power of the state. Theirs is a positive view, that the state is still strong but configured differently.

Colin Crouch in Reading 8 looks at the complex relationship between the state and economic governance. As he points out, maintaining the free market economy, espoused by neo-liberals, requires a strong state to underwrite its unfettered operation. The different forms of the state and its changing role has to be understood in the context of complex systems of governance if the social democracy is to survive the challenges posed by globalization and the general subscription to market solutions to public policy process.

The greatest challenge to attempts, like Drache's, to re-define and re-affirm the public domain is how the inroads of globalization can be managed within local and national conditions and environments. But what *is* this elusive spectre that now haunts most discussions of public policy and governance renewal? Reading 9, *Globalization: What's New? What's Not? (And So What?)*, dissects this much hyped concept. The authors usefully distinguish four forms of globalism: *economic globalism; military globalism; environmental globalism; and social and cultural globalism*. They also point to globalization's long history, distinguishing 'thin' and 'thick' globalization in terms of the degree of connectedness and interdependence in the world. In the former case, the trading relations between Britain and its empire in the 18th and 19th centuries could be characterised as a 'thin' form of globalization. In the latter case, the scale and scope of global financial markets and their interactions with the regulatory duties of the state is suggested as a 'thick' form of globalization. Together these concepts bring some analytic clarity to the discussion, as well as suggesting implications for governance on a global scale.

In Reading 10, *Taking Embedded Liberalism Global: the Corporate Connection*, John Ruggie looks at the inclusion of the corporate sectors in networks of governance for addressing global issues and problems. 'Embedded liberalism' refers to the institutional basis of the Bretton Woods system of international economic and financial transactions which lasted from the end of World War 2 until the early 1970s. Essentially, this was a 'social bargain' whereby in return for the general acceptance of the discipline of economic liberalism in international trade, nation-states provided comprehensive welfare systems for their citizenry. So liberal economic policies were embedded in (and tempered by) national systems of social security. This social bargain was associated with a long period of stable economic growth, full employment and low inflation – but gradually unravelled, giving way to the neo-liberal project of the Reagan and Thatcher years. Ruggie – who coined the term embedded liberalism – explores the prospects for incorporating international business interests into policy networks that could be the basis of more stable and long-lasting institutions of global governance. He looks at developments in corporate social responsibility (CSR) and how this concept has increasingly informed the practice of large trans-national and multinational corporations. Top-down governance, in this view, could be balanced by grassroots activism over environmental and employment rights on a global scale, through the medium of CSR.

This raises the question of how public participation can be incorporated into these complex forms of governance, a theme developed more explicitly and in very different ways by Readings 11 and 12. Pierre and Peters' discussion centres on three different philosophies of citizen involvement in governance – communitarianism, deliberative democracy and direct democracy. They focus on the principles of each and their solution for the problems of governance, as well as their relative strengths and weaknesses. Although they are all difficult to realize in practice, particularly at the level of societies as a whole, the discussion clarifies important issues in the debates about reforming policy processes in order to bring about more active citizen involvement. Beresford's discussion of public participation hones in on the role of public and service users in social policy and, in particular, the 'ownership' of social policy and 'who, and what play a central part in conceiving and constructing it'. As a long-term user of mental health services himself, Beresford has written extensively and critically on this subject and in this reading, he critiques both government policy and academic writing on social policy and user involvement in the UK. Despite attention to issues of participation, partnership and empowerment in government policy, he questions the extent to which this is happening in practice and also the language used to describe service users, patients and the public.

The common starting point for all the readings in this part is that governance is a broader concept than government, one that encompasses distributed, multi-level and indirect forms of coordination and control. Understood in these terms, the structures and processes of governance provide the context for policy work. They determine who is involved, and on what basis – and thus they are vital in providing the continuity and societal legitimacy for policy processes. Yet, as these readings all also make clear, at the same time and perhaps as never before, these governance contexts are themselves evolving, uncertain and contested.

REFERENCE

Kay, J. (2003) *The Truth About Markets: their genius, their limits, their follies*. London: Allen Lane.

Daniel Drache

THE RETURN OF THE PUBLIC
DOMAIN AFTER THE TRIUMPH
OF MARKETS

From: Drache, D. (2001) 'The return of the public domain', *The Market or the Public Domain, Global Governance and the Asymmetry of Power*, Chapter 1, Routledge

Rethinking governance

IT APPEARS THAT NOT only the state, as an organizing entity, but the public domain – the non-tradable social goods sector that exists in every society – is ready to make a come-back (Albert 1993). The current crisis of neo-liberalism has put on the agenda the need to move beyond the Washington consensus and its belief in the frictionless operation of markets. What needs specification and development is the modern notion of the public as an instrument of governance. Even if governments in the past have been reluctant to share decision-making with the public, at the present time government needs to find ways to empower citizens in order to improve public services, reduce public bads and introduce new regulatory instruments to act as a counterweight to global instability.

[. . .]

In theory, modern states have long recognized the social-binding importance of maintaining strong public domains. However for many experts, the public domain is not seen in these terms and is confused with the drive to reduce, in stark ways, the public sector. Specifically, they accept the requirement to curtail public expenditure, limit the perceived increase of government regulation of the economy and look to enhance the performance of the economy by a dramatically smaller, competitive-minded state presence (Schultze 1977).

[. . .]

The question that merits examination is the very notion of the public domain as an incipient concept with its overlapping and multiple dimensions (see Figure 6.1). In the public mind at the neighbourhood level, the public domain is synonymous with the public park, the skating rink, the local library, music halls, art galleries, bus and subway routes and the local post office. Beyond the local community exist other and more important sets of interdependencies. The most important are the public spheres, which are the sites of political life, democratic values, institutions and debate, as well as the provider of public services that form a broad notion of citizenship entitlement with the corresponding legal, political and social rights. The assets that are shared and used in common cover a diverse group of subjects, including the environment, information, health and education. It also includes civic engagements of responsibility, none of these are simple commodities to be bought and sold. In the new world order, conventional measures of government intervention often fail to capture the complexities of mixed economies and, particularly, ignore the contribution of this 'wider public domain' in maintaining political stability and economic growth in the face of significantly expanded markets and declining regulatory measures (Albert 1993).

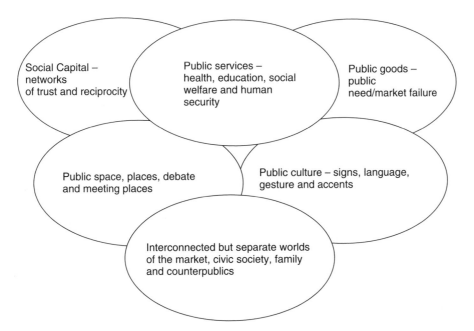

Figure 6.1 The overlapping and multiple boundaries of the public domain
Source: Drache 1999.

Political economists have as yet to find a way out of this impasse despite an impressive array of evidence that there is a *very large terrain between atomized civil society and state dominated public practice.* Public authority also needs to adopt a more realistic view of governance, one that is not premised on simplistic ideas about the power of markets. At a time of unprecedented interdependence, governments have to promote collective goals and revitalize public institutions.

[. . .]

The basic issues are, what are the public domain's chief characteristics after the apparent triumph of markets? Why has it re-emerged at a time of globalization? What is its genealogy in the literature of political science, economics and urban sociology? Why does its expansion and reinforcement matter? And finally, what are its prospects as a strategy of public policy in a post-Washington consensus era?

[. . .]

The return of the public domain: an older valued concept of policy-making

Despite the triumph of markets, there is nothing inevitable in the return of the public domain. If a revitalized notion of the public domain seems not on the radar screen of the public, the more pressing problem is that there is no clear consensus any longer of what the public is or consists of. At one time there was broad agreement when one said 'this concerns the people as a whole', 'done or existing openly', 'provided by or concerning local or central government', as in public money; public records; public expenditures or 'involved in the affairs of the community, especially in government' but no longer. Increasingly, the public is a permanent entanglement of bureaucratic and private interest, as in 'becoming a public company'. The regulatory role of public authority is much diminished with respect to health, education, finance, trade and culture.

[. . .]

So at a time when the public is at an all time low esteem, what is the public domain? Is there a case for reviving a concept? Do we need it at all? Political theorists have long recognized the importance of the public as a constitutive part of public policy-making. However, I do not intend to use public domain as a term of art to be defined mainly by reference to authoritative texts. Rather it needs to be thought of as an incipient but evolving concept which requires constant redefinition. It is important to stress that the 'public domain' is not a synonym for 'state', though sometimes the state is, in fact, the most obvious means of advancing public purposes. Instead it is meant to underline the fact that by whatever means they are achieved, many purposes, values and social goals – are inescapably *public.*

Conceptually consider it as follows. The public domain is the fourth element that abuts on civil society. It is the legal creation of the state when markets exceed their existing boundaries and it provides society with basic and complex needs. Its pedigree is long, having its roots in modern economic, political, social and legal thought. If one were to try to envision where the public domain is in relationship to the rest of the social order, we can see its place quite clearly. It is one of the centres of decision-making that allows society to organize itself, plan for consumption and support a mix between non-negotiable goods, mixed goods and negotiable goods. From it emanates the set of processes essential to a stable social order and a cohesive society.

If the state, market and civil society remain the great institutional markers of modernity, the public domain is at the intersection between civil society – largely norm-based, decentralized and hierarchically flat, the market – subject to the constraints and opportunities of the universal price mechanism, private property rights and corporate profit-taking and the modern administrative state – dependent on its full-bodied bureaucracy, large-scale financial resources and vast legal powers. It is a large irregular space covering a range of activity and organizations that belong to the public, as a whole, having flexible borders, expanding and contracting in size, driven most by need rather than by any fixed notion of rights.

[. . .]

For political theorists, it speaks of the ethic of public responsibility – community networks of trust and social solidarity are some of the distinguishing features that have been attributed to it. The public domain is about assets that are shared, and hence, there is also a strong redistributive imperative defining the boundary between the state and the market. These collective assets, outside the reach of private property and the market price mechanism, have been part of the standard tool kit of modern economics and political science. [. . .] Mainstream economics identifies the public domain merely with the consumption of public goods (Stiglitz 1988; Buchanan 1975). What makes this concept of public goods limited is that it undervalues the intricacies needed for the creation and consumption of such complex goods by all citizens and stakeholders. Since these 'social goods' belong to all members of society, in theory, their benefits are to be shared by all irrespective of private need.

[. . .]

Economists are only now beginning to rethink this fundamental issue. [. . .] While many economists do believe that these kinds of equity/governance issues are part of economics, public distributional questions need their own theoretical reiteration. It is for this crucial reason that we must realize that the notion of the public domain derives from an older view of the market economy, one premised on the idea that markets are not all encompassing and that civil society involves a critical non-market sector; part private and part public.

[. . .]

For political economists, the concept of public goods demands an equally powerful explanation. The rapid growth in public goods for infrastructure, and later education and health, in all countries, is due principally to the growth of complex public needs rather than the exigencies of market failure. [. . .] Outside of the industrial world, the state is not the instrument of last resort but is a primary mover, in developing countries and social market ones as well (Schonfield 1964; Prebisch 1971; Crouch and Streeck 1997). The fact is that state-provided services are most frequently a response to the need to curb the socially destructive rent-seeking behaviour of private actors (Coase 1960). The state is required to use its unique powers to organize the provision of social goods and resolve problems of collective action that private property regimes, with their short-term interests, cannot address.

[. . .]

The return of the public: some empirical evidence

For governments who are looking at new policy ideas and principles to better grasp the contradictory dynamics of markets and to find ways to strengthen the international order, the strategic notion of the public domain is not to be confused with the Keynesian welfare state that boldly appropriated the public domain as a governance instrument. During the four decades following the Great Depression, governments had little difficulty demonstrating their capacity to regulate markets, promote growth and keep social inequality within strict limits. At present, markets are taking their revenge. Financial institutions decide which state policies are acceptable and which are not (Boyer and Drache 1996).

It is no accident that new global players have made efficiency the universal belief of all major corporations and most leading industrial powers. In this view, capital has to be free to move across national boundaries if the world economy is to recover its past *élan* (OECD 1998). Firms have to learn to reorganize their production to take advantage of the new opportunities. People are expected to adapt and accept new employment conditions, to accommodate a world where business is no longer bound by national borders. With all these dramatic changes to the social fabric of nations, governments have used market-like incentives, such as taxes, transfer arrangements, as well as fiscal policy to convert 'public goals into private interests' (Schultze 1977).

[. . .]

Government spending, as a percentage of GDP, has grown and has kept on growing even in those countries where government spending is not large. The trend is towards bigger government, not statelessness, and this trend has been almost universal (*The Economist*, 20 September 1997). When one examines where governments are spending in industrial countries as a group, public spending only fell in one category – that of public investment – from an average of 3 per cent of GDP to 2 per cent. By contrast, transfers to persons rose consistently; transfers to business increased as well and spending on interest and debt doubled. What these numbers tell us is that in all jurisdictions, public services are a primary site of public culture. Income support benefits to the unemployed, the disabled, single parents and the elderly are the most important causes for state expansion. Services such as education, health and social transfers, as well as defence and law and order, remain the work of government.

[. . .]

In the aggregate, government outlays of the most powerful countries have not declined as predicted, averaging 50 per cent of GDP in 1995. Only in 1990 was there a significant decline when the global crisis brought national growth to a standstill. Government spending in the aggregate recovered by 1995 when markets were supposed to be triumphant and the state in full retreat. [. . .] In this complex world of state–market relations, the social market economies Austria, France, Germany, Italy and Sweden have not experienced any contradiction between their commitment to trade liberalization and their long-standing domestic institutions. [. . .] The Netherlands and Belgium have the most open economies in the world and their government spending has increased as they remain committed to their social programmes.

[. . .]

A larger but smarter state?

Market driven globalization has paradoxically created a larger state and also the need for a smarter one with more institutional capacity. So when one looks closely at the increased government expenditures, where is the money going? Debt interest repayment is the first reason that governments are spending more. The second is that social security spending has increased almost everywhere. In the case of Sweden, social spending rose modestly from 22 per cent to 25 per cent and this contrasts sharply with the UK, where spending shrunk by 3 per cent over this period. Contrary to popular perception US spending actually rose from almost 20 per cent to 23 per cent of total government outlays. Sometimes governments are cutting back their individual contributions to certain pro-grammes, such as unemployment insurance, as in the case of Canada, but in other areas they continue to maintain their programmes.

[. . .]

The big picture story is that most of the variance among OECD countries is explained by one factor, namely social transfers to the working age population, which represents on average 7.25 per cent of GDP, more than double what they were in 1960.

[. . .]

The system differences between social market, Anglo-Saxon and developing countries are large and, in fact, larger than indicated by even these state spend-ing patterns or other conventional economic indicators. Experience demon-strates that markets have to be supported by extensive public interventions of a complex variety. Markets left on their own cannot deliver optimal results, except for standard kinds of commodities and then only under certain conditions. It is not easy to correct for the so-called externalities that enable firms to produce goods without paying the full costs.[1]

Society needs public institutions with the capacity to ensure that private actors disclose the needed information for corrective action. Without strong regulatory enforcement there is little evidence that new competitive conditions are likely to correct this market deficiency (Boyer 1999). Finding the vital ingredients for a sustainable social order requires a different kind of engagement at the state level.

[. . .]

Public services/market opportunities

For many, the public domain is often identified narrowly with state-provided services, but for good reason. The welfare state reform changed forever our perception of what is public and what is private. [. . .] Private refers to the property rights of the market and domestic personal and intimate matters. By contrast, 'the public' denotes state services accessible to everyone; the institutionalization of shared common social concerns and, most importantly, the public interest or common good. The revolutionary ideal of Keynesianism was that the public sphere would establish relations of solidarity through redistribution and a large role for the state in the economy and it aimed to create a unified public realm primarily around the delivery of services. For this, the state had to grow and have the resources at its command to deliver universal health care, full employment and a range of other social policies and safety nets.

[. . .]

Still, compared to its immediate predecessor the Washington consensus has failed at a more basic level.[2] It drove a large policy wedge between the public and the private and promised much in terms of economic benefits with few political costs. Its most important claim is that countries which open their borders, regardless of the cost and consequences, will derive a high standard of living, due to cheaper goods, stronger industries and more jobs. In theory all of this results in strong efficiency gains from better economic performance of industry and economy. Countries will automatically move up-market and produce more sophisticated products that require skilled labour, which in turn commands higher wages. Consumers will benefit because goods will be cheaper and hence disposable income will go further and effective demand will strengthen. The reality for many countries has not been these dynamic gains from trade but the asymmetrical benefits from participating in the world economy.

[. . .]

So the pivotal belief has proven more often wrong than right. The incentives of free market price signals have not promoted the virtuous cycle of individual, self-seeking behaviour that neo-classical economies had predicted.

[. . .]

The policy implication of the above is that cutting back the welfare state or labour market deregulation is unnecessary to remain competitive in the new era. So the welfare state is being transformed not dismantled from a European perspective, the contrast with the Anglo-American experience is stark. The deficit reduction targets followed by Canada, Australia, New Zealand and the US have led to an under-investment in health, education and infrastructural spending and has precipitated a supply-side crisis in public and collective goods. This crisis of confidence is far from being resolved in the industrialized world and in the developing countries the return to a pre-Keynesian past of social disparity in access to income, wealth, power and public goods has reached new heights. Structural reforms have increased the influence of creditors, shareholders and international financial institutions to the detriment of workers, governments and communities (Mattoso 2000).

[. . .]

It is during a period of unprecedented globalization that the state always has a unique role in the provision of public services, particularly those critical for promoting social and economic development. The modern welfare state was born, in the first great wave of globalization, at the turn of the twentieth century. As Marquand notes, the great achievement of modern state craft has been to carve out from the private and market domain a public domain and 'to erect strong barriers against inevitable excursions into it'.

[. . .]

Critically, a new public space and an even larger private world are emerging as jobs and work culture adapt to the new competitive circumstances. So is the explosion of private wealth, epitomized by the chaotic activity on the trading floor of the stock exchange, itself the most public of places, regulated by the state and driven by the passions of untrammelled individual self-interest. Most commentators focus only on these transnational actors and their demand for investment entitlements but equally important are questions about the reconstitution of citizenship, globalization and relations with civic society.

[. . .]

Public space/private worlds

For many, the public domain is synonymous with public space, a set of real places, a code of public conduct with concrete forms and places. It is the terrain left between private holdings and the connective tissue of social agreements that bind people together (Kuntsler 1996). Specifically, urban space belongs to particular groups of people. [. . .] All public space requires a large degree of public subsidization to be maintained and to pay the wages of police, gardeners and maintenance personnel of all kinds. Without this service infrastructure public space deteriorates (Walzer 1986; Zukin 1995; Mumford 1986). In Lefebvre's terms, public space has to strike and maintain a proper balance between its use value for citizens and its exchange or commercial value for business. This is also why public space is never solely public but is always a mix between public and private use.

[...]

In recent times, strong public domains have been a powerful instrument against globally anchored forces in order to preserve ethnic, working-class and counter-cultural neighbourhoods. Cultural and commercial life will always exist side by side. Elites with their vast resources always have the greatest possibility to mould public culture. In cities, the shape of public culture is largely effected through the building and development of the city's public spaces in stone, concrete, steel and glass. As well, public culture is linked, through the architectural design of buildings, in many different ways to social identity and the social control of space (Zukin 1995).

[...]

In this contest to appropriate public space for private need, the modern city inevitably becomes a site of policy contest and confrontation. It has to choose between mega-shopping centres and malls in the suburbs or more freeways – the exit option – or full-scale urban renewal of the commercial and city centre – the voice and identity option. In terms of infrastructure, modern cities can favour industrial zones and parks, as well as satellite business districts outside the city centre linked to airports and auto-routes.

[...]

Municipal and sub-national state centres of decision-making have to determine their priorities too. They can contract out public maintenance provision, such as garbage and other vital services; impose user fees and tougher welfare rules that mean fewer recipients and lower benefits to low income families, as well as impose additional personal and property taxes. In this vision, the city becomes the dominant site of a powerful commuter culture dependent on the freeway and the private car with the suburbs weakly linked to downtown. It will be an urban environment with few social services or public housing.

[...]

The manifold meanings of the public have particular importance both nationally and for the great capital cities. In the singular, it is always synonymous with the primacy of public life in all its complexity. Public space is one of the essential sites of political community, defined as the common activity of urban/national life in all its different facets – commerce, the family and work – connected by the shared experience that these communities construct and establish. Political community is also held together by the substantive idea of the common good. Common goods and services, shared values and democratic commitments resulting from city and national planning, local resources and the provision of public goods and services by local and national authorities are part of this. The public sphere also has its own defining characteristics. It is the idea of communal space for shared activity with common values and commitments. At a time of globalization the city is the prototype of social interaction in which commercial need is forced to accommodate the democratic life of the city.

It requires the co-existence of the public and private realm and this interdependence masks the separate spheres of private need and public interest.

[...]

Public discourse/a strong or weak public

In political theory, the public sphere is the site of debate, political life and public discourse.

[...]

Fukuyama defines civil society as the 'realm of spontaneously created social structures, separate from the state, that underlie democratic institutions. "Culture" is defined as phenomenona such as family structure, religion, moral values, ethnic consciousness, "civic-ness" and particularistic historical traditions' (Fukuyama 1995).

[...]

These transnational networks of competing moral values, environmental conciousness, civicness have not resulted in over-arching agreement about the public realm and the common good. In part this is because there is no single coherent left–right political agenda in the way there once was. The political spectrum used to be organized around left and right poles. On income distribution, the left wanted a lot and the right as little as politically feasible; on the role of the state versus private ownership, the left believed in a large role for government and the right advocated a large and expanding role for private ownership. With respect to labour protection, the left advocated strong labour enhancing measures and entitlements, while the right wanted only minimal standards and practices.

[...]

So what has changed? In many forums, identity politics now cuts across this once fixed and rock-solid political, undercutting any sharp left/right divide of times past. Identity politics is organized around a different set of issues and concerns. The most important are the group versus the individual with respect to gender, race and ethnicity. Identity politics is about minorities seeking self-determination against established majorities, as in Quebec, Scotland and Spain. In a global context, identity politics has redefined cultural policy along with the rights of people to restrict the movement of global capital and halt the intrusiveness of trade agreements, regionally and globally.

[...]

Social capital – collective networks of trust and reciprocity

In the post-national state of the 1990s, social capital is increasingly considered to be a 'new' public good. However, the collective engagement of responsibility has long been part of Western democratic values. Many of these non-traded goods are non-transferable public freedoms, rights and public accountability (Albert 1993). Social capital, including collective engagements of solidarity, trust and legitimacy, epitomizes the commitment of the collective need to enhance social cohesion. Rights of the citizen, delimiting trade agreements and divergent social practices, at a time of increased social polarization, are part of the social process globalizing the *civitas*. Devolution of decision-making, the delivery of services at the city level and new information flows at a time of spatial and class polarization, all depend on networks. Putnam defines social capital as 'referring to features of social organization, such as networks, norms, and trust, that facilitates coordination and cooperation for mutual benefit' (Putnam 1993: 35–6).

[. . .]

The generic idea of the public domain has always been a powerful mainstream and alternative discourse that empowers individuals and groups. It is a narrative of potentiality and collective action because of the assets, experiences, places and concerns people share in common. The public domain is a key factor protecting and reinforcing social cohesion in the face of relentless market demands, which intrude on the world outside the market. In a primary sense, it always has a strong element of delimiting investment rights and ensuring that markets have a broad social purpose. As well, it highlights a view of public life and action that is not state-centred but is quite independent of it, even if the moving boundaries of the public domain are often dependent on the state for public services paid for out of public revenues. At a time when big government has appropriated the concept of the public for its own needs and agendas, the public domain represents a new grammar of policy conduct or what has been called 'tougher notions of public space'.

[. . .]

Society has always had need of well-constructed institutions where the rules and principles of contending interests can reconcile conflicting parties without giving any single group the power to make their views and interests always prevail over those of all others. Today there are many areas of public life where the need to limit the intrusion of markets is already on the public's agenda.

[. . .]

In many domains the fundamental notion of the citizen has been transformed into a passive, consuming client of state services. This transformation distorts democratic expectations and obligations in serious ways. Increasingly, electorates are critical of their government's failure to reform its practices and address the costs of social exclusion (Hutton 1996; Dahrendorf 1995). The dysfunctional behaviour of markets and the need to reinforce the role of intermediary institutions that limit the power of markets over people brings us full circle.

As an economic principle, the public domain emerges as a robust idea involving public goods problems, despite the fact they have fared poorly at the hands of the neo-classical framework. Public goods have always been a social necessity and socially constructed, but the precise relationship between non-negotiable goods, mixed goods and negotiable goods is inevitably complex, difficult to untangle and not well understood. Market failure is but one catalyst for action and explains little about public goods and the need for effective public goods structures (Cornes and Sandler 1994).

[. . .]

The public domain has not always existed in its present form. It was created in the nineteenth century as part of a larger political project that was to enhance the security of the elites and be a privileged site of the middle classes. With the passage of time it has been democratized and transformed in ways that few could have predicted. The pivotal question for today is what determines where the markers lie between the public and private? Historically, the public domain has always expanded and contracted as civil society and the market have each sought to appropriate the assets held in common for strikingly different ends.

[. . .]

Today there is no agreement to replace the Washington consensus. [. . .] Yet, as we have seen, there is not one, but a range of alternatives on offer. As policy-makers revisit the fundamentals of governance through the prism of the public domain, there are some grounds for optimism. The public domain is an older concept of political economy that supplies civil society with its vitality and much of its organizational capacity. Building state capacity, revitalizing public institutions, promoting collective goals and empowering citizens, all require an activist state model.

[. . .]

Notes

[. . .]

1   Of course, there are major differences between national regimes and between high and low spenders. What seems to be the determinant are eligibility requirements. A full-scale welfare regime defines this broadly and a more narrowly conceived one makes the individual responsible for his economic well-being. In 1992, in The Netherlands, 12.7 per cent of trend GDP was spent on transfers to the working-age population; in sharp contrast the figure for Japan was 1.2 per cent. Even these figures have to be taken with a grain of salt because tax systems also have a strong redistributive effect on low-income and high-income earners.

2   The Washington consensus was seen to be comprehensive but it left open many critical areas of macro-management where countries could pursue their own policies. Areas of non-agreement included the stabilization of the business cycle, the proportion of the GDP spent by the public sector and social policy, the need to eliminate indexation and the usefulness of incomes policy and wage/price freezes. Not surprising public authority chose to interpret its broad objectives so dissimilarly.

Bibliography

Albert, Michael (1993) *Capitalism vs Capitalism*, New York: Four Wall Eight Windows.
Benjamin, Roger W. (1980) *The Limits of Politics: Collective Goods and Political Change in Postindustrial Societies*, Chicago, IL: University of Chicago Press.

Boyer, Robert (1998) 'Etat, Marche et Développement: Une Nouvelle Synthèse Pour le XXI siècle?', *CEPREMAP, CNRS Paris*, 98 (Novembre).

Boyer, Robert and Drache, Daniel (eds) (1996) *States Against Markets: The Limits of Globalization*, London: Routledge.

Breton, Albert (1995) *Competitive Governments: An Economic Theory of Politics and Public Finance*, New York: Cambridge University Press.

Buchanan, James M. (1975) *The Limits of Liberty: Between Anarchy and Leviathan*, Chicago, IL: The University of Chicago Press.

Coase, Ronald H. (1960) 'The Problem of Social Cast', *Journal of Law and Economics*, 3: 1–44.

Cornes, Richard and Sandler, Todd (1994) 'Are Public Goods Myths?', *Journal of Theoretical Politics*, 6, 3: 369–85.

Crouch, Colin and Streeck, Wolfgang (eds) (1997) *Political Economy of Modern Capitalism: Mapping Convergence and Diversity*, London: Sage.

Dahrendorf, Ralf (1995) 'A Precarious Balance: Economic Opportunity, Civil Society and Political Liberty', *The Responsive Community*, Summer: 13–38.

ECLAC (2000) *Social Panorama*, Santiago: United Nations.

Employment in Europe (1998) Brussels: EU, L/2985.

Evans, Peter (1997) 'The Eclipse of the State? Reflections on Stateness in an Era of Globalization', *World Politics*, 50 (October): 62–87.

Fukuyama, Francis (1995) 'The Primacy of Culture', *Journal of Democracy*, January.

Hanson, Albert Henry (1959) *Public Enterprise and Economic Development*, London: Routledge and Kegan Paul.

Hutton, Will (ed.) (1996) *The Stakeholder Society: The Ideas that Shaped Post War Britain*, London: Fontana.

Jenson, Jane (1998) 'Mapping Social Cohesion', CPRN Study No. F\03 Ottawa.

Keane, John (1998) *Civil Society Old Images, New Visions*, London: Polity Press.

Krasinitz, Philip (ed.) (1995) *Metropolis: Centre and Symbol of Our Times*, New York: New York University Press.

Kuntsler, J. H. (1996) *Home From Nowhere*, New York: Simon Schuster.

Marquand, David (1988) *The Unprincipled Society*, London: Jonathan Cape.

Mattoso, Jorge (2000) 'Globalization, Deregulation and Labour: A Challenge for Work and Social Citizenship in Brazil', *Work and Social Citizenship in a Global Economy*, Madison, WI, November.

Mumford, Lewis (1986) *The Lewis Mumford Reader*, Donald L. Miller (ed.), New York: Pantheon.

OECD (1998) *Open Markets Matter: The Benefits of Trade and Investment Liberalization*, Paris: OECD.

Prebisch, R. (1971) *Change and Development: Latin America's Great Task. Report to the Inter-American Development Bank*, New York: Praeger.

Putnam, Robert (1993) 'The Prosperous Community: Social Capital and Public Life', *The American Prospect*, 4, 13, Washington.

Rosecrance, Richard (1996) 'The Rise of the Virtual State', *Foreign Affairs*, 75, 4 (July/August): 45–61.

Ruigrok, Winfried and Tulder, Rob van (1995) *The Logic of International Restructuring*, London/New York: Routledge.

Samuelson, Paul A. (1954) 'The Pure Theory of Public Expenditure', *Review of Economics and Statistics*, 37 (4): 387–9.

Schonfield, Andrew (1964) *Modern Capitalism*, London: Oxford University Press.

Schultze, Charles L. (1977) *The Public Use of Private Interest*, Washington, DC: Brookings Institution.

Sennett, Richard (1977) *The Fall of Public Man*, New York: Alfred A. Knopf.

Squires, Judith (1994) Ordering the City Public Spaces and Public Participation. *The Lesser Evil and the Greater Good: The Theory and Politics of Social Diversity*. Weeks, Jeffrey, Rivers Oram Press: 79–99.

Stiglitz, Joseph E. (1988) *The Economics of the Public Sector*, New York: W.W. Norton and Company.

—— (1991) 'Government, Financial Markets, and Economic Development', *NBER Working Paper*, 3669 (April).

United Nations, Department of Technical Co-operation for Development (1986) *Economic Performance of Public Enterprises: Major Issues and Strategies for Action*, New York: United Nations.

Villa, Dana R. (1992) 'Postmodernism and the Public Sphere', *American Political Science Review*, 86 (3): 712–21.

Walzer, Michael (1986) 'Pleasures and Costs of Urbanity', *Dissent*, fall; reprinted (1995) in Philip Krasinitz (ed.), *Metropolis: Centre and Symbol of Our Times*, New York: New York University Press, pp. 320–30.

Weintraub, Jeff (1995) 'Varieties and Vicissitudes of Public Space', in Philip Krasinitz (ed.), *Metropolis: Centre and Symbol of Our Times*, New York: New York University Press, pp. 280–319.

Williamson, John (1999) 'What Should the Bank Think About the Washington Consensus?', prepared as a background to the World Bank's World Development Report 2000, World Bank, July 1999, Institute for International Economics, www.iie.com/testi-mony/bankwc.htm (accessed – 03.05.01).

Zukin, Sharon (1995) *The Cultures of Cities*, Cambridge, MA: Blackwell.

Jon Pierre and B. Guy Peters

GOVERNANCE AT THREE LEVELS

From: Pierre, J. and Peters, B. G. (2000) 'Governance at three levels', *Governance, Politics and the State*, Chapter 4, Macmillan

[...]

THIS CHAPTER LOOKS AT three different types of displacement of state power and control: upward, towards international actors and organizations; downward, towards regions, cities and communities; and outward, to institutions operating under considerable discretion from the state. These three types of shifts in institutional capacity are combinations of planned and spontaneous changes.

[...]

A key argument which will be elaborated later in this chapter is that the displacement of political control between different institutional levels is not necessarily a zero-sum game, that is, institutions at one level can have their influence increased without institutions at other levels necessarily seeing their control decreasing. There are many reasons why this is the case but the most important explanation is that by granting more powers and autonomy to, for instance, subnational governments, the state loses some of its control but not as much as subnational governments increase their control.

[...]

Thus, contrary to much of what has been written about the alleged 'decline of the state', the emergence of governance could well in fact increase public control over society instead of decreasing it. The main difference between the conventional, zero-sum-game view on these issues and the governance perspective lies ultimately in the conception of what constitutes political and institutional power and capability. In a legal, constitutional sense, all displacement of power is a zero-sum game; you can only increase one institution's power by taking that power from some other institution. But that conception of power looks only at the legal powers these institutions have *in relationship to each other* – as is the case in state–local relationships – and not at the capabilities these institutions will have (or be enabled to generate) in relation to other societal actors.

[. . .]

The conventional view on government

[. . .]

The standard, idealized image of government is the only reasonably useful benchmark against which we can observe what differences the emergence of governance makes to the state's capacity to steer society.

[. . .]

Conventional techniques and processes of state steering, we maintain, are still extremely important. The new, less complying, governance strategies which we see emerging are not alternative but complementary strategies to the previous models of governance. [. . .] Contrasting the new governance with the traditional image of government helps us uncover what differences emerging modes of governance make and what are the likely consequences of these developments.

[. . .]

The conventional view on government could be summarized in four general points: state-centrism, institutional insulation and homogeneity, state sovereignty and superiority, and a focus on constitutional arrangements. The state-centric view on government sees the state as the undisputed locus of power. The extent to which the state intervenes in markets, changes the structure of ownership in the industry, redistributes wealth among different social groups, or expands or contracts its services is a matter of policy choice. The state, in this perspective, is a set of powerful institutions which can be employed to enforce the political will of the dominant political constituency.

This view on government, in turn, is predicated on an assumption of institutional insulation and homogeneity. Institutions do not have to engage in bargaining or joint ventures with other societal actors to attain their goals and tasks but can rely on their legally defined jurisdiction. Furthermore, the conventional view on government holds that institutions are not impaired by internal tensions and conflicts. The Weberian view on the bureaucracy is, in fact, an important component in this image of government.

The third defining characteristic of the conventional view on government – state sovereignty and superiority – is to some degree derived from the previous points. The state is seen as sovereign, meaning that its powers and capabilities are absolute rather than something relative, contextual and negotiable. It is much more a matter of 'power over' than 'power to'. This also means that the state to a considerable extent could define its own powers. The state certainly has extensive exchanges with the surrounding society but conducts those exchanges largely on its own terms. Also, in the conventional view on government there was little concern with legitimacy problems or critique against taxes and involvement which could undermine the effective capabilities of the state.

The focus on constitutional issues and arrangements, finally, is an important element of the conventional view on the state because constitutions and other legal frameworks governed state actions with little or no discrepancies between rules and behaviour. Given the powerful role of written rules, constitutions – conceived of as the rules of the political game – never allowed to develop organically but were assessed more in terms of their internal logic than to what extent they were *de facto* shaping political life.

The governance perspective challenges these conceptions of the state and the sources of state capabilities. [. . .] The governance approach, as outlined here, shares a state-centric perspective with the state–society literature of the 1980s but focuses more narrowly on public–private exchange, contextual and entrepreneurial styles of politically driven social and political change, and the ways in which these exchanges reverberate on the state. As we shift perspective from government to governance, state-centrism is a matter of analytical choice to a much greater extent than in the conventional view of government. In our view of the new governance, the state thus remains the key player albeit for slightly different reasons. The state exercises influence through coordination and steering in combination with the employment of its resources in various projects. The main difference between the two perspectives is that in the conventional view the centrality of the state is taken for granted whereas in the governance perspective the state is a *primus inter pares* actor whose capabilities are contingent on its ability to mobilize other societal actors for its purposes.

The institutional insulation and homogeneity which is the second feature of the conventional view on government does not find much support in governance theory. The monolithic view on the state is substituted for a model of the state which assumes much more institutional fragmentation and incoherence, perhaps even contradiction and tensions between and within institutions. To be sure, in order to meet the challenge of governance, most states have deliberately relaxed their organizational cohesion in order to enable different segments of the state to develop their own forms of exchange with societal actors. Furthermore, different institutions of the state – and sometimes even segments within institutions – have their own views about what should be the goals of governance. In addition to the institutional fragmentation and deconcentration, another typical feature of the contemporary state in governance is the relaxation of political steering and control. Thus, states frequently play both internally as well as externally coordinating roles. In some Third World countries it seems clear that states cannot engage in successful governance until they bring about some degree of internal institutional coherence and capacities, in the modern western advanced democracies there is a tendency to move in the opposite direction in order to increase the points of contact with the surrounding society.

The third assumption in the conventional view on government, state sovereignty and superiority, does not receive much support in theories of governance. There is a consensus that states control some types of resources which no other actors have access to, such as the legal enforcement of authoritative decisions. The main difference is that these types of resources are becoming less critical for most societal actors. Private businesses seem to be less dependent on national policies just as organized interests are less inclined to engage in close cooperation with an increasingly resource-constrained state. There still exist delicate dependencies between the state and powerful societal actors but the direction of those dependencies has shifted. Previously, industrial leaders were anxious to have a good dialogue with policy-makers and senior civil servants; now it is elected politicians who seek contact with private industry. Similarly, in the heyday of corporatism, organized interests were eager to secure access and participation in the state's decision-making processes. Today, it is the state which seeks to engage the third sector in public service delivery.

The focus on constitutional arrangements, finally, has been significantly downplayed in governance theory. In the conventional view, the constitution was the ultimate source of the state's powers. Today, constitutions define archaic borders between state and society which are seen as obstacles to governance. Also, systems of rules tend to impair political institutions in their exchange with societal actors which are more free to move resources without public monitoring. Also, since political capabilities in governance are derived from political entrepreneurialism and a political ability to read and exploit unique contexts, constitutions tell us less and less about what states can and cannot do.

Moving up: the emerging role of international organizations

One of the most profound and conspicuous developments since the Second World War with regard to alterations in state powers is the growing importance of international groups of actors or organizations. States have chosen to surrender parts of their sovereignty to such transnational arrangements in a number of policy sectors.

[. . .]

Our primary concern here is not so much with international organizations aiming at governing the global community of sovereign states but more on recent international actors with a different and broader agenda.

The development in international trade regulation is a good example of the consolidation of international institutions. Regulating trade, particularly ensuring free trade and the abolition of trade barriers, is a core concern for all exporting industrialized states. In the early postwar period, western states agreed on a General Agreement on Tariffs and Trade (GATT) which other states soon signed as well. The agreement was renegotiated at regular intervals but there was very limited continuous monitoring of states' trade policies. As part of the *régime économique* in the 1980s and early 1990s, however, GATT was increasingly seen as an ineffective instrument to regulate international trade. As a result, GATT was replaced by the World Trade Organization (WTO) which assumed the same roles as GATT played but, more importantly, also serves as a controller, investigator, and court for international trade disputes. In order to join the WTO, states have to demonstrate that they, in policy as well as in action, subscribe to the principles of free trade and non-state intervention in private industry (Hoekman and Kostecki, 1995).

Another perhaps even more intriguing example of the growing importance of international organizations is the Agenda 21 project. Laid down at the 1992 Rio Summit, the basic idea of Agenda 21 is that subnational governments – not states – are targeted as lead actors to develop programmes of sustainable economic development. Thus here is a case of international governance which aims at subnational political change without much control or interference by the nation state.

The emergence of these types of international actors is a very powerful challenge to the state. Indeed, it is little surprise that the project of voluntarily surrendering some of the state's sovereignty to transnational organizations has encountered fierce political resistance in many instances, as displayed not least in western Europe alongside the continued political and economic integration of the Union (Taggart, 1998). The obvious questions are: Why this tendency to move governance up to the international level? Why do states so willingly surrender their sovereignty to transnational institutions over which their influence is extremely limited? What are the costs and benefits associated with these developments? Can the process of internationalization be reversed, and what leeway do individual states have to choose whether or not they want to join these powerful international organizations? And through what mechanisms and instruments does international governance link with domestic governance?

There are many contributing explanations for the emergence of international organizations and actors but five overall hypotheses seem to offer a reasonably good account of this development. First of all, most of the significant problems confronting the contemporary political elites of the western world are not defined by national borders but are regional or even global in nature. [. . .] [T]he deregulationist regime in Europe and the United States has stripped border control of many of their authorities; hence some form of internationally coordinated efforts has become the only means of curbing international drug trade.

[. . .]

A second explanation for the growing powers of these international structures is that international coordination is necessary to accomplish deregulationist goals. Domestic economic growth and development are increasingly seen as contingent on the international performance of the nation's industry.

[. . .]

A third set of explanations is provided by the literature on the globalization of private capital. The argument is often sustained with reference to the deregulation of financial and currency markets but has a more general scope. International trade is much more important to most developed states today than it was a couple of decades ago: domestic economic growth is primarily believed to be predicated on increased exports. This is a seemingly deceptive economic development strategy, since international trade in theory at least is a zero-sum game: all countries cannot simultaneously develop and sustain a positive trade balance. However, as the history of the capitalist economy has shown, this economic system has powerful incentives not only to dominate existing markets but also to identify and exploit new markets.

Critics of the globalization argument show that for countries like Britain international trade is no bigger today in terms of the percentage of the GNP than it was in the early twentieth century (Hirst and Thompson, 1996). Also, countries like the Scandinavian countries built much of their prosperity during the 1950s, 1960s and 1970s on export revenues. For them, globalization is no news. The key difference between the 1910 or 1920s on the one hand and the 1980s and 1990s on the other is that economic policy has shifted from demand-side to supply-side economic thinking. The commitment to anti-inflation monetaristic policies forces most industrial states to keep domestic demand at a fairly low level, something which forces industry to look overseas for markets with greater demand.

A fourth reason why states support emerging international organizational structures is that policy problems are assumed to become increasingly similar among different countries and that, subsequently, developing institutions to facilitate cross-national policy learning becomes an important strategy to develop new policy concepts. The OECD has evolved into an international organization which serves to diffuse policy concepts in economic policy and administrative reform. The IMF and the World Bank increasingly often provide international loans which are contingent on specific economic reforms. Policy learning takes place at what seems to be a rapidly increasing number of international conferences for 'epistemic communities' (Haas, 1992) and a growing interest in bilateral exchange.

Finally, the argument has been made that the rapid strengthening of international organizations, or indeed globalization more generally, is a convenient excuse for nation-state governments not to address predominant political problems (Weiss, 1998). It is a legitimate political standpoint to argue that problems such as environmental protection, controlling the spread of epidemic diseases or fighting international crime can only be addressed by states acting in concert through some form of international efforts.

[. . .]

Moving down: regions, localities, and communities

The second major type of displacement of state power – the decentralization of state authority to regional and local institutions – has gained more attention than the strengthening of international structures. Decentralization, with significant differences in detail between different national contexts, has been implemented in a large number of western democracies over the past couple of decades.

[. . .]

The decentralization process has in many countries been conducted in several steps. After the institutional 'empowerment' of local governments we have seen intra-city diffusion of some powers, too. As was the case in state–local decentralization, giving neighbourhoods more influence has been coupled with greater financial responsibilities while at the same time facilitating more direct citizen participation and input on political issues. This has become important during periods of cutting back public expenditures.

This wave of decentralization has been driven by a wide range of political objectives or as responses to structural changes in the democratic state. The continued urbanization and agglomeration of cities, for instance, have necessitated financially and administratively stronger local governments. More importantly, however, the expansion of public services during the past decades have fuelled a professionalization and accumulation of expertise in subnational governments and to some extent decentralization has aimed at unleashing and capitalizing on this expertise. Another motif for decentralization is that many public services are becoming less standardized and that the need for these services to be responsive and adapted to local needs has become more important.

Decentralization has in many cases helped the nation state to bring its budget at least closer to balance and to curb the growth in public expenditure at the central government level. This has meant 'passing the buck', or displacing the problems, to subnational institutions. That said, it is interesting to note that this decentralization has not significantly been associated with an overall decrease in the size of the public sector *tout court*. Rather it is a matter of a changing division of labour within the public sector as well as changing patterns of financial and other responsibilities for public services.

[. . .]

The most important consequence of decentralization is that it has facilitated new forms of governance, both among institutions within the public sector and between local governments and the surrounding society. For societal actors there is little point in approaching local governments who have very limited powers, limited financial resources and constrained autonomy. Decentralization makes local government an attractive target for political pressures but also as a partner in different local projects, for instance within economic development and public service delivery. Thus decentralization has probably strengthened urban regimes, normally conceived of as coalitions between the local political elite and corporate actors (Elkin, 1987; Stone, 1989). [. . .]

Moving out: NGOs, corporatization and privatization

The third type of power displacement has been to move powers and capabilities traditionally controlled by the state to institutions and organizations operating at arm's length from the political elite. Most of the advanced democracies have helped set up a large number of non-governmental organizations (NGOs) in public service delivery, if they have not gone so far as to privatize such functions altogether. This idea of creating 'satellite' institutions has gained massive popularity and is currently used at all levels of government.

The exportation of policy activities takes a number of different forms. The simplest is creating quasi-autonomous 'agencies' in government to perform tasks previously performed by government departments. [...] At a second level central governments can use subnational governments for their own implementation purposes. Finally, governments can use for-profit or not-for-profit organizations to fulfil government purposes. In some cases these organizations may have existed long before the contemporary move towards greater externalization of activities. In other cases governments have fostered the creation of these organizations, and then become their major funders.

[...]

Several arguments have been used for privatization, ranging from the state's need to capitalize on its assets to reduce its debts to a more normative idea that states should not own companies which provide services. It is interesting to note that the justifications for bringing (or keeping) these services under state auspices, especially that they were collective goods which should be protected from corporate profit, has surrendered to the notion that the state is not well-equipped or designed to own such companies and that in order to make them more efficient they should be privatized.

There has also been a significant transfer of primarily implementation authority to non-public actors, not least at the local level. In some national contexts such as in Sweden, local governments have created companies owned by the local authority to deal with tasks and responsibilities which the city proper is not very well geared to, such as provision of water and electricity. This 'corporatization' has been criticized partly because it complicates public monitoring on how tax money is spent and partly on a normative level, arguing that local authorities should not own companies but that they should be privatized.

Finally, public–private partnerships have become a popular instrument for enhancing the capability of political institutions, primarily at the local level. Such a partnership could be seen as an *ad hoc* fusion of political and private resources. What critics see as questionable ways to spend public money and exercise political power in close concert with corporate interests are for others a pragmatic and efficient means of increasing the institutional 'capacity to act' (Stone, 1989).

[...]

The general idea behind these changes has been to create organizations and inter-organizational relationships that can be engaged in the policy process without some of the constraints that hinder most public sector organizations. In some instances, that may imply organizations that can function under conditions which approach market-like conditions as closely as possible, while at the same time implementing public policy. In others the organizations may operate more like private eleemosynary bodies, albeit with heavy levels of public funding. The general point is to move the activities out of the public sector.

These organizational developments are triggered in part by a need to find formats which enhance efficiency in the public sector. The inclination to experiment with different organizational solutions to these problems appears to have been much stronger at the local than at the central level. The use of private organizations is also a way of enhancing the legitimacy of certain types of activities (social work) in cases in which government has lost the respect and support of many programme recipients. These organizations also permit involving the clients of programmes to a greater extent than might be possible with public sector organizations, so that there is community involvement as well as less expense.

As has been the case with most other institutional developments described earlier, these organizational changes have been extremely important in developing new channels and instruments for public–private concerted action and exchange of resources. For most of these changes we do not believe that that aspect of organizational reform was seen as very important: it is clear that the primary goals of those reforms were cost-cutting and bringing in private-sector management philosophies. However, one of the more important consequences of the centrifugal organizational developments in the public sector has been that they have facilitated new forms of governance.

We need to think of these three shifts in formal political power – up to international regimes, down to subnational authorities and urban regimes, and out to NGOs and private organizations – in a dynamic perspective. The effective division of labour is often contextual and negotiated. In some, but far from all, cases the state still has at least a theoretical option to reclaim diffused power bases. Furthermore, different policy sectors display different patterns of power relocation. From the point of view of the state there is a risk of 'institutional stretching', that is, some of its control has been shifted upward while some of it has been displaced downward.

What's left of the state?

Looking back at the preceding discussion about the displacement of state capabilities upward, downward, and outward, the obvious question is what areas of control and resources remain under state control. The issue, however, is not so much what specific formal areas of control the state has retained as what types of instruments and capabilities it still possesses. We believe that the new emerging governance will see traditional instruments of governance being used in new contexts alongside alternative instruments. There is a growing emphasis on getting things done and less emphasis on the role of government in that process.

The developments described here lend themselves to two different, albeit not contradictory, conclusions with regard to the future of the nation state and its role in the new governance. One scenario is that the different displacements of state power and control are irreversible processes of state decline. In this perspective the state will contract until it retains only a few core societal functions. Public services will continue to be adapted to the financial condition of the state; contracting out, privatization and third sector involvement will replace state auspices in service delivery. In the international arenas, globalized capital will gain further momentum while nation states will see a further erosion of their control over private capital.

The other scenario takes a more positive view on the future of the state. Here, recent developments are interpreted not as indicators of state decline but rather as of state transformation and successive adaptation to changes in its external (domestic and international) environments. [. . .] There is also a greater degree of heterogeneity among nation states today than there was some twenty years ago due to the difference in pace and direction of administrative reform, institutional restructuring and political–economic regimes. The Anglo-American democracies seem to have gone much further than countries like Germany, France, Japan and Sweden in these respects. Thus in this scenario what we are witnessing is a process of structural and political adjustment in the state to the challenges it is now facing. Traditional sources and bases of state power are down-played since they are less efficient and appropriate instruments of governance. Instead, collaborative instruments and a more transparent and integrative state model emerge to serve as a vehicle for the pursuit of collective interests.

A key element of governance theory is that the total sum of state capabilities may well remain largely unchanged despite the relocation of traditional state authority. The emergence of international regimes suggests that the state is deprived of some of its sovereignty but that this loss to a considerable extent is matched by the state's access to the leverage controlled by such international regimes. [. . .] [D]ecentralization and subnational internationalization are 'appropriate' structural developments as the state responds and adapts to the contemporary domestic and global society in which it is embedded. What does change, however, is the selection of instruments and organizational arrangements through which the state imposes its will on society and also the nature of the points of contact between state and society.

References

Elkin, S. L. (1987) 'Twentieth-century urban regimes', *Journal of Urban Affairs*, 7, 11–28.

Haas, P. M. (1992) 'Introduction: epistemic communities and international policy coordination', *International Organization*, 46, 1–35.

Hirst, P. and G. Thompson (1996) *Globalization in Question*. Cambridge: Polity Press.

Hoekman, B. and M. Kostecki (1995) *The Political Economy of the World Trading System*. Oxford and New York: Oxford University Press.

Stone, C. N. (1989) *Governing Atlanta*. Lawrence, Kans.: University of Kansas Press.

Weiss, L. (1998) *The Myth of the Powerless State*. Cambridge and New York: Cambridge University Press.

Colin Crouch

THE STATE AND INNOVATIONS IN ECONOMIC GOVERNANCE

From: Crouch, C. (2004) 'The state and innovations in economic governance', *The Political Quarterly*, 75:1, 100–116

M Y MAIN PURPOSE IS to go beyond the polemical dichotomy of 'state versus market', and to set both within a wider framework of several different modes of governance, which come together in varying combinations. I want to show how appreciation of the diversity of these modes enables us to see a broad range of institutional possibilities with which governments and others can experiment in economic policy.

[. . .]

A striking example may be taken from recent comments on the British National Health Service by Julian Le Grand, now a central figure in government policy in this area. Initially, he was unable to distinguish governance of the NHS and similar social democratic institutions from the mechanisms of the Soviet state.[1] In the later of the two contributions cited, he explicitly moderates this view, but in a significant way. He acknowledges a major role for what he calls 'networks and trust' alongside 'command and control' in the NHS. But he then identifies networks and trust with subordination to the judgement of public service professionals. The overall aim of his argument is then to advocate the role of markets as the sole reliable approach to public service. [. . .]

Highly paradoxically, this same commitment to the market has also led New Labour to be very state-centric, further constraining its capacity to encourage diversity. It is important to address this particular paradox at an early stage. It can be done by way of dealing with another currently popular dichotomy, which appears whenever one discusses governance: that between government and governance. Many observers are suspicious of this, seeing in 'governance' an unnecessary grandiloquence on the part of those who find 'government' simply too straightforward.

[...]

Problems of the Third Way approach to governance

The first group contrast government and governance by seeing the former as hard-edged, rigid and rather nasty, and the latter as soft, flexible, and responsive. [...] As Anthony Giddens expressed it, in social democracy the state was pervasive and dominated over civil society.[2] The Third Way state, in contrast, would be benign: it was 'the state without enemies', 'doubly' democratic, transparent, working in partnership with civil society and harnessing local initiatives.[3]

These are all clear, coherent arguments, and there is a nugget of truth somewhere in them. But they make strange reading after several years of a New Labour government that has been secretive, centralising, at least as reliant as its Old Labour and Conservative predecessors on exclusive cliques of insiders, and also determinedly military. There are strong reasons why the Third Way project has not seen the state deconstruct itself into a non-coercive type of governance; and these need to be understood.

First, whatever changes are made to the forms of government and its interventions in economy and society, at the centre lies the fact of political power, possession of and closeness to which always bring reward and privilege. The mid-twentieth-century Keynesian welfare state was distinguished from other forms by the broad, even universal, swathes of population able to share in the state's capacity to provide benefits, not by the phenomenon of state benefit itself. Political power and influence remain objects of struggle just as intensely when the social state declines; it is just that the circles involved in political struggle and its fruits become more limited. Elites will always remain vitally interested in the state, as they will be served first by whatever is available. Business sectors, individual firms, and other groups able to achieve personal access to officers of state continue to lobby, whatever the general role of government in society. If the early twenty-first-century US neo-conservative polity represents some kind of paradigm case of the new residual state, it is certainly not one where business interests consider that government has become so limited that there is little need to seek access to it. [...]

Second, as Andrew Gamble demonstrated early during the neo-liberal Thatcher years, producing the 'free economy' *required* a 'strong state' – in particular a strong central one.[4] To the extent that New Labour stands for a continuation of the market-making agenda, it is subject to the same logic.

There are highly important historical precedents for the dependence of the free economy on the strong state. The original emergence of capitalism out of medieval political economy had involved a similar process. The premodern polity had been at least as complex as any image of early twenty-first-century governance. The emperor, kings, local nobility, professional corporations, towns, church authorities, all laid claim to different elements of political power, and to different interventions in economic behaviour. Capitalism developed most easily when this rich diversity had been simplified following the emergence of sovereign nation-states, which gathered this parcelised sovereignty into themselves. Thus simplified, it was necessary to convince only this one authority in a given national territory to accept a limited role for political intervention and to provide and guarantee the conditions for free markets and enforceable contracts.

[...]

In the 1980s British neo-liberals did not deny Gamble's observations; but – like the Bolsheviks after the 1917 Russian Revolution – they believed that the strong state was a temporary necessity, needed to clean out the accretions of social democracy. Once that had been achieved, free markets would blossom and the strong state could wither away. They were naive. First, they forgot that people like to enjoy political power for purposes other than liberalising economies, and concentrated power is even more enjoyable as well as less vulnerable to checks and balances than dispersed power and compromises. Second, they believed that the creation of markets was somehow a once-and-for-all-time activity.

Now, a quarter of a century later, we know that neo-liberal governments keep finding it necessary to take new initiatives to keep markets pure and extend their scope. This is partly because dynamic, sophisticated economies present an endless stream of issues that require attention and that cannot simply be read off from some free-market calculus.

[...]

The market economy does not exist in some state of nature, to which we all naturally turn unless the state inhibits us. Those who believed that the collapse of the Soviet system was all that was needed to release the 'natural' capitalist instincts of the people of Russia and Eastern Europe were distressed to find that mafia rather than markets flourished.

[...]

We have to be directed and shaped to make us pursue our goals through market means alone. Although it is often defined in terms of its offer of freedom of choice, the market offers only choices of certain kinds. Before we participate in markets we have to be disciplined so that we use its means and no others. This is not only the case in the struggle against corruption. People often also seek to protect areas of their life from the market: for example, their religious practices, their leisure time, or their citizenship rights. One way of seeing the political struggles of at least the past two centuries is as continuing dispute over where this line should be drawn. [...] The introduction of the market into an area where it did not exist before is not a liberation from constraints, but a replacement of one kind of constraint by another.

Neo-liberalism, neo-conservatism, and New Labourism – all versions of the market-making state – produce, despite their rhetoric, very busy, tough and demanding governments. Such a state cannot risk the compromises and bargaining that were meat and drink to the social and Christian democracy and old liberalism of the mid- to late twentieth century; its task is to purify and restore markets, not to make compromises between them and non-market forces. For example, negative and positive incentives have to be designed to persuade increasing proportions of the population to enter the labour force; it must be made absolutely clear to able-bodied adults that they can have a life free of poverty only if they work, and not necessarily even then. There is nothing soft and furry about the new governance of the market-making state.

[. . .]

The social science approach to governance

The second group of writers who see purpose in distinguishing government from governance have a more scientific than political agenda. This approach treats government as a *subset* of governance, one form that governance can take. For this second approach to talk of a move 'from government to governance' makes sense only as a move 'from government *to other types of* governance'; though, as we shall see, as a statement of historical tendency this too is problematic.

Governance is best understood as: *all means by which the behavioural regularities that constitute social institutions are maintained and enforced*. Social institutions are then to be defined as: *clusters of patterns of action and relationships which continue and reproduce themselves over time, independently of the identity of the biological individuals performing within them*. This basic idea can be applied to institutions of very different sizes and degrees of formality, from the family to certain international structures. It therefore provides a means of considering real diversity.

Government as such is clearly included within the scope of governance seen in this way, but there are also other forms, which must be considered alongside it and compared with it. Those that are mainly considered in the literature are the market, associations, communities, networks and corporate hierarchies. It is also important to distinguish between the state as government in its direct, interventionist, taxing and spending role, on the one hand; and the state as the source and guarantor of formal law, on the other.

[. . .]

The substantive state

The ideal, in the sense of pure or extreme, concept of substantive state governance is one in which its central command capacity shapes the entire environment. All resources are provided through the state, which allocates them through its administrative structure. Resources have low mobility, because change requires application to the administration. Communication is through the signalling of requests and commands; the state is not here defined as a necessarily democratic one, but simply as a state, working through a centralised and potentially coercive structure. These processes are formal; relations are vertical; and the state has in principle a high capacity for enforcement, with an extensive and general reach. When and if they ever operated according to their basic principles, the state socialist economies of the former Soviet bloc worked something like this.

The association

In the pure concept of an associational economy, all firms and individuals are members of formal organisations, which are responsible for all their relations with the external environment. Resources are all channelled through associations' administrative structure. Resources have low mobility, because change requires application to the association. Communication is through dialogue, because associations are defined as membership organisations. These processes are formal; relations are vertical; and the association has in principle a high capacity for enforcement among its members, but its reach is not general. [...] The association differs from the state in that it has an internal dialogue structure and limited external reach.

The community

In a pure community, individuals are strongly embedded in informal and usually local and enduring, multiply interlocking webs of relationships, which also govern all their contacts with the external environment. All resources come from the community, which allocates them through custom and tradition. Resources have low mobility, because they are embedded in the community. Communication is through dialogue, because communities are defined as membership structures. These processes are informal; relations are horizontal; and, through the interlocking nature of its relationships, the community has a high capacity for enforcement among its members.

[...]

The network

In a network (as in a network economy), individual units are linked loosely with each other in limited understandings concerning reciprocity. Resources are provided by the network, which allocates them through its structures. Resources have high mobility, because the binding undertakings of the network are weak. Communication is through dialogue, because networks are defined as membership structures. These processes can be either formal or informal, giving us two subtypes. In the former case, there is an explicit agreement among the members concerning the inception, conduct and conclusion of the network; in the latter, understandings develop in a similar way as in community, but always in a more limited and less embedded way. In both forms, relations are horizontal; and the network has a low capacity for enforcement among its members, because their relations are weak. It also has no reach beyond the members.

[. . .]

The market

In the pure concept of a neo-classical market economy, firms and individuals are linked to each other and to resources and factors of production solely by relations of supply and demand as signalled by price under conditions of perfect competition. All resources are acquired in the market, through purchase. Resources have high mobility, because they respond solely to price signals. Communication is solely through these signals; participants in the market are anonymous and therefore cannot participate in dialogue. Processes are formal, because calculations have to be precise for the market to work efficiently. Relations are horizontal; and the market has a low capacity for autonomous enforcement because of the criterion of anonymity. However, if its functioning can be guaranteed, its reach is extensive, all transactions being in principle commensurable. The market differs from the network in its dependence on price rather than allocation as its mode of acquisition of resources, its similar dependence on price signals rather than dialogue, and its extensive reach.

The procedural state

In the procedural state, individuals make contracts with each other, these contracts taking a form prescribed (or permitted) by either statute or case law. All resources are acquired by means of the contract, through either allocation or purchase. Resources may have high or low mobility, depending on the legal processes involved. Communication is solely through contract signals and judicial decision. Contract processes are highly formal; and relations are horizontal. There is in principle a high capacity for enforcement through legal process, and this capacity has extensive reach throughout the society. The contract differs from the market in its strong capacity for enforcement.

The corporate hierarchy

In the corporate hierarchy, all resource questions are handled through the internal managerial structure of large firms, including hierarchical relations between firms at different stages of the production process. All resources are endogenous to this hierarchy, and are allocated within it by administrative decision. Resources have high mobility, because they are at the disposal of the central management. Communication is through both signals and dialogue as this management chooses, these processes being formal. Relations are by definition vertical. There is a high capacity for enforcement, because of the authority of management, but reach is limited to the hierarchy itself.

[. . .]

The essentially hybrid nature of governance

It is clear from such an inspection of true ideal types of these modes of governance that hardly any of them is likely to be fully autonomous, certainly not in dealing with economic relations of any complexity. Some display a rigidity of resource allocation that makes it difficult for them to respond to changing demand among consumers (the substantive state, association, community). These modes exist only alongside market governance. This happens either openly and willingly, or (as in state socialism) in the form of black markets. Within a capitalist society the market is only absent from a few institutions, such as friendship and love relationships, and the postwar welfare state.

Some modes of governance lack autonomous external enforcement capacity (networks, markets), and have to coopt other modes when they extend beyond a narrow range. The procedural state is the main mechanism that performs this role. What is called the free market economy is always a hybrid between the pure market and the procedural state, and extension of the scope of the market often involves extension of this aspect of the state too. [. . .] In fact, what passes in most discussion for the 'market economy' is always a compound of market, procedural state and corporate hierarchy. As we have seen, hierarchy differs considerably from market as a form of governance. The compound of these three elemental forms therefore provides a governance mix of considerable potential diversity.

Within this compound form, the other governance modes operate by interposing themselves between firms and the MHP (market/hierarchy/procedural state) amalgam. For example, a firm embedded in a community within a market economy is not engaged in a subsistence economy, but reaches out through its community to a market. A substantive state within a capitalist economy changes the way in which firms subject to its interventions encounter the market, but it does not suppress markets, and has to be careful of the impact of its actions on market forces. It behaves quite differently from a state in a non-market economy, as can be seen from a comparison of the French and Russian economies during the postwar period.

It is possible to formulate other compound types. MHP will always predominate, but minority or even trace components of other governance forms can still be important, even decisive, in making niche characteristics available to certain kinds of producer in specific national or regional economies.

[. . .]

Finally, different modes of governance might prevail across different resource areas. It might be possible, for example, for an economy which has an industrial relations system dominated by corporatist (associational) structures to have vocational education located mainly in state institutions with little corporatist involvement (as in the case of Sweden).[5]

Markets and hierarchies

Relations between the market and the corporate hierarchy require some further discussion, as they are subject to considerable misunderstanding. During the 1990s it seemed that the firm as an institution, the heart of the corporate hierarchy mode, might be deconstructing itself into nothing other than a set of markets. Decision making power seemed to be passing from stable ownership groups and senior managers into the hands of constantly changing owners of shares, who related to the firm solely through market acquisition and sale of its assets. What had previously been interpreted as the power of management was seen to have become subordinated to the need to maximise shareholder value. Meanwhile, employment contracts were seen to be disappearing, as firms turned former employees into self-employed subcontractors and franchisees, with whom the firm had a purely market relationship. This account of an imminent deconstruction of the firm as organisation into a set of markets served a number of purposes. For neo-liberals it suggested that the theory of the firm and other forms of economic analysis outside the neo-classical frame were redundant; the market was the only institution in existence.

For Third Way writers, the incredible lightness of being of the new economy paralleled their general preference for 'light' institutions – as for example in Charles Leadbeater's concept of 'thin air'.[6] Also, the apparent disappearance of both management and the status of employee marked a final end to class relationships, and the replacement of the classic Old Labour figure of the employed worker by a society of entrepreneurs.

But these authors were extrapolating from a few cases, and distorting even the evidence of those. Share markets certainly did assume a new importance. The major waves of asset stripping that had accompanied the deindustrialisation of the 1980s had left large quantities of capital seeking investment opportunities. Meanwhile certain new developments, mainly in information technology, were creating such opportunities. However, most existing firms continued to rely primarily on internally generated funds rather than the markets for investment funds. Further, the move away from employment status was limited. Firms used it when they were uncertain about their future employment needs, and for marginal types of work. But for core tasks that were fundamental to the firm's own knowledge base, its public presentation and its corporate culture, they preferred to retain employees of the familiar type. There has been no general deconstruction of the corporation. In fact, globalisation has given a renewed prominence to vast multinationals.

[. . .]

Even where disintegration of employment status and of the organisational shape of the corporation did take place, this did not represent a collapse of large concentrations of capital. Rather, management used the possibilities for organisational flexibility as a strategy, deciding whether to outsource or retain in-house a function depending on the firm's needs.

[. . .]

Appreciation of the importance of corporate hierarchy and its relationship to markets is highly important to an evaluation of the frequent juxtaposition between the state and the market. The state's interactions with firms are more often than not with large corporations, which make use of the organisational resources of hierarchy as much as those of the market. This has a number of implications.

First, relations between the state and large corporate organisations have a different quality from relations within the market. In the pure neo-classical concept of the market, all transactions are anonymous, there are no enduring relations (other than series of repeated one-off transactions), and no one firm or individual is capable of setting a price or making a deal other than as determined by market forces. Political lobbying by firms cannot even be conceptualised in such a context. This is why advocates of free markets reasonably claim that such a system is corruption proof and manipulation proof. But that is not the case with corporate hierarchies, which lack all these characteristics of markets. When governments announce that they are bringing in market forces, and set about this by negotiating closely with a small number of chosen firms, they are engaged in an oxymoron. They are bringing together, not state and market, but state and corporate hierarchy.

Second, the firm as organisation has many similarities to the state as organisation, which considerably reduces some of the contrasts drawn between states and markets in polemical debate. [. . .] Large firms and governments share many characteristics, and they can and do learn from each other.

The state and complex governance

When we see the modern economy in terms of combinations of these various modes of governance, we are able to transcend the politicised dichotomy between state and market. These combinations can be used, not only at the level of analysis, but also in prescriptions for the future of the economic role of the state. During the high tide of the Keynesian and Fordist economy – broadly the third quarter of the twentieth century – there was a certain stability in economic governance. It did not comprise government alone, as some recent literature would have us see it, but a combination of at least state, market and corporate hierarchy; in some cases (such as the Nordic countries, Germany) associations were also important; in others (Italy, for example), community. Since the collapse of the Keynesian framework, there has been more experiment with governance forms. Networks have assumed an importance in several high-tech sectors. Governments have experimented with encouraging new combinations of links among networks, firms, local governments and markets.

[...]

Some particularly interesting experiments take place at the levels of cities and regions.[7] This is so for two reasons. First, the low level of autonomy of formal authorities at these levels makes them less jealous of sovereignty than nation states. Second, the policy issues here are often to do with economic development, where partnerships with firms, associations and networks can be important.

[...]

We must first remember the useful division between the substantive and procedural states, differing from each other but both equally capable of steering and intervening. The state does not withdraw from the scene; it remains (often, but not solely, in its local form) an active mode of governance, and can be a vital component of experiment. Its role changes in comparison with the postwar Fordist and Keynesian state, but it changes within a context of change in other modes of governance too. In dynamic sectors networks are growing in importance at least as much as markets. Whether there is 'more' or 'less' state in an economy where the financial sector requires a close and constantly adjusting regulatory regime is also a matter for debate.

Another conclusion is that the more diverse the repertoire of potential forms of governance that there is in a particular context, the more scope those involved will have to experiment and respond to change. This may well be a principal lesson of the southern Californian high-tech economy. There is a combination here of multiple governance modes: markets; the corporate hierarchies in several sectors; the very extensive and important networks already described; and the procedural and substantive state at several levels.

[...]

Conclusions

A major problem of the present period is that during the 1980s social democrats were slower than neo-liberals to recognise that the ensemble of the postwar economy was changing. We tried to cling to the Keynesian formula after it had passed its time. This was mainly because manual workers and trade unions continued to have their centre of gravity in large manufacturing firms, and they have been central to social democratic concerns. As a result, the neo-liberal perspective achieved a hegemonic position in defining and interpreting the terms of the twenty-first-century economy. Contemporary revisionist social democrats of the Third Way type have not found a language or means of reform other than that of mimicking its message that the market is all. Corporate hierarchies are defined away, as we saw above; the other modes of governance are either ignored, stigmatised or assimilated to the market, from which they in fact differ in various ways. The rich and complex mixes of economic governance that are appearing, and which Third Way thinking seemed poised to comprehend, are appreciated only through this distorting glass.

Social democracy will only develop its own approach to the post-Fordist economy when it gains a more detailed and more accurate perspective on the diversity of governance modes. It needs to lose its inferiority complex over the state and recognise its possibilities as a creative actor. This is a role that includes but is not limited to market making, as sometimes pure market forces might destroy the fine tissue of other mechanisms. It needs therefore also to gain a perspective on market forces and to avoid reducing all springs of innovation to them. And it needs to distinguish markets from corporate hierarchies, so that it can appreciate their respective advantages and pitfalls. A social democracy that could achieve this kind of balanced appreciation in both its rhetoric and its detailed policy-making would soon leave neo-liberals behind as blinded by dogma and unable to appreciate the complex nature of economic reality.

Notes

1   J. Le Grand, 'Tales from the British National Health Service: competition, co-operation or control?', *Health Affairs*, 1999, no, 18, pp. 27–37; and *Motivation, Agency and Public Policy*, Oxford, Oxford University Press, 2003.
2   A. Giddens, *The Third Way: The Renewal of Social Democracy*, Cambridge, Polity, 1998, p. 7.
3   Ibid., pp. 77, 79.
4   A. Gamble, *The Free Economy and the Strong State*, Basingstoke, Macmillan, 1988.
5   C. Crouch, D. Finegold and M. Sako, *Are Skills the Answer?* Oxford, Oxford University Press, 1999.
6   C. Leadbeater, *Living on Thin Air*, London, Viking, 1999.
7   C. Crouch, P. Le Gales, C. Trigilia and H. Voelzkow, *Local Production Systems in Europe: Rise or Demise*, Oxford, Oxford University Press, 2001, and *Changing Governance of Local Economies: Response of European Local Production Systems*, Oxford, Oxford University Press, 2004.

Robert O. Keohane and Joseph S. Nye Jr

GLOBALIZATION: WHAT'S NEW? WHAT'S NOT? (AND SO WHAT?)

From: Keohane, R. S. and Nye, J. S. Jr (2000) 'Globalization: What's new? What's not (And so what?)' in D. Held and A. McGrew (eds) *The Global Transformation Reader*, Polity Press

"**G**LOBALIZATION" EMERGED AS A buzzword in the 1990s, just as "interdependence" did in the 1970s, but the phenomena it refers to are not entirely new. Our characterization of interdependence more than 20 years ago now applies to globalization at the turn of the millennium: "This vague phrase expresses a poorly understood but widespread feeling that the very nature of world politics is changing." Some skeptics believe such terms are beyond redemption for analytic use. Yet the public understands the image of the globe, and the new word conveys an increased sense of vulnerability to distant causes. [. . .]

Like all popular concepts meant to cover a variety of phenomena, both "interdependence" and "globalization" have many meanings. To understand what people are talking about when they use the terms and to make them useful for analysis, we must begin by asking whether interdependence and globalization are simply two words for the same thing, or whether there is something new going on.

The dimensions of globalism

The two words are not exactly parallel. Interdependence refers to a condition, a state of affairs. It can increase, as it has been doing on most dimensions since the end of World War II; or it can decline, as it did, at least in economic terms, during the Great Depression of the 1930s. Globalization implies that something is increasing: There is more of it. Hence, our definitions start not with globalization but with "globalism," a condition that can increase or decrease.

Globalism is a state of the world involving networks of interdependence at multi-continental distances. The linkages occur through flows and influences of capital and goods, information and ideas, and people and forces, as well as environmentally and biologically relevant substances (such as acid rain or pathogens). Globalization and deglobalization refer to the increase or decline of globalism.

Interdependence refers to situations characterized by reciprocal effects among countries or among actors in different countries. Hence, globalism is a type of interdependence, but with two special characteristics. First, globalism refers to networks of connections (multiple relationships), not to single linkages. We would refer to economic or military interdependence between the United States and Japan, but not to globalism between the United States and Japan. U.S.–Japanese interdependence is part of contemporary globalism, but is not by itself globalism.

Second, for a network of relationships to be considered "global," it must include multicontinental distances, not simply regional networks. Distance is a continuous variable, ranging from adjacency (between, say, the United States and Canada) to opposite sides of the globe (for instance, Great Britain and Australia). Any sharp distinction between long-distance and regional interdependence is therefore arbitrary, and there is no point in deciding whether intermediate relationships – say, between Japan and India or between Egypt and South Africa – would qualify. Yet globalism would be an odd word for proximate regional relationships. Globalization refers to the shrinkage of distance on a large scale [. . .]. It can be contrasted with localization, nationalization, or regionalization.

Some examples may help. Islam's rapid diffusion from Arabia across Asia to what is now Indonesia was a clear instance of globalization, but the initial movement of Hinduism across the Indian subcontinent was not. Ties among the countries of the Asia Pacific Economic Cooperation forum qualify as multicontinental interdependence, because these countries include the Americas as well as Asia and Australia; but ties among members of the Association of Southeast Asian Nations are regional.

Globalism does not imply universality. At the turn of the millennium, more than a quarter of the American population used the World Wide Web compared with one hundredth of 1 percent of the population of South Asia. Most people in the world today do not have telephones; hundreds of millions live as peasants in remote villages with only slight connections to world markets or the global flow of ideas. Indeed, globalization is accompanied by increasing gaps, in many respects, between the rich and the poor. It implies neither homogenization nor equity.

Interdependence and globalism are both multidimensional phenomena. All too often, they are defined in strictly economic terms, as if the world economy defined globalism. But there are several, equally important forms of globalism:

- *Economic globalism* involves long-distance flows of goods, services, and capital, as well as the information and perceptions that accompany market exchange. It also involves the organization of the processes that are linked to these flows, such as the organization of low-wage production in Asia for the U.S. and European markets.
- *Military globalism* refers to long-distance networks of interdependence in which force, and the threat or promise of force, are employed. A good example of military globalism is the "balance of terror" between the United States and the Soviet Union during the cold war. The two countries' strategic interdependence was acute and well recognized.

  [. . .]

- *Environmental globalism* refers to the long-distance transport of materials in the atmosphere or oceans, or of biological substances such as pathogens or genetic materials, that affect human health and well-being. The depletion of the stratospheric ozone layer as a result of ozone-depleting chemicals is an example of environmental globalism, as is the spread of the AIDS virus from west equatorial Africa around the world since the end of the 1970s. Some environmental globalism may be entirely natural, but much of the recent change has been induced by human activity.
- *Social and cultural globalism* involves the movement of ideas, information, images, and people (who, of course, carry ideas and information with them). Examples include the movement of religions or the diffusion of scientific knowledge. An important facet of social globalism involves the imitation of one society's practices and institutions by others: what some sociologists refer to as "isomorphism." Often, however, social globalism has followed military and economic globalism. Ideas, information, and people follow armies and economic flows, and in doing so, transform societies and markets. At its most profound level, social globalism affects the consciousness of individuals and their attitudes toward culture, politics, and personal identity.

  [. . .]

This division of globalism into separate dimensions is inevitably somewhat arbitrary. Nonetheless, it is useful for analysis, because changes in the various dimensions of globalization do not necessarily occur simultaneously. One can sensibly say, for instance, that economic globalization took place between approximately 1850 and 1914, manifested in imperialism and increased trade and capital flows between politically independent countries; and that such globalization was largely reversed between 1914 and 1945. That is, economic globalism rose between 1850 and 1914 and fell between 1914 and 1945.

However, military globalism rose to new heights during the two world wars, as did many aspects of social globalism. The worldwide influenza epidemic of 1918–19, which took 30 million lives, was propagated in part by the flows of soldiers around the world. So did globalism decline or rise between 1914 and 1945? It depends on what dimension of globalism one is examining.

Contemporary globalism

When people speak colloquially about globalization, they typically refer to recent increases in globalism. In this context, comments such as "globalization is fundamentally new" make sense but are nevertheless misleading. We prefer to speak of globalism as a phenomenon with ancient roots and of globalization as the process of increasing globalism, now or in the past.

The issue is not how old globalism is, but rather how "thin" or "thick" it is at any given time. As an example of "thin globalization," the Silk Road provided an economic and cultural link between ancient Europe and Asia, but the route was plied by a small group of hardy traders, and the goods that were traded back and forth had a direct impact primarily on a small (and relatively elite) stratum of consumers along the road. In contrast, "thick" relations of globalization involve many relationships that are intensive as well as extensive: long-distance flows that are large and continuous, affecting the lives of many people. The operations of global financial markets today, for instance, affect people from Peoria to Penang. Globalization is the process by which globalism becomes increasingly thick.

Globalism today is different from globalism of the 19th century, when European imperialism provided much of its political structure, and higher transport and communications costs meant fewer people were directly involved. But is there anything about globalism today that is fundamentally different from just 20 years ago? To say that something is "fundamentally" different is always problematic, since absolute discontinuities do not exist in human history. Every era builds on others, and historians can always find precursors for phenomena of the present.

[. . .]

Density of networks

Economists use the term "network effects" to refer to situations where a product becomes more valuable once many people use it – take, for example, the Internet. Joseph Stiglitz, former chief economist of the World Bank, has argued that a knowledge-based economy generates "powerful spillover effects, often spreading like fire and triggering further innovation and setting off chain reactions of new inventions." Moreover, as interdependence and globalism have become thicker, systemic relationships among different networks have become more important. There are more interconnections. Intensive economic interdependence affects social and environmental interdependence; awareness of these connections in turn affects economic relationships. For instance, the expansion of trade can generate industrial activity in countries with low environmental standards, mobilizing environmental activists to carry their message to these newly industrializing but environmentally lax countries. The resulting activities may affect environmental interdependence (for instance, by reducing cross-boundary pollution) but may generate resentment in the newly industrializing countries, affecting social and economic relations.

The worldwide impact of the financial crisis that began in Thailand in July 1997 illustrates the extent of these network interconnections. Unexpectedly, what first appeared as an isolated banking and currency crisis in a small "emerging market" country had severe global effects. It generated financial panic elsewhere in Asia, particularly in South Korea and Indonesia; prompted emergency meetings at the highest level of world finance and huge "bail-out" packages orchestrated by the International Monetary Fund (IMF); and led eventually to a widespread loss of confidence in emerging markets and the efficacy of international financial institutions.

[. . .]

Economic globalism is nothing new. Indeed, the relative magnitude of cross-border investment in 1997 was not unprecedented. Capital markets were by some measures more integrated at the beginning than at the end of the 20th century. The net outflow of capital from Great Britain in the four decades before 1914 averaged 5 percent of gross domestic product, compared with 2 to 3 percent for Japan over the last decade. The financial crisis of 1997–99 was not the first to be global in scale: "Black Tuesday" on Wall Street in 1929 and the collapse of Austria's Creditanstalt bank in 1931 triggered a worldwide financial crisis and depression. In the 1970s, skyrocketing oil prices prompted the Organization of Petroleum Exporting Countries to lend surplus funds to developed nations, and banks in those countries made a profit by relending that money to developing countries in Latin America and Africa (which needed the money to fund expansionary fiscal policies). But the money dried up with the global recession of 1981–83: by late 1986, more than 40 countries worldwide were mired in severe external debt.

But some features of the 1997–99 crisis distinguish it from previous ones. Most economists, governments, and international financial institutions failed to anticipate the crisis, and complex new financial instruments made it difficult to understand. Even countries that had previously been praised for their sound economic policies and performance were no less susceptible to the financial contagion triggered by speculative attacks and unpredictable changes in market sentiment. The World Bank had recently published a report entitled "The East Asian Miracle" (1993), and investment flows to Asia had risen rapidly to a new peak in 1997, remaining high until the crisis hit. In December 1998, Federal Reserve Board Chairman Alan Greenspan said: "I have learned more about how this new international financial system works in the last 12 months than in the previous 20 years." Sheer magnitude, complexity, and speed distinguish contemporary globalization from earlier periods: Whereas the debt crisis of the 1980s was a slow-motion train wreck that took place over a period of years, the Asian meltdown struck immediately and spread over a period of months.

The point is that the increasing thickness of globalism – the density of networks of interdependence – is not just a difference in degree. Thickness means that different relationships of interdependence intersect more deeply at more points. Hence, the effects of events in one geographical area, on one dimension, can have profound effects in other geographical areas, on other dimensions.

[. . .]

Globalization, therefore, does not merely affect governance; it is affected by governance. Frequent financial crises of the magnitude of the crisis of 1997–99 could lead to popular movements to limit interdependence and to a reversal of economic globalization. Chaotic uncertainty is too high a price for most people to pay for somewhat higher average levels of prosperity. Unless some of its aspects can be effectively governed, globalization may be unsustainable in its current form.

Institutional velocity

The information revolution is at the heart of economic and social globalization. It has made possible the transnational organization of work and the expansion of markets, thereby facilitating a new international division of labor. As Adam Smith famously declared in *The Wealth of Nations*, "the division of labor is limited by the extent of the market." Military globalism predated the information revolution, reaching its height during World War II and the cold war; but the nature of military interdependence has been transformed by information technology. The pollution that has contributed to environmental globalism has its sources in the coal-oil-steel-auto-chemical economy that was largely created between the middle of the 19th and 20th centuries and has become globalized only recently; but the information revolution may have a major impact on attempts to counter and reverse the negative effects of this form of globalism.

Sometimes these changes are incorrectly viewed in terms of the velocity of information flows. The biggest change in velocity came with the steamship and especially the telegraph: the transatlantic cable of 1866 reduced the time of transmission of information between London and New York by over a week – hence, by a factor of about a thousand. The telephone, by contrast, increased the velocity of such messages by a few minutes (since telephone messages do not require decoding), and the Internet, as compared with the telephone, by not much at all. The real difference lies in the reduced cost of communicating, not in the velocity of any individual communication. And the effects are therefore felt in the increased intensity rather than the extensity of globalism. In 1877 it was expensive to send telegrams across the Atlantic, and in 1927 or even 1977 it was expensive to telephone transcontinentally. Corporations and the rich used transcontinental telephones, but ordinary people wrote letters unless there was an emergency. But in 2000, if you have access to a computer, the Internet is virtually free and transpacific telephone calls may cost only a few cents per minute. The volume of communications has increased by many orders of magnitude, and the intensity of globalism has been able to expand exponentially.

Markets react more quickly than before, because information diffuses so much more rapidly and huge sums of capital can be moved at a moment's notice. Multinational enterprises have changed their organizational structures, integrating production more closely on a transnational basis and entering into more networks and alliances, as global capitalism has become more competitive and more subject to rapid change. Nongovernmental organizations (NGOs) have vastly expanded their levels of activity.

With respect to globalism and velocity, therefore, one can distinguish between the velocity of a given communication – "message velocity" – and "institutional velocity." Message velocity has changed little for the population centers of relatively rich countries since the telegraph became more or less universal toward the end of the 19th century. But institutional velocity – how rapidly a system and the units within it change – is a function not so much of message velocity than of the intensity of contact – the "thickness" of globalism. In the late 1970s, the news cycle was the same as it had been for decades: people found out the day's headlines by watching the evening news and got the more complete story and analysis from the morning paper. But the introduction of 24-hour cable news in 1980 and the subsequent emergence of the Internet have made news cycles shorter and have put a larger premium on small advantages in speed.

[. . .]

Transnational participation and complex interdependence

Reduced costs of communications have increased the number of participating actors and increased the relevance of "complex interdependence." This concept describes a hypothetical world with three characteristics: multiple channels between societies, with multiple actors, not just states; multiple issues, not arranged in any clear hierarchy; and the irrelevance of the threat or use of force among states linked by complex interdependence.

We used the concept of complex interdependence in the 1970s principally to describe emerging relationships among pluralist democracies. Manifestly it did not characterize relations between the United States and the Soviet Union, nor did it typify the politics of the Middle East, East Asia, Africa, or even parts of Latin America. However, we did argue that international monetary relations approximated some aspects of complex interdependence in the 1970s and that some bilateral relationships – French–German and U.S.–Canadian, for example – approximated all three conditions of complex interdependence. In a world of complex interdependence, we argued, politics would be different. The goals and instruments of state policy – and the processes of agenda setting and issue linkage – would all be different, as would the significance of international organizations.

Translated into the language of globalism, the politics of complex interdependence would be one in which levels of economic, environmental, and social globalism are high and military globalism is low. Regional instances of security communities – where states have reliable expectations that force will not be used – include Scandinavia since the early 20th century. Arguably, intercontinental complex interdependence was limited during the cold war to areas protected by the United States, such as the Atlantic security community. Indeed, U.S. power and policy were crucial to the construction of postwar international institutions, ranging from NATO to the IMF, which protected and supported complex interdependence. Since 1989, the decline of military globalism and the extension of social and economic globalism to the former Soviet empire have implied the expansion of areas of complex interdependence, at least to the new and aspiring members of NATO in Eastern Europe. Moreover, economic and social globalism seem to have created incentives for leaders in South America to settle territorial quarrels, out of fear both of being distracted from tasks of economic and social development and of scaring away needed investment capital.

[. . .]

The information revolution and the voracious appetite of television viewers for dramatic visual images have heightened global awareness of some of these civil conflicts and made them more immediate, contributing to pressure for humanitarian intervention, as in Bosnia and Kosovo. The various dimensions of globalization – in this case, the social and military dimensions – intersect, but the results are not necessarily conducive to greater harmony. Nevertheless, inter-state use and threat of military force have virtually disappeared in certain areas of the world – notably among the advanced, information-era democracies bordering the Atlantic and the Pacific, as well as among a number of their less wealthy neighbors in Latin America and increasingly in Eastern-Central Europe.

The dimension of complex interdependence that has changed the most since the 1970s is participation in channels of contact among societies. There has been a vast expansion of such channels as a result of the dramatic fall in the costs of communication over large distances. It is no longer necessary to be a rich organization to be able to communicate on a real-time basis with people around the globe. Friedman calls this change the "democratization" of technology, finance, and information, because diminished costs have made what were once luxuries available to a much broader range of society.

"Democratization" is probably the wrong word, however, since in markets money votes, and people start out with unequal stakes. There is no equality, for example, in capital markets, despite the new financial instruments that permit more people to participate. "Pluralization" might be a better word, suggesting the vast increase in the number and variety of participants in global networks. The number of international NGOs more than quadrupled from about 6,000 to over 26,000 in the 1990s alone. Whether they are large organizations such as Greenpeace or Amnesty International, or the proverbial "three kooks with modems and a fax machine," NGOs can now raise their voices as never before. In 1999, NGOs worldwide used the Internet to coordinate a massive protest against the World Trade Organization meeting in Seattle. Whether these organizations can forge a coherent and credible coalition has become the key political question.

[. . .]

So what really is new in contemporary globalism? Intensive, or thick, network interconnections that have systemic effects, often unanticipated. But such thick globalism is not uniform: it varies by region, locality, and issue area. It is less a matter of communications message velocity than of declining cost, which does speed up what we call systemic and institutional velocity. Globalization shrinks distance, but it does not make distance irrelevant. And the filters provided by domestic politics and political institutions play a major role in determining what effects globalization really has and how well various countries adapt to it. Finally, reduced costs have enabled more actors to participate in world politics at greater distances, leading larger areas of world politics to approximate the ideal type of complex interdependence.

Although the system of sovereign states is likely to continue as the dominant structure in the world, the content of world politics is changing. More dimensions than ever – but not all – are beginning to approach our idealized concept of complex interdependence. Such trends can be set back, perhaps even reversed, by cataclysmic events, as happened in earlier phases of globalization. History always has surprises. But history's surprises always occur against the background of what has gone before. The surprises of the early 21st century will, no doubt, be profoundly affected by the processes of contemporary globalization that we have tried to analyze here.

John Gerard Ruggie

TAKING EMBEDDED LIBERALISM GLOBAL: THE CORPORATE CONNECTION

From: Ruggie, J. G. (2003) 'Taking embedded liberalism global: the corporate connection' in D. Held and M. Koenig (eds) *Taming Globalization: Frontiers of Governance*, Polity Press, Blackwell

TWENTY YEARS AGO I published a scholarly article that introduced the concept of embedded liberalism. It told the story of how the capitalist countries learned to reconcile the efficiency of markets with the values of social community that markets themselves require in order to survive and thrive. That lesson did not come to them easily.

In the Victorian era, policy concern with the level of domestic employment and price stability was subordinated to maintaining the external value of currencies and, less consistently, to the strictures of free trade. But the growing democratization of national political life made that posture increasingly unsustainable, and the first so-called golden age of globalization unraveled. In the period between the two world wars the opposite was true: the unfettered quest for national policy autonomy – pushed by the political left, right and center alike – steadily undermined and ultimately destroyed an already fragile international economic order.

When a workable balance finally was struck it took on somewhat different forms in different countries, reflecting national political realities: in the US, the New Deal or Keynesian state, and in Europe social democracy or the social market economy. But the underlying idea was the same: a grand social bargain whereby all sectors of society agreed to open markets, which in some cases had become heavily administered if not autarchic in the 1930s, but also to contain and share the social adjustment costs that open markets inevitably produce. That was the essence of the embedded liberalism compromise: economic liberalization was embedded in social community.

Governments played a key role in enacting and sustaining this compromise: moderating the volatility of transaction flows across borders and providing social investments, safety nets and adjustment assistance – yet all the while pushing international liberalization. In the industrialized countries, this grand bargain formed the basis of the longest and most equitable economic expansion in human history.

So what is the problem today? For the industrialized countries, it is the fact that embedded liberalism presupposed an *international* world. It presupposed the existence of *national* economies, engaged in *external* transactions, conducted at *arm's length*, which governments could mediate at the *border* by tariffs and exchange rates, among other tools. The globalization of financial markets and production chains, however, challenges each of these premises and threatens to leave behind merely national social bargains.

The developing countries, of course, never enjoyed the privilege of cushioning the adverse domestic effects of market exposure in the first place. The majority lack the resources, institutional capacity, international support and, in some instances, the political interest on the part of their ruling elites. As a result, large parts of the developing world have been unable to exploit the opportunities offered by globalization for achieving poverty reduction and sustainable development.

[. . .]

Embedding the global market within shared social values and institutional practices represents a task of historic magnitude. The reason is obvious: there is no govern*ment* at the global level to act on behalf of the common good, as there is at the national level. And international institutions are far too weak to fully compensate.

[. . .]

First, I describe some of the main drivers of the anti-globalization backlash, especially the growing anxieties in the industrialized countries that the social embeddedness side of the equation is losing out to the dictates of globalization. Then I examine the evolution of voluntary initiatives involving civil society and the global business community to promote corporate social responsibility as one means of responding to the many challenges of globalization. In that context, I also summarize the key features of Annan's Global Compact, a UN initiative to engage the corporate community, in partnership with civil society and labor, to implement human rights, labor standards and environmental sustainability in its global domain. The burden of my argument is that the corporate sector, which has done more than any other to create the growing gaps between global economy and national communities, is being pulled into playing a key bridging role between them. In the process, a global public domain is emerging, which cannot substitute for effective action by states but may help produce it.

The backlash

The globalization backlash has many sources. [. . .] But three negative attributes of the recent era of global market integration stand out as having animated particular concern.

First, the benefits of globalization are distributed highly unequally. As the IMF's Managing Director, Horst Köhler, has conceded, "the disparities between the world's richest and poorest nations are wider than ever."[1] Large parts of the developing world are left behind entirely.

[. . .]

Moreover, apart from China, income disparities among the world's people, as, distinguished from countries, either have not improved significantly during the past three decades or actually may have become worse, depending on how they are measured. Much the same holds for global poverty rates. Even in the United States, the unprecedented boom of the 1990s barely budged the income shares of the bottom 20 percent of households, and then only briefly.

[. . .]

Second, the backlash is triggered by a growing imbalance in global rule making. Those rules that favor global market expansion have become more robust and enforceable in the last decade or two – intellectual property rights, for example, or trade dispute resolution through the World Trade Organization. But rules intended to promote equally valid social objectives, be they labor standards, human rights, environmental quality or poverty reduction, lag behind and in some instances actually have become weaker.[2] One result is the situation where considerations of patent rights have trumped fundamental human rights and even pandemic threats to human life – at least until that clash became unbearable for the world's conscience over the HIV/AIDS treatment issue in Africa.[3]

Third, for many people globalization has come to mean greater vulnerability to unfamiliar and unpredictable forces that can bring on economic instability and social dislocation, sometimes at lightning speed. The Asian financial crisis of 1997–8 was such a force – the fourth but not the last major international financial crisis in just two decades. Indeed, the integrity of cultures and sovereignty of states increasingly are seen to be at risk.

[. . .]

The long struggle that ultimately resulted in the embedded liberalism compromise suggests that disparities of this sort are socially unsustainable. [. . .] What is more, the backlash against globalization has particular bite because it is driven not only, or even primarily, by the poor and the weak. Its vanguard includes large numbers of people in the most privileged societies the world has ever known.

[. . .]

Public expenditure

Vito Tanzi and Ludger Schuknecht document the evolution of public expenditure in the industrialized countries going back to 1870.[4] Over the course of the subsequent 125 years, spending grew from an average of 10.7 percent of gross domestic product, to 45.6 percent. The two world wars and the Great Depression accounted for significant increases. But the most dramatic expansion took place between 1960 and 1980, and in that period social expenditures – for education, health, pensions, unemployment benefits and the like – more than doubled on average. This was also the period of the most significant reductions in barriers to trade and monetary flows by the industrialized countries. Research by political scientists as long ago as the late 1970s demonstrated a relationship between the two: the most open economies also tended to lead in social spending.

[. . .]

The 1980s and 1990s saw the emergence of growing skepticism about the role of the state, especially in the United Kingdom and the United States. For a variety of reasons, some substantive, others political, prevailing economic theory and public attitudes began to shift in a neoliberal (the preferred term for neo-laissez-faire) direction. Though public spending continued to increase, it was at a slower pace. And it was purchasing fewer social services, in part due to the declining cost-effectiveness of some interventions, and in part because a rapidly rising public sector debt burden consumed an ever greater fraction of overall government spending. A period of reform and retrenchment ensued.

Tanzi and Schuknecht predict a reduction in public expenditure relative to GDP in the years ahead, reflecting less favorable attitudes toward the role of the state (which may be partially off-set in the United States by the effects of 9/11 and corporate malfeasance), coupled with greater fiscal constraints due to demographic shifts, among other factors.

But what exactly is the relationship between these trends and globalization? An increasingly widespread view holds that global market integration induces governments to pursue greater fiscal austerity, ease regulatory and tax burdens on business, and strongly discourage certain policy options if not ruling them out altogether.[5]

[. . .]

The magnitude of these changes remains small and patterns of variation among countries, and across different market segments for the same country, are exceedingly complex. Nevertheless, they may signal a gradual shift in the political economy of industrialized countries, away from an earlier "compensatory" approach to managing the effects of increased openness, toward more of a "competitiveness" model. This would confirm that popular anxiety about globalization, though possibly exaggerated, is not without any basis in fact.

[. . .]

Income and employment

In the United States, organized labor has been among the most ardent opponents of globalization, especially of further trade liberalization.

[. . .]

There is little dispute that median family income in the United States has been stagnant for two decades while worker productivity has been growing. And there can be no disagreement that this gap coincides with large increases in trade exposure.

But there any consensus ends. Edward Leamer has developed a sophisticated economic model and presents country-based evidence partly supporting the globalization hypothesis.[6]

[. . .]

Disentangling and establishing these and other factors with any degree of certainty, Dani Rodrik suggests that the link between globalization and its labor market effects may be largely indirect, through shifts in relative bargaining power.[7] Globalization makes the services of large numbers of workers more easily substitutable across national boundaries, Rodrik argues, as a result of which the leverage of immobile labor vis-à-vis mobile capital erodes. Thus, in the neoliberal countries workers are obliged to accept greater instability in earnings and hours worked, if not lower wages altogether; to pay a larger share of their own benefits (as has become all too evident in the area of pensions and health care) as well as improvements in working conditions; and to accept more frequent job changes. [. . .] In the more traditional social democracies and social market economies where income levels and employment are more secure, labor is obliged to accept higher rates of chronic unemployment and lack of job creation.

Thus, the impact of globalization on wage stagnation in the US and high unemployment in Europe remains at minimum an open question for the economy as a whole. Of course, it is not an open question for workers in the industries affected most directly by job-displacing imports, who may have to accept lower-paying work.

[. . .]

Voluntary initiatives

Once upon a time, governance at the international level was entirely a statist affair. Whether the instruments were international alliances, regimes, law and organizations, or transnational networks of national bureaucracies, states both monopolized the conduct of governance and were the primary objects of their joint decisions and actions. That was the foundational premise of the traditional system.

In recent decades, actors and forces for which the territorial state is not the cardinal organizing principle have begun to outflank the state externally and to gnaw away at its governance monopoly from the inside. They may be driven by universal values or factional greed, by profit and efficiency considerations or the search for salvation. They include global financial markets and production chains, civil society organizations and such uncivil entities as transnational terrorist and criminal networks.

The place of non-state actors and movements remains poorly understood in the mainstream literature.

[. . .]

Nevertheless, significant institutional developments *are* evolving at the global level, among them the emergence of what we might call a global public domain: an arena of discourse, contestation and action organized around global rule making – a transnational space that is not exclusively inhabited by states, and which permits the direct expression and pursuit of human interests, not merely those mediated by the state. One of its major drivers is the expanding role of civil society, and the interplay between civil society organizations and the global corporate sector. This institutional development does not and cannot take the place of states, but it introduces new elements and new dynamics into the processes of global governance.

Civil society organizations

Real world players have come to recognize the involvement of civil society organizations (CSOs) in several areas related to global rule making – where by "recognize" I mean that the other players regard CSOs' participation as more or less legitimate, and in varying degrees they actually count on them to play those roles.[8] In other words, the roles have become institutionalized – much as, for example, the environmental movement did within the industrialized countries a generation ago.

To begin with, civil society organizations have become the main international providers of direct assistance to people in developing countries, be it foreign aid, humanitarian relief or a variety of other internationally provided services. Governmental entities, such as the United States Agency for International Development, largely have become contracting agencies while CSOs deliver the goods.

[. . .]

CSO coalitions also have become a significant, if still episodic, force in blocking or promoting international agreements. Two exemplars have acquired iconic status. The most celebrated blockage was of the Multilateral Agreement on Investment (MAI), negotiated at the Organization for Economic Cooperation and Development (OECD), which would have been the high water mark of the neoliberal quest in the 1990s. And the most dramatic instance of successfully promoting a new agreement – even participating fully in its negotiation – is the land-mines ban, which was begun, literally, by two people with a fax machine, and ended up helping to produce an international treaty over the opposition of the most powerful bureaucracy in the world's most powerful state: the US Pentagon.

[...]

Coalitions of domestic and transnational civil society networks also perform indispensable roles in the defense of human and labor rights, environmental standards and other social concerns within countries where the normal political process impedes or opposes progress in those areas.

[...]

Finally, civil society organizations have become a major force to induce greater social responsibility in the global corporate sector, by creating transparency in the overseas behavior of companies and their suppliers and creating links to consumers back home.

Corporate social responsibility

The rights enjoyed by transnational corporations have increased manyfold over the past two decades, as a result of multilateral trade agreements, bilateral investment pacts and domestic liberalization. Along with those rights, however, have come demands, led largely by civil society, that corporations accept commensurate obligations. To oversimplify only slightly, as governments were creating the space for transnational corporations (TNCs) to operate globally, other social actors have sought to infuse that space with greater corporate social responsibility.

Civil society organizations have joined issue with the global corporate sector for several reasons. First, individual companies have made themselves targets by doing "bad" things in the past: Shell in Nigeria, Nike in Indonesia, Nestlé in relation to its breast milk substitute products, unsafe practices in the chemical industry as symbolized by Union Carbide's Bhopal disaster, upscale apparel retailers purchasing from sweatshop suppliers, unsustainable forestry practices by the timber industry, and so on. Even where companies may be breaking no laws, they have been targeted by activist groups for violating the companies' own self-proclaimed standards or broader community norms in such areas as human rights, labor practices and environmental sustainability. CSOs seek to induce companies to undertake verifiable change.

Second, the growing imbalance between corporate rights and obligations itself has become a major factor driving CSO campaigns and, as I suggested earlier, it has particular resonance where it touches on life-and-death issues like HIV/AIDS treatment and related public health crises.

[...]

Gradually, however, the sheer fact that the corporate sector, unlike states and international organizations, has global reach and capacity has become its most compelling attraction to other social actors, together with its ability to make and implement decisions at a pace that neither governments nor intergovernmental agencies can possibly match. In the face of global governance gaps and governance failures, civil society – and increasingly other actors as well, including states – seeks to engage the corporate world's global platform to advance broader social objectives. Kofi Annan's Global Compact, discussed below, is based entirely on this rationale.

The universe of transnational corporations consists roughly of 63,000 firms, with more than 800,000 subsidiaries and millions of suppliers. Improving those companies' social and environmental performance has direct benefits for their employees and the communities in which they operate.

[. . .]

In sum, as a result of pressure from civil society, companies and business associations began to accept, on a voluntary basis and at a modest pace, new corporate social responsibilities in their own corporate domains, and more recently vis-à-vis society at large. The decision by firms to engage is driven by a variety of factors, but above all by the sensitivity of their corporate brands to consumer attitudes.

Certification institutions

Transnational corporations have adopted scores of codes of conduct and negotiated others within industry associations and with CSOs. Gary Gereffi and his colleagues call these "certification institutions." By now they exist in most major economic sectors, including mining, petroleum, chemicals, forest products, automobiles as well as textiles, apparel and footwear. A recent OECD survey inventoried 246 codes, though the total number remains unknown. In that survey, labor standards (heavy concentration in the apparel industry) and environmental concerns (high in the extractive sector) dominate other issues addressed (148 and 145 cases respectively), with some codes including both.

[. . .]

The most ambitious and typically the most transparent certification arrangements tend to be sectoral in scope, and to involve several companies and/or business associations along with civil society participants. Their aims range from ensuring that the price paid to cooperatives of small-scale family farmers growing coffee beans in Costa Rica includes a premium for growing the beans in an environmentally sustainable manner (Fair Trade Certified coffee); to ensuring that plywood ending up at Home Depot and other participating home improvement outlets is produced in accordance with sustainable forestry practices (Forest Stewardship Council); to certifying that sweatshirts sold in college bookstores or cashmere sweaters destined for Fifth Avenue department stores and upscale suburban malls are knitted in conditions that meet agreed labor standards and conditions (Workers Rights Consortium, and either the Fair Labor Association or an individual company code with compliance audited by SA8000). A certification institution called Responsible Care – triggered by Bhopal – now operates in the US chemical industry, while the Global Mining Initiative was recently launched in that sector.

[. . .]

The Global Compact

Kofi Annan coupled his 1999 warning to the world's business leaders about the fragility of globalization with an initiative called the Global Compact (GC). It is *not* a code of conduct – which has been a major point of contention vis-à-vis anti-globalization activist groups. A partnership between the United Nations, business, international labor and major transnational civil society organizations, the Compact instead seeks to engage companies in the promotion of certain UN principles within corporate domains.[9] The principles themselves are drawn from the Universal Declaration of Human Rights, the International Labor Organization's Fundamental Principles on Rights at Work and the Rio Principles on Environment and Development. Companies are encouraged to move toward "good practices" as defined through multi-stakeholder dialogue and partnership rather than relying on their often superior bargaining position vis-à-vis national authorities, especially in small and poor states, to get away with less. The Compact employs three instruments to achieve its aims.

Through its "learning forum," it is designed to generate consensus-based understandings of how a company's commitment to the nine principles can be translated most effectively into corporate management practices.

[. . .]

By means of its "policy dialogues," the Compact generates shared understandings about, for example, the socially responsible posture for companies when operating in countries afflicted by conflict.

[. . .]

Finally, through its "partnership projects" in developing countries the Compact contributes to capacity building where it is needed most. Ongoing cases include support for microlending, investment promotion, HIV/AIDS awareness programs for employees in sub-Saharan Africa, devising sustainable alternatives to child labor, and a host of initiatives in ecoefficiency and other dimensions of environmental management.

[. . .]

Companies initiate participation in the Compact with a letter of commitment from their Chief Executive Officer to the Secretary-General, a step that often requires board approval. Since a kickoff event in July 2000, some 400 companies worldwide – based in Europe, the United States, Japan, Hong Kong, India, Brazil, Thailand and elsewhere – have done so.

Organizationally, the Compact comprises a series of nested networks. The Secretary-General's office provides strategic direction, policy coherence and quality control. The participating UN agencies, companies, international labor, transnational NGOs, and university-based research centers do the heavy lifting in the learning forum, policy dialogues and partnership projects.

The Global Compact has triggered several complementary regional, national, and sectoral initiatives. Typically, they take a subset of interested GC participants beyond its minimum commitments.

[. . .]

As noted, the Compact is not a code of conduct but a social learning network. It operates on the premise that socially legitimated good practices will help drive out bad ones through the power of transparency and competition. The UN General Assembly could not generate a meaningful code of conduct at this time even if that were deemed desirable; the only countries that would be eager to launch such an effort are equally unfriendly to the private sector, human rights, labor standards and the environment. In any event, many of the GC's principles cannot be defined at this time with the precision required for a viable inter-governmental code. No consensus exists on precisely what comprises a "precautionary approach."

[. . .]

Moreover, ex ante standards often become performance ceilings that are difficult to change – witness the inability of the US Senate to muster the political will to improve automobile fuel efficiency standards that have not been altered since 1985, long before the prevalence of so-called sports utility vehicles. In contrast, the Compact seeks to peg company performance globally to evolving international community-based "good practices," thereby potentially "ratcheting up" performance on an ongoing basis.[10]

The Global Compact is based on principles that were universally endorsed by governments, thus stipulating aspirational goals of the entire international community. It enlists partners in the corporate sector and civil society to help bridge the gap between aspiration and reality – to become agencies for the promotion of community norms. Thus, the Compact is a heterodox addition to the growing menu of responses to globalization's challenges that engage the private sector – including corporate codes of conduct, social and environmental reporting initiatives, and various other means to promote and monitor corporate social responsibility.

A global public domain

Despite the great progress that has been achieved in promoting voluntary initiatives, their scope remains limited. [. . .] Of the 700 companies subscribing to the Global Compact, perhaps no more than a quarter are deeply engaged. And so on, throughout other industry sectors. By themselves, therefore, they do not and cannot constitute the entirety of solutions.

At the same time, these company-based initiatives are significant not only for what they achieve directly, but also because they are triggering broader second-order consequences. Consider some of the main elements and actors.

First, the investment community has shown growing interest, which brings large amounts of capital into play.

[. . .]

Second, the public sector is slowly entering the picture. Several OECD countries – the UK, France and the Netherlands – have begun to encourage or require companies to engage in social reporting, for example, and to promote corporate social responsibility through other means.

[. . .]

Where labor is included in voluntary initiatives – as in the Global Compact – it gains a global platform that may help compensate for, and possibly overcome, its stagnant and even shrinking platform at the national level. Indeed, no social partner has made more effective use of the Global Compact than labor.

Perhaps the most significant development politically is the emergence of a new advocate for a more effective global public sector: business itself. Corporate leaders at the frontier of corporate social responsibility issues have begun to realize that the concept is infinitely elastic: the more they do, the more they will be asked to do. As a result, business leaders themselves have begun to ask, "*Where is the public sector?*" Three elite global business groups – the World Economic Forum, International Chamber of Commerce, and World Business Council for Sustainable Development – recently launched governance initiatives, not to curtail the public sector but to clarify where private sector responsibility ends and public responsibility begins.[11]

[. . .]

Finally, at the end of the day the accumulation of experience inevitably will lead to a desire for greater benchmarking, for moving from "good" to "best" practices and even formal codification, so that some of the "soft law" products of voluntary initiatives are likely to become "harder" law down the road. The advocates will include industry leaders to lock in their own first-mover advantages, or wanting a level playing field vis-à-vis laggards – as happened when several major energy companies lobbied the US Congress for some form of greenhouse-gas limits after President Bush rejected the Kyoto Protocol. Laggards have a harder time opposing standards based on actual achievements by their peers than ex ante standards.

This terrain is fraught with strategic manipulation and the potential for shirking. But it also opens the door to more firmly institutionalizing an emerging global public domain by bringing the public sector into it. Globalization was a one-way bet for the business community: governments were needed to create the space within which business could expand and integrate, but they were not otherwise welcome. The combination of global governance gaps and governance failures, however, created an organizational niche that civil society actors began to occupy, and from which they have been engaging the global business community in the attempt to balance its newly acquired rights with new social responsibilities.

[...]

Conclusion

When we reflect on how hard it was and how long it took to institute the original embedded liberalism compromise at the national level, the prospect of achieving a similar social framing of global market forces seems exponentially more daunting. But if there is one similarity between the two eras, and the two levels of social organization, it is in the respective roles of the private sector as an inadvertent transformational force – be it the hegemony of the great "trusts" in the late nineteenth century, the abysmal failure of financial institutions in the interwar period, or the spread of multinational corporate empires today. The international political arena differs radically, characterized as it is by the absence of government. And so at the global level there will be many more zigs, many more zags, and quite probably many more failures. But our discussion has outlined both a dynamic of possible change and a possible trajectory.

I have argued that, as a result of the expansion of civil society and its engagement with the corporate sector, a global public domain is emerging. I take that to mean an arena inhabited by various actors for whom the territorial state is not the cardinal organizing principle, as well as by states; and wherein a variety of human interests are expressed and pursued directly, not merely those mediated – promoted, filtered, interpreted – by the state. Indeed, some areas of global public policy would barely exist were it not for non-state actors. And in addition to the traditional machinery of interstate governance, the likes of essentially private certification institutions are becoming significant components of global rule making. But private governance produces only partial solutions, and its own unfolding brings the public sector back in.

[...]

Moreover, the skewed distribution of agential capacity between North and South is too pronounced, accountability problems too pervasive and the distributional consequences of these kinds of global governance instruments too poorly understood for us to believe that they reflect some new stable equilibrium.

What we can say is that a fundamental recalibration is going on of the public–private sector balance, and it is occurring at the global level no less than the domestic. Haltingly and erratically, something akin to an embedded liberalism compromise is being pulled and pushed into the global arena, and the corporate connection is a key element in that process.

Notes

1   "Working for a Better Globalization," remarks by Horst Köhler at the Conference on Humanizing the Global Economy, Washington DC, Jan. 28, 2002.

2   For detailed surveys of what gets "regulated" at the global level, and how, see P.J. Simmons and Chantal de Jonge Oudraat (eds), *Managing Global Issues* (Washington DC: Carnegie Endowment, 2001), and John Braithwaite and Peter Drahos, *Global Business Regulation* (New York: Cambridge University Press, 2000).

3   The business community itself felt that the big pharmaceutical companies put themselves in an untenable position. Gardiner Harris and Laurie McGinely, "AIDS Gaffers in Africa Come Back to Haunt Drug Industry at Home," *Wall Street Journal*, Apr. 23, 2001.

4   Vito Tanzi and Ludger Schuknecht, *Public Spending in the 20th Century* (New York: Cambridge University Press, 2000).

5   Clearly financial market integration has increased the cost of utilizing capital controls. For example, when Malaysia imposed targeted and time-bound controls to limit domestic spillover from the Asian financial crisis, for which it had no responsibility, all the major credit rating agencies downgraded Malaysia's sovereign risk rating – Fitch IBCA to "junk bond" status. Said a spokesperson for Fitch: "We are in no doubt about Malaysia's ability to service its debt. It is a question of willingness to do so" – even though the Malaysian government had done nothing to indicate any such unwillingness. See Rawi Abdelal and Laura Alfaro, "Malaysia: Capital and Control," Harvard Business School, Case 9-702-040 (June 4, 2002), p. 12.

6   Edward E. Leamer, "Wage Inequality from International Competition and Technological Change: Theory and Country Experience," American Economics Association, *Papers and Proceedings*, May 1996.

7   Dani Rodrik, *Has Globalization Gone Too Far?* (Washington DC: Institute for International Economics, 1997).

8   For useful introductions, see Sanjeev Khagram, James V. Riker and Kathryn Sikkink (eds), *Restructuring World Politics: Transnational Social Movements, Networks and Norms* (Minneapolis: University of Minnesota Press, 2002); Ann M. Florini (ed.), *The Third Force: The Rise of Transnational Civil Society* (Washington DC: Carnegie Endowment for International Peace, 2000); and Jessica Mathews, "Power Shift," *Foreign Affairs*, 76 (Jan./Feb. 1997).

9   The GC participants include the UN (the Secretary-General's Office, Office of the High Commissioner for Human Rights, International Labor Organization, UN Environment Program and the UN Development Program); the International Confederation of Free Trade Unions (ICFTU); more than a dozen transnational NGOs in the three areas covered by the GC, such as Amnesty International, the International Union for the Conservation of Nature, and Oxfam; as well as individual companies and international business associations. For up-to-date information, see www.unglobalcompact.org.

10   This concept is due to Charles Sabel, Dara O'Rourke and Archon Fung, "Ratcheting Labor Standards: Regulation for Continuous Improvement in the Global Workplace," John F. Kennedy School of Government, Harvard University, KSG Working Paper no. 00–010, May 2, 2000.

11   The World Economic Forum plans to publish an annual Global Governance Report, which will assess the respective contributions that various sectors of society are making to solving global problems; www.weforum.org/site/homepublic.nsf/Content/Global+Governance+Task+Force.

Jon Pierre and B. Guy Peters

COMMUNITARIANISM, DELIBERATION, DIRECT DEMOCRACY AND GOVERNANCE

From: Pierre, J. and Peters, B. G. (2000) 'Communitarianism, deliberation, direct democracy and governance', *Governance, Politics and the State*, Chapter 7, Macmillan

IN ADDITION TO CHALLENGES to traditional patterns of governance arising from globalization and from the power of networks, there is yet another set of challenges that would produce very different styles of governing. This collection of related challenges all endeavour to deinstitutionalize governance and to more directly involve citizens in making binding policy decisions. The assumption undergirding these ideas is that the public can – and more especially should – have more direct influence over decisions than they can exercise in representative democracy. These ideas go beyond the 'new governance' ideas of using groups, networks and other intermediate social structures as mechanisms for governance to focus on citizens themselves as the principal source of governance.

These ideas then represent a populist challenge to 'big government', and seek to return governance to 'the people'. Unlike the market challenge to large-scale government involvement in the economy, however, the normative inclination here is collectivist rather than individualistic. Its purpose is not so much to permit the individual to retain earnings and wealth as to permit the individual to participate in a legitimate political community and to make effective decisions about their future through collective action.

These populist challenges are then more closely linked to traditional governance ideas than is the market vision of reform. In particular, these views are linked to a traditional conception of *democratic* governance. The assumption is that to govern appropriately a democratic political system must be capable of linking the demands and wishes of the public directly to policies (Rose, 1976). Further, the traditional governance view often argues that most representative institutions do not permit adequate debate and discussion but rather depend more on one side prevailing over the other with as little discussion as possible.

For both the market and the collectivist challenges the status quo of governance is considered deeply flawed, but the prescriptions tend to be diametrically opposed. Rather than dismantling most governance structures in favour of an atomistic market many of these populist reformers would build even more inclusive structures, and would require most citizens to devote greater time and energy than they now spend to the processes of collective governance. Even those collectivist reformers who do not desire to build structures *per se* do want to use a political (voting) device, rather than an economic device, to make choices for the collectivity.

Although we are discussing alternatives to governance through the public sector, the critique of government embedded within this populist challenge is actually targeted more broadly. It is a generalized critique of virtually all representative and intermediate structures in industrialized societies, including political parties and even the interest group networks that are so central to much of the 'new governance' literature. [. . .] The ideas being advocated are to reform all social institutions and to develop alternatives that will either replace or complement the more traditional structures.

There are three major variants of this populist challenge to the traditional conceptions of governance. All three versions would deinstitutionalize existing government structures, or at least would seek to augment them with more direct citizen involvement. Within the three there are still some differences in the degree to which government structures and representative democracy would be de-emphasized. The least movement away from the status quo in governance appears to be represented by communitarianism.

[. . .]

The basic tenet of communitarianism is that large-scale society and government have outlived much of their utility and they need to be replaced by smaller units of governing. The more appropriate basis for governing is considered to be the 'community', although this term itself is open to some interpretation. In this view some of the basic mechanisms of governance by political means are not incorrect; the difficulty is with the scale on which those devices are being implemented. Large-scale decision-making, it is argued, forces the same sort of individualism associated with economic models of policy; individuals need to have their self-interest modulated by less selfish commitments to community.

The second alternative to the existing patterns of government is deliberative democracy. This [. . .] has a somewhat stronger emphasis on the immediate reform of decision-making institutions. The logic of this approach is that representative democracy does not permit average citizens to exert adequate influence over policy decisions. Rather than being the apathetic 'couch potatoes' assumed in some contemporary discussions of governing, the public is assumed to desire to be more involved in political life. Advocates of deliberative democracy argue that citizens feel, however, that they are effectively excluded by the current institutional arrangements used for governing. This view represents one of the standard sociological definitions of alienation – the existence of ends with the absence of effective means to achieve those ends.

Establishing mechanisms for greater direct public involvement in policy-making are hypothesized to be essential for reviving democracy. This contribution to enhanced democracy is especially valid if those methods can create more numerous opportunities for the public to discuss issues and to develop more complete and nuanced understandings of those issues than is possible within existing representative institutions. Developing these institutions for discussion and deliberation is deemed to be especially important (and feasible) at the local level, having this conception in common with the communitarians. The lower level of government is believed to be a more suitable locus for developing 'genuine' deliberative democracy than are other levels of government.

Finally, direct democracy constitutes another alternative to representative democracy. Even more than the other two alternative approaches, this method of governance would supplant the existing representative institutions in favour of the public making its own decisions through mechanisms such as initiatives and referendums. In the literature supporting this alternative the assumption is that the public does not really need to have the elaborate discussion and deliberation inherent in the deliberative democracy approach. Rather, the public is argued to be capable and ready to make important policy decisions through a simple vote on the issues. Even more than that, there is an assumption in some of this literature (and practice) that the public is capable of setting the agenda for governing, as when initiatives permit the public (through petitions) to place an issue on the ballot for subsequent resolution.

[. . .]

The discussion will attempt to demonstrate some of the strengths of each alternative, but also to portray some of its weaknesses. The fundamental argument developed here is that none of these three is capable of supplying governance in the coherent and integrated manner that is required. There are some common problems in all these models that we will identify, but there are also some very particular issues that arise for each of the three. In some instances, a strength of one of these three alternatives may be a major weakness of one of the others.

We will also point out that each of the three alternatives represents useful complements to existing patterns of governance, although they are almost certainly not adequate replacements in all instances. [. . .] The advocates of each of these approaches tend to consider it as a general solution for the problems of governance, but our views will be contingent and more modulated. There are in our view a large number of instances in which the traditional patterns of governance are preferable, and in which the use of one of the alternatives will produce a positive loss of governance capacity.

The diagnosis

Before we embark on the detailed examination of each of the three alternatives, however, we should examine some general points of diagnosis — what do these approaches to governance believe is amiss in the conventional patterns of governing? [. . .] This portion of the discussion will remain rather general, with the more particularistic points discussed in reference to each of the three alternatives. The critique of the existing patterns of governance rests on four main problems in the present governing systems: size, remoteness, displacement of goals and the adversarial nature of the institutions.

[. . .]

Size

The first critique is that existing governance structures are too large. This is true of the geographical and social space that they cover. It is also true of the range of issues about which they attempt to exercise governance, and also about their ambitions in governing. That is, governments in many industrialized democracies are argued to have taken on too many responsibilities and promised too much to their citizens, and have not been able to deliver the goods and services promised. [. . .] The disjuncture between promises and performance has been one component of the disaffection of many citizens with their governments.

[. . .]

The larger scale of discourse tends, in turn, to make individuals less responsible for their own governing and less likely to be able to conceptualize solutions. [. . .] Seeing themselves at the mercy of forces, well beyond their control, citizens are assumed simply to opt out of political participation. The other option is that a definition of political life is developed that tends to exclude those who do not accept a particular civic virtue, or who do not fit the prevailing conception of appropriate behaviour.

[. . .]

Even if viable 'public spaces' for discussion are maintained in a large-scale representative democracy, deliberation becomes relatively useless: there is little or no way that meaningful discussions can occur at that larger scale of governance (Habermas, 1984). Only at the face-to-face level, in small units, is there likely to be discussion and dialogue over policy, other than in the most superficial manner.

[. . .]

Another aspect of this critique of large-scale government is that size prevents governments from developing the types of policies that are increasingly required in a 'post-industrial democracy' (Bell, 1976). [. . .] Having to cope with large numbers of clients, and large numbers of service providers, makes 'empowerment politics' more difficult to implement.

Remoteness

Another common complaint about the contemporary system of governance is that it is too remote from the average citizen. That average citizen encounters a very difficult time in influencing policy or setting the terms of debate about policy. Given the number of citizens that each elected delegate must represent, he or she cannot really be said to reflect those views very closely or even be aware of most of them. This scale means that the representatives are able to make decisions on their own with little or no reference to the wishes of their publics. Further, the views in any constituency, may be so diverse that the representative can pick and choose among interests and views, rather than seek to form any consensus among those ideas.

[. . .]

Citizens often have information that is not possessed by official sources but is more 'street-level' knowledge that even for some technical policy issues may be crucial for making the most appropriate decisions.

Even with interest groups, as components of the networks that are so central to the 'new governance', there is a gap between the average member and the group leadership.

[. . .]

Displacement of goals

Finally, given the remoteness of leadership in both political institutions and interest groups, there is a capacity for the leaders to pursue their own goals rather than those of the citizens or their membership. This is in part because the large-scale structures, and the low levels of information conveyed by voting, and even by occasional public meetings, are insufficient to provide guidance for even the most conscientious politician.

The above view is, however, in contrast to one of the other critiques of modern politicians that they are unwilling to make stands on their own but rather depend too heavily on public opinion polls. [. . .] And for the less than conscientious among them there is ample latitude for self-aggrandizement, whether legal or extra-legal.

[. . .]

The pursuit of individual goals by political elites while in office is seen in these critiques simply as a continuation of the same individualistic norms inherent in contemporary governance structures. Rather than being part of a community of any variety, the individual citizen is simply one lone individual attempting to make his or her way through this vale of tears as skilfully as possible. This perceived focus on the individual politician as a utility maximizer in matters of governance may be a case of life imitating art, as the methodological individualism of rational choice theory has come to dominate analysis in the social sciences (Green and Shapiro, 1994). This view can be contrasted to a variety of more collectivist theories about social life.

[. . .]

Adversarial governance

The fourth general problem with representative government institutions identified by the three alternative conceptions of governance is that these institutions tend to be adversarial. Steven Kelman (1992) has argued that one of the most important differences among various political systems is the extent to which they are adversarial, with the Westminster systems being particularly combative while more corporatist systems (Scandinavia) being more consensual. For the proponents of these alternatives [. . .] the differences are perhaps not worth considering, and representative institutions in general are excessively oriented toward conflict and a winner-take-all style of conflict resolution. It is perhaps not surprising, therefore, that most advocates of the alternative visions of governance are from Anglo-American systems.

The problem being identified here is that government through adversarial mechanisms divides members of the public rather than permitting the development of policies that can satisfy all of the public, at least minimally. In some instances it may be difficult to find such a policy, but the process of negotiation itself may be a significant way in which to expose fundamental issues and at least to identify the reasons for the disagreement. Further, representative institutions are almost designed to enhance adversarial and competitive behaviours, rather than consensus-building. The idea of securing a majority in parliament in order to govern, for example, is an inherently adversarial concept and, especially when a single party can win control (as in Westminster systems), tends to institutionalize the winner-take-all mentality of those systems.

[. . .]

Communitarianism

The most general option for addressing the problems in democratic governance outlined above is communitarianism. As an option to the isolation and atomism of contemporary society and representative political institutions, these scholars and activists would create working communities and community governments (Etzioni, 1995, 1998; Bell, 1993). There is a working assumption that most socio-economic problems can be solved at lower levels of aggregation than at which they are currently addressed. Further, there is an implicit judgement that with the proper social engineering even large-scale cities and towns, if not nations, can be made into more communal decision-making systems. There is also a belief that people are inherently communal rather than individualistic, so that contemporary structures fail to fulfil some basic needs of the public.

In the communitarian view individual autonomy is important, but it can only be understood as socially constructed, as opposed to the more complete autonomy characteristic of much liberal individualistic thinking. Further, in the communitarian view, personal autonomy implies substantial respect for the autonomy of other individuals, as well as preserving the process of self-actualization. Thus, actions that may be harmful to the collective welfare are not acceptable, even if they fulfil the individualistic desires of some members of the society (Etzioni, 1995). Full personal autonomy is also found only when there is some order in society, so that some mechanisms must be found to blend individual with collective desires.

[. . .]

Another way to conceptualize the communitarian solution to governing is to consider the now wide-spread arguments about social capital (Putnam, 1993; Perez-Diaz, 1994). When attempting to understand why democracy has flourished in some settings and not in others scholars have concluded that the existence of 'social capital' is crucial to its success. Social capital is indicated by the existence of large numbers of social groups formed outside the family or the immediate clan. The formation of such groups indicates that individuals are able to identify with social entities outside the family and are willing to make some commitment to such non-familial groups. That level of social trust enables people to be involved in politics.

It is not clear just how the communitarian argument would conform with the idea of social capital. On the one hand there is a commitment to participating in some types of social organization outside the family. On the other hand, however, the communities under discussion could be quite localized and also highly particularistic and may therefore not be the type of social groupings that figure in Putnam's models of building democracy. That is, membership in the community may be tightly circumscribed, so that not just anyone may be a member.

[. . .]

The governance implications of communitarianism

By this point the implications of this pattern of thinking for governance should be clear. Their implicit, and at times explicit, plan is to decentralize government as far as possible and to make smaller 'communities' responsible for more aspects of public policy.

[. . .]

Communitarianism proceeds well beyond the simple desire to devolve governing to smaller governments and communities as defined in a common-sense manner. It involves as much as anything else a shift away from individualism towards a more collective sense of governing. This involves rethinking the basis on which public policy is made: rather than individual utility maximization, policy is to be made on the basis of community values, presumably held by all participants.

[. . .]

If we move away from the existing structures, communitarianism would advocate creating mechanisms that would enhance participation and facilitate the development of meaning in government.

[. . .]

Problems in communitarianism

As appealing as some aspects of communitarianism are, there are some significant problems when this set of ideas is taken as an approach to governance. Perhaps the most fundamental is that the theory makes assumptions about human nature that are perhaps not sustainable. There is an assumption that the average citizen wants to participate in government and to invest a great deal of time and effort in governing. It further assumes that human beings are cooperative and not the self-aggrandizing individualists that are assumed in a good deal of contemporary social and political theory.

[. . .]

The problems of communitarianism are exacerbated when there is no clear definition of the community for which the political system is to function. That is, in a homogenous society the community and the society may be coterminous. In many contemporary countries that correspondence may not exist, and people who live next to each other may not think of themselves as belonging to the same community. A genuine sense of community appears necessary for sharing and for making the redistributive decisions necessary for most public policies.

[. . .]

Can political community be created? One of the assumptions of the communitarian approach is that even when there is no natural or preexisting community, it be created. This is in part a 'field of dreams' argument, with the assumption that if there are opportunities for community policy-making created, then the public will find it desirable to take part. In this view community can come out of interaction, rather than interaction coming from community.

[. . .]

Communitarian theory also assumes that important problems can be solved at relatively low levels of aggregation. In reality, the important problems may not be solvable in very small units. For example, poverty can be seen at a low level but its causes may be economic and social forces that have their origins well outside the local community.

[. . .]

Deliberative democracy

In some ways ideas about deliberative democracy comprise a subset of communitarian thinking. The basic idea of creating a locus for making decisions at a low level of aggregation appears compatible with communitarian thinking. What is most fundamental to the practice of deliberative democracy, however, is a *process* of involving the public in making decisions through open debate and dialogue. This process is in contrast to representative democracy in which the public is involved only as voters selecting the elites who will later make the decisions. It is also in contrast to direct democracy in which the public make decisions themselves, but do so with little or no collective deliberation or confrontation of alternative views on the issues.

[...]

There are several conditions that can be used to judge the extent to which any particular attempt at deliberative democracy corresponds to an 'ideal type' model. The first question is whether the process of deliberation is empowered to make the final decision on a policy, or whether it is only advisory to a formalized decision-making body.

[...]

A second criterion is whether the discussion is ongoing or is a simple one-time chance to express views. The better deliberative process is one in which there is an opportunity for discussion over some length of time, with opportunities to consider and address lacunae of information and to counter opposing arguments (Bessette, 1994). Without some continued possibilities for interaction among the participants, a deliberative process may become reduced to a simple opportunity to vent feelings rather than a genuine opportunity to make decisions.

[...]

Third, adequate deliberation also hinges upon how the participants are selected, or rather not selected. The ideal type of a deliberative process is one in which anyone can participate, as opposed to being selected as a representative of some interest or some segment of society. The advocates of deliberation argue that the more selective process prevents the full range of opinion from being heard and tends to bias outcomes in favour of more or less 'tame' interests. This view is especially common in feminist analyses of policy, arguing that women are often excluded from the process of decision-making within representative institutions.

[...]

Finally, deliberative systems vary in the extent to which the range of options available to the participants is constrained *a priori* or not. In some deliberative processes there is a simple question to be considered and decided, with the process thereby constrained, no matter who is entitled to participate and for how long. [...] Clearly the need to make a certain type of decision will initiate policy-making, but the advocates of deliberation tend to want to have fewer constraints once the process is initiated.

This ideal model of the deliberative process is rarely, if ever, achieved in the real world. If the standard could be achieved the assumption of the advocates of deliberation is that the process would have several positive effects. One would be to enhance the actual quality of the decisions made in the process. [. . .] More importantly, this type of process should enhance the legitimacy of the decisions that are made. The idea that this is a more genuine form of democracy than representative systems, and that face-to-face participation will enhance citizen efficacy, is fundamental to the advocacy of deliberative democracy.

Even if the ideal model is not attainable, there may be some approximations that are functioning. Even if not ideal, they may have some of the positive effects assumed to obtain from the more perfect version. The familiar public hearing is a very limited, if still effective, version of deliberative democracy and could easily be extended to a wider range of policy issues. It could also be enhanced to more closely approximate the ideal type.

[. . .]

The democratic and populist values inherent in deliberative democracy are appealing in many ways, but there are also a number of problems inherent in the model. Some of these problems are not dissimilar to the questions already raised concerning communitarianism, in particular how can advocates make this model premised on small (and generally homogenous) groups of people function in larger and more diverse political settings? Once the deliberative process is moved beyond the small organization or the small community, not only do the physical problems of engaging in meaningful dialogue become more evident, but also the social basis of communication may be insufficient to permit that meaningful dialogue. As the community becomes more heterogeneous the different premises for arguments and the different goals of the actors diminish the possibilities for effective dialogue.

[. . .]

Following from the above is the question of whether the general public really has much to add to a discussion of nuclear power or one on biotechnology. [. . .] The advocates of deliberative democracy would, of course, argue that these questions are too important to be left to the experts.

[. . .]

Finally, there are important questions about how any final decision can be reached through such a deliberative process. The underlying model appears to be that of discussion and bargaining until a consensus is reached. The model therefore assumes first that there is a consensus to be reached, and second that confronting social problems with evidence and creating understanding will make people operate against what may well be their true self-interests.

[. . .]

Direct democracy

The third populist challenge to the conventional forms of governance is direct democracy. This is by far the simplest of the three alternative approaches, and lacks much of the philosophical underpinnings of the other two approaches. The argument is simply that the public should be empowered to make decisions about policy themselves. For the referendum option in direct democracy, the legislature, or perhaps the executive, may ask the public to consider a piece of legislation for which they do not want to be responsible themselves. It may be that the legislature does not want to take a stand on contentious moral issues such as abortion or divorce: Italy and Ireland, as predominantly Roman Catholic countries, have had several referendums on these issues. Or the issue may be perceived to be in essence constitutional: a number of countries in the European Union have dealt with proposals for major changes in the European Union basic law by calling referendums and the Maastricht and Amsterdam treaties were sent to referendums in a number of countries including Denmark, France and Sweden. Finally, the legislature may be required constitutionally to submit the issue to the people. For example, in some states in the United States, any increase in the bonded, indebtedness of the state or any change in the state constitution will have to go to the people.

The initiative option is somewhat more complex, with the public having to mobilize first in order to get an issue on the ballot, and then again during the campaign before the election. This opportunity removes the elected legislature and executive from the process of governing almost entirely, with the public being empowered to set the agenda as well as make the final policy determination. In the relatively few localities that provide for the initiative, members of the public appear willing to tackle difficult and controversial issues that a legislature might want to avoid. These are also issues that many ordinary citizens might also want to avoid having to discuss and decide upon, but their more activist neighbours will not permit that. They do not have to vote (in most locales) or pay attention to the issues, but with political advertising through broadcast media they may not be able to avoid being bombarded with information about them.

The justification for direct democracy is simple, clear and apparently very democratic. It is that the people should be able to decide themselves on significant issues that will affect them. The definition of significance may vary in different political systems, but the basic principle is that of preventing a remote decision-making body (even if elected democratically) from determining matters of lasting importance for the public. In this conception of democracy the public is at least as capable as their elected representatives of making difficult (and the most difficult) decisions. Further, it appears that they will be expected to make those decisions on the basis of limited information and debate.

Although appealing to all our democratic sentiments there are a number of extremely difficult questions about direct democracy as a form of governance, although we should remember that this method is still phrased as a complement to the traditional mechanisms of representative democracy. The first question is how questions get on a ballot for determination. When that process is automatic, then there may be little difficulty, but when some form of signature campaign (the initiative) is required then many of the same problems of representative democracy appear to arise. That is, organizing a campaign of that sort involves the same organizational skills and the same financial resources that tend to make access to legislatures unequal. Further, the emphasis tends to be on single-issue politics, with very intense minorities tending to have a disproportionate influence over the agenda of the public sector. This may be especially true of the agenda-setting process in which those single-issue groups can focus attention on a campaign with little concern for overall governance capacities.

A second concern about direct democracy involves the generally limited information and discussion that tend to characterize the campaigns for these referendums. Again, this places a premium on the ability to get a message out through the media, and hence on financial resources.

[. . .]

Both of these crtical perspectives oppose the conventional representative institutions of governance, but may themselves have very different ideas about what the most desirable options for change would be. Because of the restricted information and general discussion, any policy decisions made through referendums may well be decided on the basis of simple, stereotypical views of the issues and may even produce anomalous results.

[. . .]

There are also questions of whether the most important issues can be phrased in the simple 'yes or no' style inherent in resolution through popular voting. A part of the critique of the remoteness of contemporary institutions is that their members make issues excessively complex and also are not committed to values that would motivate their voting in the ways that their constituents would have them vote. That may be true at least in part, but it also masks something of the underlying complexity of issues. The public is given to assume that there are simple answers to complex issues, while anyone who works on these issues for any time soon learns that those simple answers are more often than not misleading.

[. . .]

Nor is direct democracy likely to be conducive to making economic redistributive decisions that would take away from the majority and give to a minority. If voters vote their self-interest, generally not a bad prediction, they are not likely to choose to give away resources readily. Interestingly, however, the other two alternatives to conventional forms of governing may be well-suited to making redistributive decisions and to coping with minority rights. The opportunity to discuss the need for such policies, and the development of community, may make it possible to adopt those difficult policies. This is especially true for redistribution *within* a community, although the opportunities for redistribution *across* communities may be much more limited.

The democratic character of direct democracy can also be questioned because of the manner in which the public appears to consider these opportunities for participation. In general, turn-out in referendums is very low unless there is an election for public office occurring at the same time. The public appears still to believe that selecting their representatives is a more important activity than deciding on particular policy issues themselves. The lack of any personal identification with the issue may be one part of the problem. It could also be argued that the absence of real opportunities to discuss the issues involved in that referendum tends to depress participation: if the public does not understand issues fully they are unlikely to participate. If this lack of understanding is an issue, then it argues for creating a hybrid model of governance in which there are opportunities for dialogue in conjunction with the opportunity to make the final decision through the referendum.

The concepts contained in 'deliberative polling' may be a means through which to overcome at least one of the problems raised by direct democracy and to create the discussion of issues needed before a referendum. In deliberative polling, instead of having the public simply respond to survey questions without any preparation, they are provided an opportunity to discuss the issues among themselves, and perhaps also with experts, before expressing their own opinion. Deliberative polling is as yet not a method of decision-making but rather a more sophisticated mechanism for public opinion polling. It certainly has the potential of augmenting the usual mechanisms of direct democracy, but as was the case with discussion and deliberation and communitarianism, finding a means to conduct these exercises for more than a small group appears difficult and perhaps extremely expensive.

[. . .]

Summary and conclusion

These three alternatives to governing represent possible departures from the institutions common in most democratic political systems. They all assume that the current institutions of governing are flawed in important ways, and need to be reformed in ways that will permit the public to be more active participants in governing themselves. Further, two of the three are interested in promoting more genuine debate and discussion on policy issues and making policy only once the public has had the chance to think and talk about the issues.

The most fundamental point to be made about these alternatives is that the process by which decisions are made may determine the policy decisions. The representative institutions that are the targets of criticism for these three alternatives may be good at making some types of decisions, but they are not necessarily good at making all types. Further, even if the representative institutions are capable of making the decisions, the standard processes tend to privilege certain outcomes and to disadvantage other opportunities. For example, the deliberationists and the advocates of direct democracy think that a lack of inclusiveness tends to produce decisions that favour the better-organized elements of society and disadvantage the ordinary citizens. The argument is not so much that the process *qua* process has this biasing effect. Rather it is argued that the manner of selecting the participants in the process tends to bias the outcomes in favour of powerful interests in society.

[. . .]

There are certainly very important problems with existing governance systems, and the critics are successful in identifying those deficiencies. That having been said, the proposals offered for reform appear to have some genuine deficiencies of their own. The principal problems appear to be in the practicalities of taking ideas about governance that can work in small settings and attempting to make them perform equally well for mass democracy. There is no real evidence that this can be successful.

As with so many particulars in social and political life, we are faced with making a trade-off of values when discussing approaches to governance. Among other things that are being traded off are the (relative) divisiveness of representative democracy against the deliberation and due consideration of all points of view argued to characterize deliberative democracy, and to some extent communitarianism. On the other hand, however, direct democracy may be more decisive than current representative systems, and some advocates favour it because it allows a clear decision on a point of policy, without all the amendments and ambiguities that may be built into a policy by a legislative body.

References

Bell, D. (1976) *The Coming of Post-Industrial Society: A Venture in Social Forecasting*. 2nd edn. Harmondsworth: Penguin.

Bell, D. (1993) *Communitarianism and its Critics*. Oxford: Oxford University Press.

Bessette, J. R. (1994) *The Mild Voice of Reason*. Chicago, Ill.: University of Chicago Press.

Etzioni, A. (1995) *New Communitarian Thinking: Persons, Virtues, Institutions and Communities*. Charlottesville: University Press of Virginia.

Green, D. P. and I. Shapiro (1994) *Pathologies of Rational Choice Theory: A Critique of Applications in Political Science*. New Haven, Conn.: Yale University Press.

Habermas, J. (1984) *Theory of Communicative Action: Reason and Rationalization in Society*. London: Heinemann.

Kelman, S. (1992) 'Adversary and co-operationist institutions for conflict resolution in public policymaking', *Journal of Policy Analysis and Management*, 11, 178–206.

Perez-Diaz, V. (1994) *The Return of Civil Society*. Cambridge, Mass.: Harvard University Press.

Putnam, R. D. (1993) *Making Democracy Work: Civic Traditions in Modern Italy*. Princeton, NJ: Princeton University Press.

Rose, R. (1976) *The Problem of Party Government*. London: Macmillan.

Peter Beresford

SERVICE USERS, SOCIAL POLICY AND THE FUTURE OF WELFARE

From: Beresford, P. (2004) 'Service users, social policy and the future of welfare', *Critical Social Theory*, 21:4, 494–512

T HIS IS A DISCUSSION about the ownership of social policy and the effects of who owns it on its nature, objectives and possibilities. The owner- ship of social policy, that is to say, who and what play a central part in conceiving and constructing it, influencing its shape and controlling it, has been significantly neglected or treated as taken for granted in modern social policy discussions as it relates to the role played by service users and their organisations. Here though, it will be argued that such ownership and control play a key role in determining social policy's regressive and liberatory potential. In this discussion, social policy is taken to include both the *discipline* of social policy, with its concern with study, teaching, analysis and interpretation, and the *practice* of social policy – the political process of policy making and implementation. The aim is to explore the implications of ownership for both of these, with particular reference to issues of ownership, involvement and influence by people as welfare service users.[1]

Back to the future

[...]

During the last 20–30 years we have seen the emergence and growth of new movements of welfare service users: of older people, disabled people, mental health service users/survivors, people living with HIV/AIDS, people with learning difficulties, looked after young people and so on. These movements have worked to transform the terms of discussion, the ideas underpinning policy, approaches to theory and research in social policy (Campbell, 1996; Campbell and Oliver, 1996). Government has sought to incorporate these movements and has had to respond to them. For me they are the most genuinely new development affecting social policy and offer some of the most significant insights for the future of social policy.

While the emergence of these movements has begun to impact on social policy, until recently a pattern of 'provider-led' policy and provision has dominated social policy, with a range of key interests including politicians, managers, academics, planners and practitioners shaping them, with service users and citizens more generally having little or no say in them. This has not meant that there has been one shared interest at work shaping and developing policy and services. Instead, as has been discussed in the context of social care, they have been the result of conflicts, compromises and negotiations among a number of interest groups including central and local state, politicians, ideologues, workers and trade unions. The point is, though, that the people who use them have traditionally had little or no ownership or control over them (Open University, 1997).

New Labour social policy

It is very difficult to come to conclusive judgements about New Labour and its social policy. Ambiguity and contradiction are central features of both its philosophy and practice. [. . .] There is little formal agreement about New Labour social policy. The only point on which there does seem to be some consensus is that it is distinct from its predecessors. The social policy commentator, Howard Glennerster, for example, is overall positive and optimistic about it. [. . .] He concludes:

> I am forced to give Blair's social policy an alpha minus. Alpha for the strategy, gamma for presentation, beta for some of the detail.
> The Blair administration, against all my pre 1997 predictions I must say, has put together a coherent package that is distinct both from its Conservative and Labour predecessors and different from other European countries . . . It has contained the demands of an ageing population on the tax payer but shifted much of the burden into people's own pockets . . . It has a commendable policy of distribution to the lower income working poor and their children . . . The attack on inequality may still look small in comparison to the powerful economic forces at work but it does move in the opposite direction to nearly two decades of budget policy.
>
> (Glennerster, 2001: 402)

For Carey Oppenheim, former scourge of Tory poverty policy, now working in the Prime Minister's Policy Unit, while there are also still some big questions, the general verdict is again positive:

> The government's strategy on welfare reform and the labour market does indeed represent a new and imaginative attempt to rethink strategies to tackle poverty and social exclusion in the light of a transformed economic, social and political context.
>
> (Oppenheim, 2001: 90)

Ian Butler and Mark Drakeford, however, in a critique of contemporary social work and social care, offer a much less generous view of New Labour social policy, concluding that:

> Social work has, under the New Labour Government (1997–), become part of an incorporative agenda whereby the function of social work is predominantly to ensure that difficult and troublesome individuals are made to accept prevailing social norms, rather than inclusive in a way that permits a radical practice to better serve the recipients of social work services . . . it is our contention that the same tendency to align social work with authoritarian, rather than libertarian policies is characteristic of this government's wider thinking.
>
> (Butler and Drakeford, 2001: 7–15)

While, as we are told, New Labour social policy may be very different from that of previous Labour and Tory administrations, its emphasis on 'sticks and carrots', on the 'deserving' and 'undeserving', on social control as well as support, on social policy as a moral and political project, would not be unfamiliar to a Rip Van Winkle awaking from a sleep that had lasted since the nineteenth-century New Poor Law. Many elements of it would also be very familiar to anyone acquainted with US welfare rhetoric and traditions of the second half of the twentieth century generally, and particularly of more recent post-welfarist attitudes and policies of both the Democratic and Republican parties.

A new psychology of welfare state service users

Psychological profiling seems to be a key underpinning idea in New Labour social policy. [. . .] It is this interpretation of welfare state service users, this view of them as unreliable, untruthful and suspect, as much as practical politics and policy, which seems to lie at the heart of the new emphasis on 'conditionality' and responsibilities before rights. It suggests the same kind of suspicion that dominant groups always tend to have of subordinated and disempowered ones, whether the latter's oppression relates to their gender, 'race', age, disability, sexuality, religion, culture or class. Such people can expect to be conceived of as devious, irresponsible and untrustworthy. This has become a preoccupation of welfare policy.

[...]

At the heart of this social policy seems to be the idea of *changing* people (welfare service users). The focus seems to be on reforming, regulating, redeeming and regenerating them. An explicit example of this is the 'Change a life' campaign to discourage people from giving money to beggars, to help force beggars to change their way of life (Vasagar, 2000). This approach raises two significant issues for this discussion. First, while social policy has in this sense become, in part at least, a psychological policy, with the perceived aim of internalising different values, attitudes and ways of behaving in welfare service users, it has done little to involve them in this project. Yet we might expect that such involvement would be a prerequisite for success, by encouraging a sense of ownership in policy, which might facilitate the acceptance and adoption of official values.

Second, much of the social policy seen as most important and positive by government supporters is based on such a model of primarily reforming *people, rather than* policy, economy, social institutions or society. Thus the emphasis is on improving 'supply side' and 'employability', rather than on 'full (and equal) employment'. Such an approach seems to rest on an inherently negative view of its candidates as either unable or unwilling to act as expected and required.

[...]

While welfare to work policies are presented as the modern version of the helping welfare state, we know that they are not necessarily experienced like this by those on the receiving end (Duffy, 2001). Instead they are associated with explicit provisions for compulsion, the restriction of choices and removal of benefit. On the ground, their broad-brush philosophy is mediated by over-burdened agencies and officials, required to meet targets, and inculcated with negative stereotypes of and attitudes towards welfare claimants. They rest in principle on an assimiliationist rather than integrationist approach to social inclusion, which prioritises having a job as a central individual obligation (Levitas, 1998; Butler and Drakeford, 2001). For many service users the New Deal and 'jobseekers' culture can mean compulsory interviews, having to change their appearance and being expected to take *any* job, regardless of their experience and the job's conditions, quality or meaning. Such policy does not seem to take account of how people may react to the instrumental and negative interpretations it places upon them and the alienating effects this is likely to have. While it prioritises 'agency' in one way, it seems to ignore it in another.

Many disabled people, for example, are left wondering:

.... whether we are seen as an 'easy target', or as a political movement that has become too powerful and needing to be 'taught a lesson'. Whether by design or 'coincidence', disabled Britons have been the target of repeated press reports, suggesting that the disability benefit system is beset by scroungers and fraudsters.

(DAA, 1999)

[. . .]

Social policy practice and participation

[. . .]

It is also not clear whether New Labour has been any more successful than its 'old' Labour predecessors in involving and engaging people in its social policy project. New Labour has highlighted participation, partnership and empower-ment in social policy (and indeed in public policy more generally). There are now legal requirements, statutory guidance and detailed policy statements requiring and encouraging user involvement and partnership across policies. But the reality is complex and ambiguous.

Service users and their organisations distinguish between increasing demands to 'get involved' and the resulting 'consultation fatigue' and what say and involvement they actually have. So far, welfare service users have had mini-mal involvement in welfare reform despite the significance attached to such reform and the massive impact it is having. What involvement there has been has tended to come from outside (rather than being supported from within). This includes initiatives like the Citizens' Commission on the Future of the Welfare State, supported by the Baring Foundation, reporting welfare state service users' views of existing policy and provision and their proposals for the future (Beresford and Turner, 1997; Citizens' Commission, 1998) and the Our Voice In Our Future Project being undertaken by the user controlled Shaping Our Lives Project and supported by the Joseph Rowntree Foundation, which is currently seeking social care service users' views about welfare reform nationally and locally as a basis for lobbying and campaigning. Change in welfare reform, for example, over pensions and disability benefits, has generally been achieved by external campaigning, political and trade union pressure, rather than through the existence of new arrangements for participation.

[. . .]

Emphasising the 'otherness' of welfare users

This issue brings us to another key concern, the relationship between 'patients' or 'service users' and the wider public or publics. The tendency is often to treat the two in discussions superficially as if they were similar or synonymous. Clearly there are links and crossovers. Later we will explore discussions where the emphasis is on highlighting such overlaps and interrelations. But first we need to consider discussions where the implicit or explicit agenda is to do the opposite and to highlight *distinctions* between 'users' and 'citizens/public'. This activity has dominated welfare politics and discussions in the west for the last 20 years. It is epitomised by the New Right's conceptualisation of *welfare users* as wealth *consuming*, and a cost to *public/citizens*, who are contrasted as wealth *creating*.

This division has dominated popular as well as academic discussions. It has generated concepts like 'dependency culture', 'underclass' and 'the socially excluded'. It has laid stress on the different values, morality and ways of life of those included in such categories, highlighting their perceived deviance and rejection of 'accepted values'. Such stereotyping has not been significantly challenged by New Labour, which instead has maintained and reinforced it. It has been associated particularly with refugees and asylum seekers, lone parents, disabled people, mental health service users and other groups reliant on benefits. This approach to social policy is based on stressing the gap between 'them' and 'us' in welfare, encouraging 'us' to devalue, reject and discriminate against these groups as 'other' and to deny that which connects 'us' to 'them' in ourselves.

Government approaches to mental health service users offer a key case study of this approach. These are located within an overarching framework of 'public safety', which prioritises the protection of 'the public' from 'service users' (Beresford, 2000; Sayce, 2000). This has followed from the presentation of service users as dangerous and their association with an increase in homicides following the move to 'care in the community', regardless of the contra-indications from existing evidence (Taylor and Gunn, 1999). Research has highlighted the destructive effects which service users report such stigmatisation as having (Mind, 2000).

The importance of populism

The scapegoating of welfare service users can be seen as both a cause and effect of populist approaches to social policy. If *CSP*'s early contributors were aware of the significance of populism for policy in the early 1980s (expressing their concern that people would turn to New Right populism if social policy did not include their interests), populism's importance, if anything, seems to have increased rather than decreased over the years. It seems to have become more and more explicitly part of both the general and specifically social policy process. This is reflected in the significance attached to opinion and 'message' polls, reliance on focus groups and emphasis on the presentation and language of policy rather than its detailed content and principles on the part of *both* main political parties. Effective populism is advanced as a solution rather than a problem in competing electorally and Tory electoral failure in 2001 has been associated with its reliance on 'the wrong kind' of populism (see, for example, Ivens, 2001).

[. . .]

Not only has the role of the tabloid press increased in social policy agenda setting, but also its own extended direct political role; the complex relations that governments and politicians have developed with it and its proprietors, and the electoral importance that they attach to it, all combine to give the tabloid press an enlarged importance. In the context of mental health policy, for example, at a conference on mental health and the media, David Brindle, editor of *Guardian Society*, stated that while publicly government ministers rejected the association of mental health service users, dangerousness and homicide, at private briefings, they and their spin doctors 'spun a different tune fuelling demands for a more custodial form of mental health care', as advanced by the *Sun* and *Daily Mail* (24 February 2000). The 2001 General Election was framed in particularly populist terms, with an emphasis on controlling crime, policing asylum seekers and reforming welfare.

[. . .]

While recent governments seem to have adopted populist approaches to social policy, they are also themselves vulnerable to them. Thus, whatever the sophistication of their policies and proposals, these are still mediated through the same tabloid press whose support politicians have been anxious to enlist. The version of social policy that millions of tabloid reading voters get is likely to be the tabloid one.

[. . .]

Participation and the discipline of social policy

The centrality of populism highlights the importance of participation in social policy. As has been said, we might expect that if social policy is to be owned, accepted and understood, then the people it affects would need to be involved in its process. [. . .] The signs are, though, that the discipline of social policy has yet to prioritise either the perspectives of service users or their involvement and inclusion. Relatively little interest has so far been shown in the movements of welfare service users, their theories, discussions, proposals and their now large and growing body of published work. This was reflected in the findings of a review in 1997, based on looking at key current and recent social policy texts, recent social policy conferences and journal content. These indicated that social policy's focus on and interest in these movements was very limited. The discipline did not generally discuss their ideas and activities, directly include their commentators, or reference discussions and publications that they produced. This was true for national and international texts, texts which sought to look at key directions for the future and new perspectives, and texts from all political positions: left, right, centre and new politics (*CSP* was an honourable exception) (Beresford, 1997). There is little sign that this overall situation has changed in any major way since this review was undertaken.

[. . .]

As awareness has grown of the need to address their perspectives, because of their increasing political significance, the tendency has been to focus on mediating and interpreting them, rather than on acknowledging them as discourses in their own right.

The general failure of social policy debates to attach importance to the movements of welfare service users is surprising. The reasons for it are also not immediately clear, since it seems to conflict with social policy's own declared interests and priorities. Issues of difference and diversity, fragmentation, difference, diverse subjective realities, social inclusion and social integration, which are highlighted by the movements, are among the key themes of social policy. It reflects a much longer tradition of marginalising the perspectives of service users, except as a data source, which has characterised both Fabian and New Right approaches to social policy.

[. . .]

Ignoring the difference of welfare users

While in social policy practice the tendency is often to highlight the difference between welfare service users and others, in the discipline of social policy it seems to have been the opposite, highlighting their *similarity*. Often when I and other people in service user movements raise the issue with members of what might be called the 'social policy community' of ensuring the equal involvement of people as welfare service users, we are told 'we are *all* welfare service users'. The suggestion is that this is an artificial and unhelpful distinction to draw.

But for service users' organisations and movements, it is not as simple as that. We may all be 'users', but not all in the same way. There are of course overlaps around all issues of difference and social division: biologically between men and women, around sexuality between heterosexuals and gays and around issues of 'race' and ethnicity. But we cannot say that going to your GP for routine maintenance, having a child at a state school, or paying your NI contributions, is the same as being a young black man diagnosed with 'schizophrenia' or as having 'personality disorder' who is subject routinely to racist regimens, to the forcible restriction of his rights and compulsory 'treatment'; a disabled person living in residential services that lack privacy, control or decent conditions, or who relies on ever-changing, untrained, sometimes insensitive domiciliary carers for support in the intimate tasks of daily living; someone living and bringing up children on poverty level benefits or a combination of low-grade employment and tax credits. Long-term, regulatory, intimate and segregating contact with welfare services *is* different and is associated with stigma, discrimination, poverty and exclusion. Its effects may endure long after actual contact ends. Speaking from personal experience, after eight years on poverty level benefits and 12 years using mental health services, it is not the same.

Like many identities, the identities and movements of welfare service users have grown out of discrimination and exclusion. There are still disproportionately few people who from the perspectives of direct experience of social policy, particularly of its heavier end, are involved in the construction of social policy discussion and action or are part of its 'community'. The issue is not one of service users and their organisations saying other perspectives have no legitimacy and shouldn't be included, but rather that they seek to be included themselves.

The 'them' and 'us' of social policy hasn't been engineered by welfare service users. It is the result of exclusions operating in social policy itself. The voices of disabled people, mental health service users, people with learning difficulties and older people are still largely marginal in social policy. One of the key developments in social policy in recent years has been the recognition and inclusion of difference and challenging of social divisions. This hasn't happened for service users *as service users*. If social policy as a discipline is to reflect commitments to equality and inclusion, this must change. This isn't just about the inclusion of a specific group of current service users, although this is clearly important. It also raises broader issues about everyone's inclusion in terms of being able to be open about who we actually are, our vulnerabilities, our whole identity, our full selves in social policy. This raises additional issues about the nature of social policy as an academic discipline.

[. . .]

Service users, knowledge and social policy

Service user campaigners aren't just calling for social policy to ask for and include their views. Researchers have been doing this for years – surveying service users, then analysing, interpreting and acting upon them as they see fit. Service users are demanding that social policy goes beyond seeing them as a data source (Oliver, 1996; Lindow, 2001). Service users and their organisations can and want to offer their own analyses, interpretations and plans for action. They want to develop their own practice, services and organisations instead of just being subject to other people's. One of the ironies of social policy is that while the discipline has been slow to include service users, movements like the disabled people's movement can now probably exert more political influence than the discipline can. We must now be looking to social policy's full and equal involvement of welfare service users and their organisations in its discussions and activities. This whole issue raises some big intellectual and moral questions. Service users are now calling into question the legitimacy of traditional research and the problems of bias associated with research and knowledge linked culturally, politically, organisationally and financially with the service and policy system (for example, Wilson and Beresford, 2000; Rose, 2001). This raises fundamental questions such as:

- What is the validity of knowledge that is based on experience as service users – and what is the validity of that which isn't?
- Who owns service users' knowledge? Is it unproblematic for other researchers and academics to interpret and report it, especially when they may be linked with structures and institutions which service users see as part of the problem?
- How can social policy, which doesn't fully and equally include service users, resist accusations of institutionalised discrimination, bias and presenting a partial picture?

Alternative futures for welfare

[. . .]

Only with the full and equal involvement of current service users and other citizens who may become users are we ever likely to get the kind of social policy that people want and that people will support.

But the issue goes beyond this. It is also one of resisting social policy which people *don't* want and here there is even more cause for concern.

We may all have our own scenarios for future UK politics. But whether the longer-term future lies in assimilationist New Labour welfare or cost-cutting Conservative administrations, the prospects are worrying. If social policy doesn't move beyond its current narrow base, if it hasn't seriously done more to involve service users, as well as practitioners and other citizens by this time, then populism is likely to continue to be a key determinant of policy. If social policy as a discipline is to resist the reactionary populism that has grown in strength over the years and make possible an inclusive, anti-discriminatory future for welfare, then it must now work to prefigure this in its own process and activities.

Notes

1   The terms 'service user' and 'welfare service user' are used in this discussion to describe people who receive or are eligible to receive social care and welfare services. This embraces people included in a wide range of categories, including mental health service users/survivors, lone parents, people living with HIV/AIDS, children and young people in state 'care' or who are fostered or adopted, disabled people, older people, people living on low income, low wages and/or receiving or entitled to state benefits or tax credits, people with learning difficulties, people with addictions to alcohol and proscribed drugs, etc. People may receive welfare and social care services voluntarily or involuntarily. The term 'service users' is problematic, because it conceives of people primarily in terms of their use of services, which may well not be how they would define themselves. However, there is no other umbrella term which can help-fully be used to include all these overlapping groups. For example, some may include themselves as and be included as disabled, but others would not. Therefore the term 'service user' is used here, recognising its inadequacies, as a shorthand to describe the subjects of welfare and social care, without seeking to impose any other meanings or interpretations upon it or them.

CSP – *Critical Social Policy*, a journal launched in 1980.

References

Beresford, P. (1997) 'The Last Social Division?: Revisiting the relationship between social policy, its producers and consumers', in M. May, E. Brunsdon and G. Craig (eds) *Social Policy Review 9*, pp. 203–26. London: Social Policy Association.

Beresford, P. (2000) *Mental Health Issues, our Voice in our Future*. London: Shaping Our Lives/National Institute for Social Work.

Beresford, P. and Turner, M. (1997) *It's Our Welfare: Report of the Citizens' Commission on the Future of the Welfare State*. London: National Institute for Social Work.

Blair, T. (1997) 'The Will to Win', Speech at the Aylesbury Estate, Southwark, 2 June.

Butler, I. and Drakeford, M. (2001) 'Which Blair Project: Communitarianism, social authoritarianism and social work', *Journal of Social Work* 1(1): 7–19.

Campbell, J. and Oliver, M. (1996) *Disability Politics: Understanding our past, changing our future*. Basingstoke: Macmillan.

Campbell, P. (1996) 'The History of the User Movement in the United Kingdom', in T. Heller, J. Reynolds, R. Gomm, R. Muston and S. Pattison (eds) *Mental Health Matters*. Basingstoke: Macmillan.

Cecil, N. (2001) 'Fury At Blair's "Yob Tokens" ', *The Sun*, 25 April, p. 2.

Charlton, J. I. (2000) *Nothing About Us Without Us: Disability, oppression and empowerment*. Berkeley: University of California Press.

Citizens' Commission on the Future of the Welfare State (1998) *Response of the Citizens' Commission on the Future of the Welfare State to the Green Paper: New Ambitions for Our Country: A New Contract for Welfare*. London: Citizens' Commission on the Future of the Welfare State.

Coles, J. (2001) '8 Kids from 6 Dads: . . . So the council rewards single mum with 5-bed £130,000 dream home', *The Sun*, 14 May, pp. 1,4,5,8.

DAA (1999) 'Changes to Disability-Related Benefits Causes Damaging Revolt in the Ranks of the UK Government', *Disability Awareness In Action*, Newsletter No. 73, June, pp. 1–3.

Duffy, J. (2001) 'New Labour and Disabled People', *Coalition*, pp. 9–11.

Dunn, S. (1999) *Creating Accepting Communities: Report of the Mind Inquiry into social exclusion and mental health problems*. London: Mind.

Glennerster, H. (2001) 'Social Policy', in A. Seldon (ed.) *The Blair Effect: The Blair Government 1997–2001*, pp. 383–403. London: Little, Brown.

Ivens, M. (2001) 'The World Tells the Tories: Get populist', *The Sunday Times*, 13 May, p. 16.

Levitas, R. (1998) *The Inclusive Society?: Social exclusion and New Labour*. Basingstoke: Macmillan.

Lindow, V. (2001) 'Survivor Research', in C. Newnes, G. Holmes and C. Dunn (eds) *This Is Madness Too*, pp. 135–146. Ross on Wye: PCCS Books.

Mind (2000) *The Daily Stigma: Counting the cost, mental health in the media*. London: Mind.

Oliver, M. (1996) *Understanding Disability: From theory to practice*. Basingstoke: Macmillan.

Open University (1997) *Community Care: Workbook 3; Provision and practice in community care*. Milton Keynes: The Open University.

Oppenheim, C. (2001) 'Enabling Participation?: New Labour's Welfare-to-Work Policies', in S. White (ed.) *New Labour: The progressive future?*, pp. 77–92. Basingstoke: Palgrave.

Rose, D. (2001) 'Some Reflections on Epistemology in Relation to User-Led Research', paper presented to the Survivors Research Network, February. London: Mental Health Foundation.

Sayce, L. (2000) *From Psychiatric Patient to Citizen: Overcoming discrimination and social exclusion*. Basingstoke: Macmillan.

Spicker, P. (1996) 'Understanding Particularism', in D. Taylor (ed.) *Critical Social Policy: A reader*. London: Sage.

Taylor, P. and Gunn, J. (1999) 'Homicides by People with Mental Illness: Myth and reality', *British Journal of Psychiatry* 174: 9–14.

Vasagar, J. (2000) 'Homeless Campaign Raises Just £10,000', *Guardian Society*, 20 March.

White, M. (2001) 'Blair's CD Ploy to Reclaim Streets', *Guardian*, 25 April, p. 11.

Wilson, A. and Beresford, P. (2000) ' "Anti-Oppressive Practice": Emancipation or appropriation?', *British Journal of Social Work* 30: 553–73.

PART THREE

Instruments and discourses

INTRODUCTION

THIS PART TURNS TOWARDS the form and content of actual policies. This does not mean looking at particular proposals for specific fields, of course, but rather at the generic concepts and approaches out of which any such public policies are fashioned. We call these instruments and discourses because they range from the relatively concrete (you know when a tax regime changes) through to those that may appear more rhetorical and whose impacts are less immediate and clear cut. In the latter case, characteristically, some among both academics and practitioners will say it is 'just talk' and makes little if any difference, while others will claim language matters, working subtly to re-shape thinking, priorities and professional identities. In any event, these are the tools of the policy workers' trade: those who would influence policy need to know what these instruments amount to, what the currently fashionable policy concepts do and do not offer, and what is likely to be involved in translating them into particular policy arrangements and practices.

We start in Reading 13 with a magisterial overview of approaches to regulation – it is composed of extracts from Baldwin and Cave's comprehensive review of regulation strategies and issues. Their discussion of different strategies is neatly summarized and could give the illusion of a straightforward choice – but of course the world of regulation is far messier than this. Those engaged in policy work will find this a useful starting point for understanding where, and how, different approaches are likely to be more or less justifiable, and the issues they may raise. The authors then unravel the constituent elements of 'good' regulation and the basis for judgements about regulators' approaches and performance. The result is a map of regulatory practice which combines clarity about underlying principles with a robust appreciation of the ambiguities and uncertainties that are bound to be encountered in practice.

The readings in the previous two sections of this book have highlighted the influences of globalization and changes in governance arrangements on policy work. One of the consequences has been that under a variety of banners ('re-inventing government', 'New Public Management', 'modernization', etc.), public sector reform has been at the top of the public agenda in many nation-states for at least two decades. Arguably, it is now and will continue to be a permanent agenda item for governments around the world. Readings 14 and 15 examine different aspects of these changes and what they are entailing. Christopher Pollitt has written extensively on 'new public management' and he provides an assessment of the evidence for the impacts of this particular bundle of reform ideas. Of course, we should not expect such high-level design ideas to have immediate and direct consequences. The agencies of government are embedded in wider institutional networks and have developed in relation to other bodies with which they are necessarily linked. New design principles and roles (e.g., a purchaser–provider split) can shape behaviour, but not necessarily in the ways expected, because they are subject to many other influences as well. Pollitt's analysis highlights the fact that although the aims of creating more efficient and effective public services seem relatively widespread, there is considerable variation in where the starting points are, and the capacities and strategies of governments. Using existing research by others as a basis, he concludes that there is some convincing evidence for improvements in efficiency, effectiveness, processes and flexibility but that this is not the full story of the impact of reform due to ambiguity in conducting such research and the need to look at the *downside* too.

Bureaucracy has, from the beginning, been the core instrument of government – both its necessary tool and the source of most criticism. The state functionary for whom following the rules becomes a *raison d'être* is the epitome of bureaucratic dysfunction. But without rules, and rules that are taken very seriously, governments cannot be in control of their actions, nor accountable for them. Hence, Kernaghan's depiction of the contrasts between bureaucratic and the emerging post-bureaucratic forms of public organization offers a clear overview of a key issue – one that is all the more valuable for *not* presenting these complex developments in terms of the new form simply and rightly supplanting the old. He then goes on to discuss the role of public service values – and the efforts being made around the world to bolster them against commercial erosion – in the new arrangements.

Perhaps more than any other over the last decade, 'partnership' is the policy idea that has been most obviously 'in good currency'. It can be presented as part of the answer to many of the governance and process issues discussed in earlier readings. The next two readings look more explicitly at what this has meant in terms of organizing and delivering public services. First, in Reading 16, Janet Newman explores the dynamics of partnership in governance and the ways in which the Labour Government in the UK has encouraged this mode of working. She develops a model of how to understand the dilemmas for, and influences on, partnership working and the pulls towards different partnership positions. However, she guards against seeing these as neat categories and that the focus and emphasis can shift over time and in different contexts. Then in Reading 17, Jane Broadbent and Richard Laughlin tackle one of the most controversial implementations of the idea – the development of public private partnerships (PPPs). In the UK, PPPs have tended to cluster around the Private Finance Initiative, but in an unusually wide-ranging overview the authors highlight the different models of PPPs used in other countries, drawing attention to definitions of 'public' and 'private' and whether relationships between public and private sector organizations are merely contractual or more collaborative in nature. The authors also review the purpose and development of the Private Finance Initiative in the UK and the concerns that have been raised about the potential mismatch of values of private and public sector organizations engaged in these relationships.

Performance is another concept that has been important and pervasive in policy work in recent years. It is a term that takes no prisoners. Through its lenses, the world is straightforward, situations are or should be controlled, the issues are clear, the criteria are unambiguous. The usual uncertainty, patchiness, riders and qualifications – all these can be read as excuses. Performance sounds categorical – that is precisely its attraction. It has been closely associated with two other trends – the rise of new modes of oversight (what has been called 'the audit society') and the use of targets and measurement. In Reading 18, John Clarke examines the first of these, focusing on the expansion of scrutiny to accommodate the new and complex organizational structures for delivering public services. He shows how audit has expanded both in scope and scale in order to provide a full evaluation of performance. Audit and inspection has also increased competition between organizations as the attention to evaluation has inevitably resulted in the publication of 'league tables', highlighting comparative performance. Clarke highlights the challenges to such scrutiny: its methodological problems (reliability and replicability of knowledge; identification of variables; the nature and amount of data and documentation required – and the use of resources in producing it); concerns about representation and accountability in scrutiny agencies and practices; and finally, whether these agencies and processes can uncover organizational performance (given the failure of audit in the private sector). In Reading 19, Rob Paton reviews the literature on measurement and what lessons can be drawn from this, especially for nonprofit organizations and social enterprises. Like Clarke, he highlights well-documented costs, difficulties, dysfunctions and limitations of this practice. The aim is to encourage realism about its use and abuse – and thus to restrain the technocratic fantasies of control to which it often seems to give rise.

Robert Baldwin and Martin Cave

REGULATION CHOICES

From: Baldwin, R. and Cave, M. (1999) *Understanding Regulation. Theory, Strategy and Practice*, pp. 9–17, 34–35, 58–62, 76–84, 334–336, Oxford University Press

Why regulate?

MOTIVES FOR REGULATING CAN be distinguished from technical justifications for regulating. Governments may regulate for a number of motives – for example they may be influenced by the economically powerful and may act in the interests of the regulated industry or they may see a particular regulatory stance as a means to re-election. [. . .] To begin, though, we should consider the technical justifications for regulating that may be given by a government that is assumed to be acting in pursuit of the public interest.

Many of the rationales for regulating [see Table 13.1] can be described as instances of 'market failure'. Regulation in such cases is argued to be justified because the uncontrolled market place will, for some reason, fail to produce behaviour or results in accordance with the public interest. In some sectors or circumstances there may also be 'market absence' – there may be no effective market – because, for example, households cannot buy clean air or peace and quiet in their localities.

Regulatory strategies

If the state wants to control, say, the pollution of a river it may use a number of strategies.

[. . .]

Table 13.1 Rationales for regulating

Rationale	Main aims of regulation	Example
Monopolies and natural monopolies	Counter tendency to raise prices and lower output Harness benefits of scale economies Identify areas genuinely monopolistic	Utilities
Windfall profits	Transfer benefits of windfalls from firms to consumers or taxpayers	Firm discovers unusually cheap source of supply
Externalities	Compel producer or consumer to bear full costs of production rather than pass on to third parties or society	Pollution of river by factory
Information inadequacies	Inform consumers to allow market to operate	Pharmaceuticals Food and drinks labelling
Continuity and availability of service	Ensure socially desired (or protect minimal) level of 'essential' service	Transport service to remote region
Anti-competitive and behaviour predatory pricing	Prevent anti-competitive behaviour	Below-cost pricing in transport
Public goods and moral hazard	Share costs where benefits of activity are shared but free-rider problems exist	Defence and security services. Health Services
Unequal bargaining power	Protect vulnerable interests where market fails to do so	Health and Safety at Work
Scarcity and rationing	Public interest allocation of scarce commodities	Petrol shortage
Distribution justice and social policy	Distribute according to public interest Prevent undesirable behaviour or results	Victim protection Discrimination
Rationalization and Coordination	Secure efficient production where transaction costs prevent market from obtaining network gains or efficiencies of scale Standardization	Disparate production in agriculture and fisheries
Planning	Protect interests of future generations Coordinate altruistic intentions	Environment

Choosing the right strategy for regulating matters. A regulatory system will be difficult to justify – no matter how well it seems to be performing – if critics can argue that a different strategy would more effectively achieve relevant objectives. How, though, can we map out the array of different regulatory techniques? A starting point is to consider the basic capacities or resources that governments possess and which can be used to influence industrial, economic, or social activity. These have been described as follows:

To command – where legal authority and the command of law is used to pursue policy objectives.

To deploy wealth – where contracts, grants, loans, subsidies, or other incentives are used to influence conduct.

To harness markets – where governments channel competitive forces to particular ends (for example by using franchise auctions to achieve benefits for consumers).

To inform – where information is deployed strategically (e.g. so as to empower consumers).

To act directly – where the state takes physical action itself (e.g. to contain a hazard or nuisance).

To confer protected rights – where rights and liability rules are structured and allocated so as to create desired incentives and constraints (e.g. rights to clean water are created in order to deter polluters).

A number of basic regulatory strategies are built on the use of the above capacities or resources and can be distinguished from each other as follows [see Table 13.2].

[. . .]

What is 'good' regulation?

To decide whether a system of regulation is good, acceptable, or in need of reform it is necessary to be clear about the benchmarks that are relevant in such an evaluation.

A temptation for some economists may be to assert that regulation is good if it is efficient in the sense that it maximizes wealth. It can be objected, however, that wealth maximization provides no ethical basis for action, that it cannot justify any particular distribution of rights within society, and that, as a result, it cannot be used to measure regulatory decisions affecting rights.

This is because there is circularity in the assertion that one should distribute rights (e.g. to pollute or to be free from pollution) in a manner that maximizes wealth. For every particular, given, distribution of wealth there is a specific allocation of further rights that will maximize wealth – thus, how best to allocate the new supply of petrol would be governed by who owns the machinery that burns petrol. Deciding distributional issues on the basis of wealth maximization, accordingly, assumes a given distribution from the start. Similarly, it is circular to state that rights should be allocated to those who value them most – valuation

Table 13.2 Regulatory strategies: posited strengths and weaknesses

Strategy	Example	Strengths	Weaknesses
1 *Command & Control*	Health and Safety at Work	Force of law Fixed standards set minimum acceptable levels of behaviour Screens entry Prohibits unacceptable behaviour immediately Seen as highly protective of public Use of penalties indicates forceful stance by authorities	Intervenes in management Prone to capture Complex rules tend to multiply Inflexible Informational requirements severe Expensive to administer Setting standards is difficult and costly Anti-competitive effects Incentive is to meet the standard, not go better Enforcement costly Compliance costs high Inhibits desirable behaviour
2 *Self-Regulation*	Insurance Industry	High commitment to own rules Well-informed rule-making Low cost to government Coincidence of regulatory standards and the standards that industry sees as reasonable Enforcement efficiency Comprehensive rules Flexibility Effective complaints Can combine with external oversight	High cost of approving rules Rules may be self-serving Legalism not necessarily avoided Rulemaking procedures may be closed to public or consumers Enforcement may be weak or may favour the industry Public may not trust self-enforcers Legal oversight may be problematic Public may want governmental responsibility
3 *Incentives*	Differential tax on leaded and unleaded petrol	Low regulator discretion Low-cost application Low intervention in management	Rules are required Poor response to problems arising from irrational or careless behaviour

(Continued)

Table 13.2 (Continued)

Strategy	Example	Strengths	Weaknesses
		Incentive to reduce harm to zero, not just to standard Economic pressure to behave acceptably	Predicting outcome from given incentive difficult Mechanical, so inflexible Regulatory lag Politically contentious as rewards wrongdoer and fails to prohibit offence
4 *Market-Harnessing Controls* (a) *Competition Laws*	Airline Industry	Responses to market driven by firms not bureaucrats Can be applied across industries Economies of scale in use of general rules Low level of intervention Flexibility for firms	No expert agency to solve technical or commerical problem in the industry Uncertainties and transaction costs Courts slow to generate guidance Principles develop sporadically
(b) *Franchising*	Rail, Television, Radio	Enforcement is low cost to public Low level of restriction Respects managerial freedoms Allows competition for market as substitute for competition in the market Managers rather than bureaucrats respond to market preferences	Evidential difficulties Need to specify service Tension of specification and responsiveness/innovation Uncertainties impose costs on consumers Requires competition for franchise but may be few bidders Need to enforce terms of franchise
(c) *Contracting*	Local Authority refuse service	Combines control with service provision Sanctioning by economic incentive or non-renewal Easier to operate than licensing system	Potential confusion of regulatory and service roles Poor transparency and accountability Judicial control weak

(d) *Tradeable Permits*	Sulphur dioxide emissions (USA)	Pollution by greatest wealth producer Incentive to reduce harm to zero Managerial freedom considerable Regulatory discretion low Regulatory costs low	Enforcement may require inspectorate Regulatory lag, lack of rapid response in crisis No compensation for victims Requires healthy market for permits Barriers to entry may be created Some harms need to be prohibited absolutely
5 *Disclosure*	Mandatory disclosure in food/drink sector	Low intervention Allows consumer to decide issues Lower danger of capture Useful in low-risk sectors	Information users may make mistakes Economic incentives (e.g. price) may prevail over information (on e.g. risk) Cost of producing information may be high Risks may be so severe as to call for prohibition Policing of information quality and fraud may be required Information may be in form undermining its utility
6 *Direct Action*	State-supplied work premises	Can separate infrastructure provision from operation Assures acceptable level of provision Useful where small firms in poor position to behave responsibly Allows state to plan long-term investments	Fairness of subsidies may be contentious Funding costly Public sector involvement contentious Innovations may not be market driven
7 *Rights and Liabilities Laws*	Rules of tort law; right to e.g. light or clean water	Self-help Low intervention Low cost to State	May not prevent undesired events that result from accidents and irrational behaviour Individuals may not enforce due to costs

(*Continued*)

Table 13.2 (Continued)

Strategy	Example	Strengths	Weaknesses
			Evidential difficulties and legal uncertainties reduce enforcement
			Victims may lack resolve and information to proceed so deterrence sub-optimal
			Difficult for courts to deter efficiently
			Insurance may temper deterrent effects
8 Public Compensation/ Social Insurance	Workplace safety schemes (USA, Canada, Japan, New Zealand)	Insurers provide economic incentives	Incidence levels may be too low
		Low intervention in management	to allow risk discrimination
		Low danger of capture	Tension of loss-spreading and incentive to behave responsibly
		Encourages accurate reporting of incidents	Inspection and scrutiny of performance expensive
		Makes employers aware of costs of activities	May operate in very similar manner to command and control mechanism
		Good coverage, applied to all employers	
		No need to legislate for each individual harm	

itself depends on assumptions about the allocation of rights (one can only value if one has something to value with or else the valuation takes place in the realms of fantasy). Questions of justice, it follows, cannot be answered by economists' appeals to efficiency and distributional questions such as whether it is right to allow an extra unit of pollution (thus shifting the balance of rights from, say, river user A to polluting factory owner B) have to be made on the basis of grounds other than efficiency.

This is not to say that efficiency may not be a factor to be taken into account in making regulatory judgements. We may, in deciding how to allocate rights between, say, polluters and potential victims, want to take on board the wealth implications of particular distributional choices. What we should be wary of is using efficiency as a single measuring rod or justification for regulatory decisions. This will involve either circularity, as noted, or the assumption that the present distribution of wealth, together with a bias in favour of those with wealth, is acceptable.

A further moral objection to wealth maximization relates to its implication that it is right to allow B to interfere with A's rights (e.g. by polluting their river or exposing them to a hazardous substance) if B generates enough wealth to compensate A for the harm done. Human beings, the objection runs, have certain basic rights that it would be morally objectionable to put up for sale. Certain risks, it might similarly be said, should not be imposed on individuals' lives no matter what the price, compensation, or wealth gain on offer.

A more plausible approach to regulatory evaluation can be arrived at by looking at those arguments that have general currency when regulatory arrangements and performance are discussed in the public domain. Certain arguments have force in debating whether this or that regulatory action or regime is worthy of support (is 'legitimate'). These arguments involve reference to one or more of five key tests:

- Is the action or regime supported by legislative authority?
- Is there an appropriate scheme of accountability?
- Are procedures fair, accessible, and open?
- Is the regulator acting with sufficient expertise?
- Is the action or regime efficient?

The five tests, or criteria, should be explained before their role in assessing regulation is discussed further.

The legislative mandate

This criterion suggests that regulatory action deserves support when it is authorized by Parliament, the fountain of democratic authority. If the people, through Parliament, have instructed certain regulators to achieve result X, and those regulators can point to their having produced result X, then they are in a position to claim public support. They have fulfilled their mandate.

It might be very proper to judge regulators according to their success in fulfilling their mandates. Unfortunately, however, it is seldom easy to state in precise terms what this should involve. Most regulatory statutes give regulators broad discretions and implementing the mandate thus involves interpretation. A statute, for example, may order a regulator to protect the interests of consumers but it may be silent on the balance to be drawn between industrial and domestic or large and small consumers' interests.

Such statutes, moreover, often set out objectives that exist at mutual tension. Achieving certain objectives may necessarily involve trading off performance in relation to other stated objectives. Regulatory statutes, in addition, often give regulators scope for exercising judgement and devising solutions. [. . .] It is, in such cases, impossible to point to clear objectives. Legislators, furthermore, may deliberately avoid setting down precise objectives because they want regulators to have the freedom to cope with problems as they arise in the future. For all of these reasons, regulators are seldom, if ever, involved in the mechanical transmission of statutory objectives into results on the ground and the mandate benchmark, though of relevance, will rarely provide an easy answer to questions of legitimation.

Accountability or control

Regulators with imprecise mandates may, nevertheless, claim that they deserve the support of the public because they are properly accountable to, and controlled by, democratic institutions. Thus, a regulatory agency might claim that it is accountable for its interpretation of its mandate to a representative body and that this oversight renders its exercise of powers acceptable.

A difficulty with this criterion is that controversy will often attend the selection of the individuals and bodies that provide accountability. If Parliament itself or another elected institution is not the body holding the regulator to account then the arrangement may be criticized as unrepresentative. Where control is exercised by certain institutions (e.g. courts) the competence of those institutions in specialist areas may also be called into question. Issues also arise as to the appropriate degree of accountability, the resources that should properly be devoted to accountability, and the acceptability of any trade-off between accountability and the effective pursuit of regulatory objectives.

Due process

The basis of the due process claim is that public support is merited because the regulator uses procedures that are fair, accessible, and open. Thus, attention is paid to equality, fairness, and consistency of treatment but also to the levels of participation that regulatory decisions and policy processes allow to the public, to consumers, and to other affected parties. The underlying rationale of such a claim is that proper democratic influence over regulation is ensured by due process being observed and that this influence has a legitimating effect.

The criterion is, again, however, limited in so far as further guiding principles are required in order to explain, for example, who should be able to participate and in what manner. Trade-offs once more have to be made against the effective implementation of the mandate. Thus, more participation may lead to less effective decision-making and eventually to stagnation in the regulatory system. To expand participatory rights beyond a certain point may not, moreover, be consistent with the development and exercise of expertise and judgement.

Disputes may also arise concerning the appropriate *mode* of participation. Lawyers, for instance, may see certain (perhaps formal or trial-type) methods of participation as appropriate in circumstances that those from other disciplines might see as calling for quite different arrangements.

Expertise

Certain regulatory functions may require the exercise of expert judgement. This is liable to be the case where the decision-maker has to consider a number of competing options or values and come to a balanced judgement on incomplete and shifting information. In these circumstances, the regulator may claim support on the basis of his or her expertise, and the nature of the task at hand, rather than offering to give reasons, or justifications. 'Trust to my expertise' is the essence of such a claim. Experts thus assert that they will come to the most appropriate decision and achieve the best results most rapidly when freed from duties of explanation.

One problem with this test is that it may be difficult for the public to assess whether the decisions arrived at have been appropriate or effective. (It may be difficult to tell what would have happened had alternative decisions been made.) Claims of expertise may also be questionable where the expert fails to explain why *this* issue demands expert judgement (a communications failure that the expert may say flows from the lack of expertise of the lay public). A natural distrust by lay persons of those who lay claim to expertise also serves to undermine demands of support from specialists. This may be the case particularly where experts refuse to give full reasons for their actions, deny access to decision-making processes, or pursue narrow and arcane modes of analysis. Conflicts of opinion between experts again affect their credibility. Nor can it be assumed that experts are neutral – decisions involving judgements will inevitably have a political aspect as competing interests are affected by regulation and as tensions are resolved in a particular manner.

[...]

Efficiency

A regulator may claim support on the basis of acting efficiently and, in doing so, may make two kinds of claim. The first of these urges support on the basis that the legislative mandate is being implemented at the least possible level of inputs or costs and there is productive efficiency. This, of course, is a claim afflicted by all the problems discussed above in relation to the mandate – notably those arising from the imprecision of that mandate. It is particularly difficult to measure efficiency when the mandate fails to set down consistent or coherent objectives. Or where a regulator's functions intermesh with those of other agencies and departments. It is difficult, moreover, to assert that a particular method of regulating achieves 'better' results than alternative methods when the latter have not been put to the test in the relevant arena.

A second version of the efficiency claim urges support on the basis that the regulation at issue leads to results that are efficient – as judged by criteria set down with a degree of independence from the mandate. Reference might thus be made to the regulatory regime's allocative efficiency (whether it is impossible to redistribute goods to make at least one consumer better off without making another consumer worse off) and its dynamic efficiency (whether there is encouragement of desirable process and product innovation and whether the system produces flexible responses to changes in demand).

Leaving aside the problem of showing that alternative systems would not offer superior performance, such claims present difficulties because, as noted, efficiency is not a value independent of distributional considerations and efficiency in itself provides no answers on distributional issues or in defining the regulatory mandate. The pursuit of efficiency may, indeed, conflict with legislative statements on distributional matters and, accordingly, the appropriateness of efficiency claims may be especially questionable in those spheres of regulation where distributive concerns are central.

[. . .]

The role of the five criteria

The above five claims, it can be seen, are all fraught with difficulties but collectively they constitute a set of benchmarks for assessing regulatory regimes. These are the rationales that are employed and have currency in real-life debates on regulation and its reform. Arguments in support of (or arguments criticizing) regulators that do not fall under these five headings will be deemed irrelevant by most members of the public.

[. . .]

Judging the extent to which regulation is legitimate is not to offer a sociological assessment of the actual support that a regulator enjoys (this might have been achieved by good public relations or even misrepresentation); it is, rather, to offer an assessment of the legitimacy that a regulator *deserves*. What matters is the collective justificatory power of the arguments that can be made under the five headings. Strong claims across the board point to regulation that deserves support, generally weak claims indicate a low capacity to justify.

How, though, can trade-offs between claims be dealt with? How, can it be said whether a weakening of rights of participation in return for improvements in satisfying the statutory mandate is a good or a bad thing?

The answer is that, at the end of the day, the weight that individuals place on each legitimating argument will reflect their personal political philosophies and, in the absence of all persons agreeing on the nature of an ideal world, we will differ on matters of weighting. What we do seem to agree on, however, is the benchmarks themselves. Any perusal of debates on regulation will reveal their exclusive usage.

This means that, short of those discussing regulation simply exposing their political differences, much can still be said in making assessments of regulatory performance. It can be asked, notably, whether performance on one of the five fronts can be improved significantly without material loss on another. [. . .]

Where trade-offs between different kinds of claim are involved, resolution will demand reference to a political philosophy or position. Designers or reformers of regulation should bear in mind, however, that performance under some headings (e.g. the legislative mandate) may be linked, under certain conditions, to performance under other headings (e.g. fairness and openness of processes). Thus, if a regulatory regime is perceived by the public or industry to be unfair, the regulator may enjoy low levels of cooperation and this may impede performance in satisfying the mandate. This means that a reformer may not have the option of effecting an extreme trade-off between fairness or openness and more efficiency in achieving mandated ends – public reaction will stand in the way of achieving this efficiency. The implication is that, whatever the philosophy of the regulatory designer or reformer, that individual or institution should be wary of endorsing regulatory designs that score conspicuously badly on any of the five tests – performance as judged on the other criteria may be affected detrimentally.

How, then, can legitimacy be improved in the real world? The answer is by taking steps to improve ratings according to the five tests. To give some brief examples, under the mandate, measures could be taken to improve the clarity of the mandate and achieve agreement on its terms. A regulatory body could, thus, publish its vision of the mandate and hold discussions on this. Alternatively, regulators and ministers could, at periodic intervals, jointly produce statements of aims in explanation of the mandate and these could be put to Parliament for approval. Regulators' claims to be properly accountable might be improved by such steps as the creation of a specialist parliamentary select committee (a House of Commons Select Committee on Regulated Industries) or by strengthened (perhaps publicly funded) standing consumer bodies for specific industries or products. Due process claims could be improved by reforms to increase information flows and participation in regulatory decision- and policy-making and there might, for instance, be a role for statutory or court-mandated requirements that regulatory rules be disclosed whenever they are in operation. Expertise claims might be reinforced by legislative or administrative actions to designate those issues that are matters of judgement for the regulator and by improving levels of training and resources where these are inadequate. Efficiency claims might be strengthened by taking steps to clarify the mandate and by improving flows of information to the public. [. . .]

To summarize: regulatory regimes and actions can be assessed by making judgements about the merits of legitimating claims under the five headings set out. To assess in this manner is not to evaluate the moral correctness or legality of the regulatory action or regime but to make a judgement as to its worthiness of public support. In making that judgement, personal visions have to be tempered by considering the responses of other parties. Assessing regulation thus involves areas of agreement (on benchmarks) but also of divergence (on the weighting of different desiderata).

[. . .]

Conclusions

Regulation often appears to be a game in which the rules are uncertain, the method of scoring is in dispute and the distinction between players and spectators is unclear. This is because regulators' mandates tend to be imprecise; identifying good regulation involves contention and rights of participation are often subject to debate. Regulators, moreover, carry out a number of functions that are not always compatible. They not only exercise control – over, for example, monopoly power – but they also act to organize and enable the development of competitive markets. They seek to encourage efficiency but often have to take on board a variety of different social objectives. Regulators, furthermore, have constantly to balance various interests and to perform trade-offs of different values. Balances have to be made between providers and consumers; different service providers; commercial and domestic consumers; incumbents and potential new entrants; infrastructure suppliers and operators of services; and a host of other sets of divergent interests.

[. . .] Should more accountability be established at a given cost in efficiency? Should greater freedom to exercise expert judgements be given in spite of the loss of accountability involved? Should more efficient regulation be sought by reducing access to the regulatory process? These and similar questions have to be faced by regulators on a daily basis.

Nor are there any easy answers. The arguments suggest that we should be highly sceptical of regulatory solutions or designs that are couched in terms of single values – notions, for instance, that certain strategies will be efficient and therefore are justifiable and should be pursued without further debate.

It also follows that in such an uncertain and politically contentious world, any regulator will live a precarious existence. No claim to legitimacy that a regulator makes will ever be recognized as clear-cut or beyond argument and, to render life more difficult, no set of regulatory conditions or even public expectations of regulation is liable to remain static.

The regulator's world is also one in which it is difficult to deal with issues in isolation – it is a world of overlaps, interactions, and blurred boundaries. Regulation, for example, is difficult to tease apart from self-regulation; 'public' actions, decisions, policies, and rules are difficult to separate from 'private' ones; regulated spheres are not easy to distinguish from those that are unregulated; domestic systems of regulation interact with supra-national regimes; different regulatory mechanisms operate in coordination as well as in competition; and questions of enforcement cannot be completely disentangled from those concerning policies and rules.

[. . .]

Not only, therefore, is regulation a politically contentious activity, it is one that presents a host of technical and intellectual challenges. Does such a catalogue of difficulties, however, offer a counsel of despair? Does it imply that since any regulatory action will give rise to contention, anything goes? The answer to both questions is definitely 'no'. We have suggested that regulatory activities be judged according to the five benchmarks. [. . .] To recognize that judgements about regulation will give rise to contention, even if it is assumed that everyone in society agrees on the five benchmarks, is not to counsel despair but to recognize that the choices made in regulation are inevitably political ones. Being clear about those benchmarks that are relevant in evaluating regulation, and discussing regulation with reference to these yardsticks, brings clarity to the regulatory debate rather than imposing any particular political vision on participants in that conversation. Not only does it help to identify certain pitfalls of regulatory analysis (such as single benchmark evaluations) but it also assists in identifying the trade-offs that have to be considered when, for example, assessing reforms.

[. . .]

As for the future of regulation, what is clear is that the political dimension of the regulators' work will not disappear. Not only that, it may prove increasingly to be the case that direct democratic influence will be demanded not merely with respect to the decisions, actions, and policies of regulators but also with regard to those of the 'private' firms that provide regulated or public services. [. . .] Difficult political judgements will remain and will be the proper province of democratically-legitimated bodies.

The main hope for improving regulation lies not in taking such judgements away from legitimate institutions but in developing our understandings on two fronts. First, concerning the array of choices between various goals that different regulatory arrangements present us with. Second, about the potential of new regulatory arrangements to provide us with more attractive ranges of choice.

Christopher Pollitt

IS THE EMPEROR IN HIS UNDERWEAR?

AN ANALYSIS OF THE IMPACTS OF PUBLIC MANAGEMENT REFORM

From: Pollitt, C. (2000) 'Is the emperor in his underwear? An analysis of the impacts of public management reform', *Public Management*, 2:2, 181–199

Introduction

THE MAIN AIM OF this article is to assess the available evidence on the results of the public management reforms which have swept through the OECD world during the last ten to fifteen years, and which continue today. To attack such a huge subject in a single article necessarily requires the discussion to be pitched at a fairly high level of generalization. On the other hand, while the detail is both rich and occasionally paradoxical or contradictory, on the broad scale attempted here there do seem to be some larger points which are worth making.

To approach the main question of impact, some attention needs first to be devoted to three significant preliminary questions. These are, first, what kind of evidential materials are available; second, what kinds of reform are we talking about; and, third, what do we mean by 'results'? These three preliminaries will be tackled sequentially in the next three sections. Subsequently, the main part of the article will deal with the central question of what we know and what we do not know about the results of reform.

[. . .]

Characteristics of the available materials

A great deal of the available material on public management reform is either promotional or how-to-do-it. Governments produce White Papers, statements and booklets in which they attempt to convince legislatures, the media, the public and public servants themselves that their reforms are significant, well-intentioned and likely to produce a variety of improvements. Departments produce practical guidelines to help their staffs implement change. The promotional documents are intended to persuade, and, accordingly, they tend to be heavily freighted with rhetoric and rather light on self-criticism. Consultants and other advisers are also either promotional or how-to-do-it – often they are selling their patented systems (re-engineering, total quality management (TQM), benchmarking or whatever) and ultimately they are all selling their services to governments, public agencies and corporations.

[. . .]

It would be unwise, therefore, to assume that, in aggregate, these types of rhetoric and documentation afford a full and balanced picture of what is happening 'on the ground' throughout the administrative systems of the countries concerned. [. . .] In this article our main recourse will therefore be to studies which can, *prima facie*, claim a greater degree of independence than either the promotional or the how-to-do-it literature – particularly to academic studies and to evaluations or other assessments with a significant degree of independence or 'distance'.

What is happening in the world of public management reform?

A first answer which is simple but wrong

For some years now there has been a powerful story abroad. It tells that there is something new in the world of governance, termed 'the new public management' (NPM), 'reinvention', 're-engineering', 'entrepreneurial government' or some similarly dynamic title. [. . .] In their influential book *Reinventing Government*, Osborne and Gaebler (1992) put it very strongly. Referring to what they termed 'the rise of entrepreneurial government' in the USA, they claimed that 'a similar process is underway throughout the developed world' (1992: 328) and that it was 'inevitable' (1992: 325). [. . .] From this perspective particular governments or public services can be seen as being 'well ahead' or 'lagging behind' along what is basically a single route to reform. In many of the 'promotional' publications the characteristics of the reformed public sector organization have been specified. Typically, these include:

- being close to its customers;
- being performance-driven (targets, standards) not rule-bound;
- displaying a commitment to continuous quality improvement (again, targets, standards);
- being structured in a 'lean' and 'flat' way – highly decentralized, with street-level staff who are 'empowered' to be flexible and innovate;
- practising tight cost control, with the help of modern, commercial-style accounting systems;

- using performance-related systems for recruiting, posting, promoting and paying staff.

Furthermore, if these are the characteristics of *individual organizations* within a reformed public sector, 'reinvented' *governments* will also display a distinctive approach to their work in a broader way. They will:

- 'steer not row', i.e. become more concerned with strategy and less with carrying-out;
- act in anticipatory ways – for a host of public problems prevention is better than cure;
- seek to use market mechanisms wherever possible, either in the form of quasi-markets to introduce competition between public providers, or by contracting out or privatizing services which were previously undertaken directly by the state;
- seek inter-organizational partnerships, both within the public sector ('joined-up government') and with the private and voluntary sectors.

This, therefore, is the simple answer to the question 'what is happening?'. Governments are redesigning institutions and procedures so as to conform to the new model outlined above. Everyone is doing more or less the same thing, because they have little choice. Powerful forces in the environment are obliging governments to change. Some are further ahead than others.

A second, more complicated, but more accurate answer

The community of scholars conducting comparative analyses of public management reforms is not large but, over the past decade, it has produced a number of significant studies covering Western Europe, North America and Australasia. [. . .] What these show is a world in which, although the broad aims of producing more efficient, effective and responsive public services may have been widely shared, the mixtures of strategies, priorities, styles and methods adopted by different governments have varied very widely indeed. [. . .]

Part of the explanation is that countries have not *started* from the same point, either in terms of the make-up of their public sectors or in terms of the way they think about the role and character of the state. 'Path dependent' explanations fit public management reform rather well. Furthermore, governments have not all possessed the same *capacities* to implement reforms. In some countries, such as Germany, changing the central administrative structures is politically and legally very difficult. In other countries, such as New Zealand and the UK, it has been comparatively easy. [. . .] State schools, hospitals and social and community services agencies took on a variety of forms, and in many of these autonomous professionals, not bureaucrats, were the key actors (Clarke and Newman 1997).

Thus, not every country is taking the same route, and, in particular, the radical reforms implemented during the 1980s and early 1990s in New Zealand and the UK are certainly *not* universally regarded as a desirable model to emulate. In some countries leading opinion formers regard the NPM with considerable suspicion. The USA is an interesting case because, although it has been a fountain of rhetoric for reinvention and re-engineering, the federal executive's capacity for implementing coherent, broad-scope reforms is severely limited by the well-known fragmentation of the American political system (Peters 1995).

[. . .]

Defining 'results'

Before one can assess evidence about impacts, one has to decide what kind of thing is going to *count* as a result. This is by no means straightforward. For example, a result could be any one or more of the following:

- savings (reduced budget appropriations);
- improved processes (e.g. faster, more accessible complaints procedures; quicker turn-round times for repairs or the processing of licences; 'one-stop shops' offering several services in one place);
- improved efficiency (better input/output ratios, e.g. more students graduate per full-time equivalent member of staff; the same number of drivers' licences are issued with 20 per cent fewer staff);
- greater effectiveness (less crime, poverty, functional illiteracy; homelessness; drug abuse; gender or ethnic inequality; more new jobs created; more contented and trusting citizens, etc.);
- an increase in the overall capacity/flexibility/resilience of the administrative system as a whole (e.g. through the recruitment and training of more skilled, more committed public servants).

Furthermore, each of these categories contains its own conceptual puzzles, definitional problems and pitfalls in operationalization (Pollitt and Bouckaert 2000: ch. 5).

What evaluations have been done?

There have been surprisingly few independent, broad-scope evaluations of the public management reforms (Pollitt 1995, 1998). Those which have been conducted tend to suffer from some fairly fundamental conceptual and methodological limitations (which have sometimes been acknowledged, and on other occasions not).

[. . .]

The most common limitations to those studies which have been done are as follows:

- an absence of reliable base-line measures, so that before-and-after comparisons become speculative;
- an absence of benchmarking, e.g. the productivity gains of a privatized firm may be praised without it being noticed or admitted that comparable

non-privatized corporations have made similar gains over the same period (Naschold and von Otter 1996: 24–5);

- limited or no gathering of the views of service users;

- scarcity or absence of data on transitional costs. For example, the first major huge Australian evaluation acknowledges the difficulty of assigning savings to the reforms – Task Force on Management Improvement 1992. Kettl (1994: 9) makes the same point about the US NPR. Yet implementation costs can be considerable;

- scarcity or absence of data on step-changes in transactional costs and/or on other continuing 'side-effects' such as the loss of trust or a degree of value confusion;

- opinion gathering being limited to, or biased towards, senior staff (a number of surveys have shown that middle and lower-level staff are often more critical of reforms than their bosses);

- little analysis of contextual variations which may mean that a similar type of reform will work well in one situation or locality, but not in another (Pawson and Tilley 1997);

- limited or no attention to attribution problems. Often several reforms have proceeded simultaneously, and external conditions have also been changing. This makes it very hard to attribute results confidently to specific reforms.

    [. . .]

- narrow range of criteria applied to the findings (e.g. productivity measures only, with no attention to equity, to staff morale or to externalities). In effect, most of the evaluations fail to distinguish between and/or miss out altogether many of the types of 'result' listed in the previous section of this article.

There is little sign that these significant limitations to evaluation designs are being addressed. Recent evaluations (e.g. Schick 1996) appear to be just as prone to major weaknesses as those undertaken five or more years ago.

What results have been found?

The limitations – or downright absence – of evaluations discussed in the previous section mean that many important questions cannot be answered, or can only be answered tentatively or anecdotally, with many qualifications and reservations. Consequently our discussion of results may seem to have a slightly frustrating quality to it. Nevertheless, some aspects are clearer than others, and quantities of evidence lie around the world, inviting scholarly sorting and interpretation. In making a small start to that large labour, I will organize my brief comments under the same headings as were used in the defining 'results' section above. Thus we begin with the claims of reform to achieve economies in the operation of the public sector.

Savings

One German scholar attempted to test what he described as the 'OECD hypothesis': namely, that bureaucratic regimes would perform less well in macro-economic terms than regimes which had modernized themselves according to the NPM prescription. He concluded that:

> Confronting our findings with the hypothesis formulated by the OECD as to the relationship between macroeconomic performance (economic growth, productivity and unemployment), on the one hand, and the regulation regime (bureaucratic governance by rule and its alternatives) on the other, the OECD hypothesis has to be strikingly refuted: all the countries with bureaucratic governance by rule exhibit with respect to almost all the dimensions a markedly better macroeconomic performance than the other countries.
>
> (Naschold 1995: 39)

Naschold goes on to acknowledge that there are considerable difficulties in interpreting this apparent negative correlation. His caveat should be vigorously endorsed. Even if one confines one's attention to a narrower range of macro-economic indicators than those cited by Naschold, interpretation remains deeply problematic. For example, the OECD database shows that government outlays as a percentage of nominal gross domestic product (GDP) fell between 1985 and the late 1990s, at least in the majority of the countries discussed in this article. However, it would be rash indeed to attribute this shrinking proportion to management reforms.

[. . .]

A 'saving' on one dimension may have been offset by increases in expenditure elsewhere, or by quality reductions, or by scope of service reductions, or by shifting costs elsewhere in the public sector (and therefore achieving no overall advantage for the state as a whole). Yet one must not carp too much: when a reform of procurement policy frees (or obliges) public servants to purchase simple requirements (staplers, office furniture, security services) from cheaper suppliers, it requires a contortion to see this as other than an improvement.

One kind of 'saving' that appears relatively easy to count is a reduction in the number of civil servants ('downsizing' in management parlance). The OECD databank (OECD 1999) shows that some countries have been able to make large reductions in the ratio of public employment to total employment. Other countries have not (see Table 14.1).

Once again, however, there is need for great interpretive caution when deploying aggregates of this kind. The OECD statisticians do their best, but varying definitions of government employment plague their comparisons. On this basis the correlation between staff reductions and NPM-style reform appears positive, but weak. [. . .] The sometimes virulent anti-bureaucratic rhetoric of the Reagan and Bush Presidencies produced a much smaller effect on the US civil service than the apparently more federal government-friendly Clinton Presidency. An extension of these figures to other countries, such as Finland and The Netherlands, would

Table 14.1 Changes in civil service employment, the public sector and the economy as a whole (%)

	1985–90	1990–7
Australia		
Civil service	−7.1	−22.0
Public sector	–	−2.7
Economy as a whole	+16.2	–
Canada		
Civil service	+6.2	−19.0
Public sector	+9.9	−4.7
Economy as a whole	+8.8	+15.2
France		
Civil service	+1.9	+6.3
Public sector	+2.3	−4.4
Economy as a whole	+3.8	+2.9
Sweden		
Civil service	−28.9	−38.0
Public sector	+5.4	−18.1
Economy as a whole	+4.9	−11.0
UK		
Civil service	−5.8	+16.1
Public sector	−2.6	−12.9
Economy as a whole	+9.9	+9.2
USA		
Civil service	+1.7	−17.0
Public sector	+11.7	+5.3
Economy as a whole	+13.2	+12.1

Source: OECD (1999: Annex 2, p. 28).

multiply such curiosities. Despite all these qualifications, however, it seems reasonably sure that some governments have been able to make substantial reductions in the numbers of core public servants they employ.

[...]

Improved processes

Again, anecdotal evidence crowds together in the promotional literature. [...] Most of us probably also have personal experience of improvements: desk staff better trained to handle difficult requests; greater attention paid to the decor, comfort and cleanliness of waiting areas; simplified forms. Techniques such as TQM and re-engineering generate many measured process improvements, sometimes of spectacular proportions. There is now a great deal of public sector knowledge about how to improve individual processes, once the will to do so and the appropriate techniques are brought together in the same place. Modernized management has some real success stories to tell.

[...]

Improved efficiency

For two decades, the efficiency criterion has lain at the heart of many management reform initiatives. Reorganizing so as to achieve more outputs per input or the same outputs for reduced inputs is one of the core skills of good managers. Achieving a certain percentage 'efficiency gain' became an annual routine for UK government departments and agencies, and for NHS hospitals during the 1980s and early 1990s. Furthermore, in principle at least, the measurement of efficiency is somewhat less difficult than that of either quality or effectiveness. With quality measurement there is always the awkward initial step of trying to find some consensus among users as to what, for them, constitutes 'quality'. Effectiveness measurement entails research into impacts 'out there', beyond the organization, and may be both costly and methodologically complex.

[. . .]

A first point to make is that efficiency gains may be achieved at the cost of other, less desirable effects.

[. . .]

Second, while many of the claims of efficiency gains are probably perfectly reasonable and accurate, it would be prudent not to take all assertions at face value. Consider the widely accepted idea that contracting out public services (whatever its other effects may have been) has regularly led to efficiency gains:

> claims that empirical studies find 'consistently' and 'without exception' that contracting out is more efficient than municipal supply are demonstrably untrue. Even taken at face value, only around half of the studies discussed in the paper {a review of contracting out in US local government} is associated with lower spending and higher efficiency. Furthermore, many of the studies contain specific methodological flaws that cast doubt on the evidence on the impact of service contracts. . . .
> (Boyne 1998: 482)

[. . .]

A recent study of five European national audit offices showed that even Supreme Audit Institutions, when they conduct performance audits, often seem to be able to construct and apply true efficiency measures in only a minority of their studies. More often they fall back on assessing the presence or absence of good management practice.

[. . .]

Greater effectiveness

For at least thirty years civil servants and evaluators have recognized that assessing the effectiveness of many public policies and programmes is an extremely difficult task. Occasionally some particular programme will enjoy the benefit of an available, valid and relevant indicator of outcome, but often the links between programme activities and final outcomes are tentative or obscure. There are several well-documented reasons for this complexity. Politicians frequently mandate policy objectives which, in Wildavsky's famous phrase, are 'multiple, conflicting and vague' (Wildavsky 1979: 139). Thus the initial question of what outcomes are being aimed at may be hard to answer in operational terms. Then there is the problem of timescales: the final outcomes of some educational, health and environmental programmes, for example, may lie a long way down the road – longer than many politicians and citizens are willing to wait before passing judgement. A third common difficulty is that of safely attributing observed effects to the programme in question.

[. . .]

By itself, management reform alters none of these constraints. Indeed, the evaluation of the effectiveness of management reform itself is subject to precisely these challenges – the aims of the reform are often hard to operationalize, the timescales over which effects occur can be long and drawn-out and the attribution of observed effects is frequently uncertain (Pollitt 1995).

[. . .]

We should not be surprised, therefore, when we discover that cases where there is unmistakable evidence of management reform producing more effective government action are rare. The connections between management reform and the effective delivery of long-term policy goals are often both distant and complicated by factors that lie beyond the control of public managers.

More capacious/flexible/resilient administrative systems

Systems improvements, it is argued, are not to be judged on the basis of the success or failure of a single project, programme or policy, but rather in a more holistic way. For example, the transformation of a rigid, inward-looking, slow-moving bureaucratic hierarchy into a 'flat', responsive, multi-disciplinary agency could be said to have increased that system's *capacity* to cope with new developments in its environment. As in this example, system changes are broad-scope and will frequently involve both major restructurings and an engineered shift in the dominant organizational culture.

[. . .]

One problem is that the currency of systems claims is hard to cash into specific measurements or indicators. Thus claims of 'better accountability' or cultural change or greater responsiveness are relatively easy to illustrate with a sound-bite anecdote but very hard to capture in a general measure. Who has measured cultural change? Who has reliable statistics on changes in 'accountability'?

In what units may one count shifts in the 'responsiveness' or 'capacity' of a system of public administration? On those (still quite rare) occasions when systematic research has been carried out on such matters, the findings have by no means all pointed towards positive 'transformations', though they have certainly registered that change is underway.

[...]

From a strict scientific perspective, therefore, the jury is still out on 'systems transformations' – and it may be out for some time. The Emperor says he has revolutionized his entire wardrobe, but some of his workers doubt if it is entirely for the better, and many of the onlookers have not yet noticed much difference.

Conclusions

In conclusion, what can be said about the state of dress of the Emperor of NPM/NPR? First, it is hard to see him clearly: there are a lot of conceptual problems about quite what it is we are looking for, and also some methodological and interpretive puzzles about what the available data can be said to show. Second, in so far as we *can* get a good look, the Emperor does not appear to be naked. Management reform has not all been windy rhetoric, by any means. Downsizing has been accomplished in a number of countries. In many instances measured efficiency has definitely increased. The influence of published targets in prompting improvement on specific dimensions has been demonstrated time and time again. In many cases, also, specific services have certainly become more user-sympathetic and flexible. All these garments can be worn with pride. At the same time it should be conceded that their full cost – 'side-effects' and all – has frequently been obscure. Other features of services, which are not measured or publicized, may have taken a turn for the worse. Other groups – of staff or citizens – may have suffered degenerating conditions as a consequence of the drive to improve the more salient aspects of a particular service. It is only rarely that the full balance sheet is available for scrutiny.

Two other things can be said about the Emperor. While he may not be naked he is far from fully dressed. Some of the larger claims heard from time to time for NPM and the NPR must be judged either false (so far at least) or not proven. Large savings in aggregate public expenditure have seldom accrued from management reforms *per se*. [...] The correlation between the implementation of NPM reforms and macro-economic performance is hardly striking, with Germany, Japan and the USA being three of the most successful economies (by most criteria) over the last twenty years and yet none of these being among the group which has implemented the most radical reforms (indeed, Germany and Japan have been among the *least* active in this respect). Furthermore, the achievement of more *effective* (as distinct from more efficient) government is hard to demonstrate. Even in those cases where improved effectiveness *can* be demonstrated, there is usually considerable ambiguity as to what it should be attributed.

The splendid coat of many colours envisaged by some reformers – slim, fast, effective, decentralized, open, trusted government – still lies more in the realms of hope and imagination than in demonstrated and warranted reality.

Finally, we should remember that the jurisdiction of this half-clad Emperor is limited. His heartlands have never really extended beyond Australasia, North America and the UK. Although some of his methods may have been selectively borrowed by other countries – especially the Dutch and the Nordics – these countries have never unconditionally accepted his authority.

[. . .]

References

Boyne, G. (1998) 'Bureaucratic Theory Meets Reality: Public Choice and Service Contracting in US Local Government'. *Public Administration Review*, 58:6 pp. 474–84.

Clarke, J. and Newman, J. (1997) *The Managerial State*, London: Sage.

Kettl, D. (1994) *Re-inventing Government? Appraising the National Performance Review*, Washington DC: Brookings Institution.

Naschold, F. (1995) *The Modernization of the Public Sector in Europe*, Helsinki: Ministry of Labour.

Naschold, F. and von Otter, C. (1996) *Public Sector Transformation: Rethinking Markets and Hierarchies in Government*, Amsterdam: John Benjamins Publishing Company.

OECD (1999) *Structure of Civil Service Employment in Seven OECD Countries* (http://www.oecd.org/puma/mgmtres/hrm/index.htm).

Osborne, D. and Gaebler, T. (1992) *Reinventing Government: How the Entrepreneurial Spirit is Transforming the Public Sector*, Reading MA: Addison Wesley.

Pawson, R. and Tilley, N. (1997) *Realistic Evaluation*, London: Sage.

Peters, G. (1995) 'Bureaucracy in a Divided Regime: The United States' in J. Pierre (ed.) *Bureaucracy and the Modern State: An Introduction to Comparative Public Administration*, Aldershot: Edward Elgar.

Pollitt, C. (1995) 'Justification by Works or by Faith? Evaluating the New Public Management'. *Evaluation*, 1:2 pp. 133–54.

—— (1998) 'Evaluation and the New Public Management: An International Perspective'. *Evaluation Journal of Australasia*, 9:1&2 pp. 7–15.

Pollitt, C. and Bouckaert, G. (2000) *Public Management Reform: A Comparative Analysis*, Oxford: Oxford University Press.

Schick, A. (1996) *The Spirit of Reform: Managing the New Zealand State Sector in a Time of Change*, Wellington: State Services Commission.

Wildavsky, A. (1979) *Speaking Truth to Power: The Art and Craft of Policy Analysis*, Boston: Little, Brown.

Kenneth Kernaghan

THE POST-BUREAUCRATIC ORGANIZATION AND PUBLIC SERVICE VALUES

From: Kernaghan, K. (2000) 'The post-bureaucratic organization and public service values', *International Review of Administrative Sciences*, 66, 91–104

RECENT PUBLIC SECTOR REFORMS, especially those associated with the new public management (NPM) movement, have increased concern about the state of public service values. This concern has arisen in large part because some advocates of public sector reform pay little or no attention to values and others focus narrowly on the application of private sector values to the public sector. However, a growing number of reform advocates are seeking to reconcile traditional public service values with 'new' values arising from new approaches to organizing and managing public organizations, including approaches based on private sector experience. This paper, in its examination of the implications of these new approaches for public service values, makes three major arguments. The first is that reformers should take careful and systematic account of the value implications of reforms. The second is that account should be taken not only of ethical values but of other types of values as well. The third argument is that a statement of key values (often described as a code of conduct), both for the public service as a whole and for individual public organizations, facilitates an assessment of the value consequences of reforms.

[...]

Table 15.1 From the bureaucratic to the post-bureaucratic organization

Characteristics of the bureaucratic organization	Characteristics of the post-bureaucratic organization
Policy and management culture	

Organization-centred
  Emphasis on needs of the
  organization itself
	Citizen-centred
	  Quality service to citizens (and clients/
	  stakeholders)

Position power
  Control, command and
  compliance
	Participative leadership
	  Shared values and participative
	  decision making

Rule-centred
  Rules, procedures and
  constraints
	People-centred
	  An empowering and caring milieu
	  for employees

Independent action
  Little consultation, cooperation
  or coordination
	Collective action
	  Consultation, cooperation and
	  coordination

Status quo-oriented
  Avoiding risks and mistakes
	Change-oriented
	  Innovation, risk taking and
	  continuous improvement

Process oriented
  Accountability for process
	Results oriented
	  Accountability for results

Structure	

Centralized
  Hierarchy and central controls
	Decentralized
	  Decentralization of authority and control

Departmental form
  Most programmes delivered by
  operating departments
	Non-departmental form
	  Programmes delivered by wide variety
	  of mechanisms

Market orientation	

Budget driven
  Programmes financed largely
  from appropriations
	Revenue driven
	  Programmes financed as far as possible
	  on cost recovery basis

Monopolistic
  Government has monopoly
  on programme delivery
	Competitive
	  Competition with private sector for
	  programme delivery

The post-bureaucratic organization

The bureaucratic/post-bureaucratic framework shown in Table 15.1 reflects the broad scope of recent reform initiatives and proposals (Kernaghan *et al.*, 2000). It includes the major elements of NPM, but in view of the controversy over NPM's meaning and scope, it avoids the frequent practice of equating NPM with public sector reform in general. The framework takes account of several models

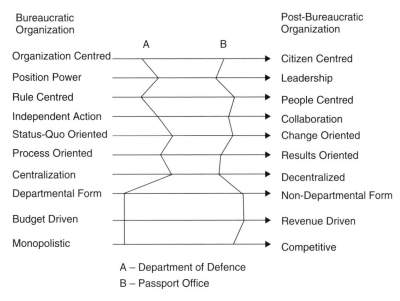

Figure 15.1 Organizational profiles

of public organization, including the market and participatory ones (Peters, 1995). The primary means by which public organizations can move toward the post-bureaucratic model have become well known to the public administration community, especially over the past decade. They include partnerships, empowerment, restructuring, re-engineering, information technology and continuous learning.

Many public organizations around the world have undergone significant reform by moving toward the post-bureaucratic model. The model is not a normative one in the sense that all public organizations are encouraged to conform as closely as possible to its several components. [. . .] Indeed, there is tension among some of the model's components, for example the emphasis on coordination and collaboration versus the emphasis on decentralized authority and control. Moreover, an organization that uses the framework to analyse the current state of its structure, culture and management may decide, for sound reasons, to move towards the bureaucratic, rather than the post-bureaucratic, pole of certain continua. An organization may, for example, put relatively greater emphasis on accountability for process (i.e. for following the rules) after an embarrassing instance of unreasonable risk-taking. The framework is intended to serve (1) an analytical purpose by including the major elements of reform in public organizations; and (2) a practical purpose by helping public organizations assess where they stand in relation to recent reform proposals.

The concept of an *organizational profile* is central to using the framework for these two purposes. Figure 15.1 shows that for each public organization a profile can be developed to depict that organization's location on each of the continua of the framework – and to compare its location to that of other organizations.

The framework can also be used to assess change in a single organization over time (e.g. a department of agriculture in 2000 compared to 1990).

[. . .]

When assessing the benefits and costs of moving along the several continua of the bureaucratic/post-bureaucratic framework, public organizations must examine not only the structural and managerial implications of such movement, but the political and value implications as well. For example, in considering a shift from an organization-centred to a citizen-centred approach, it is essential to examine the feasibility of new structures such as single window mechanisms for service delivery and new management approaches such as employee empowerment. But it is essential also to examine the implications of reform for political control of the public service and for such core public service values as accountability and integrity. While these four major dimensions of public administration cannot in practice be easily separated, for analytical purposes this paper focuses on the *value dimension*.

Public service values

Values have long been an important concept in scholarly writings on public administration, especially in the United States (Kaufman, 1956; Gilbert, 1959). In most other countries, reference to public service values has historically been much less explicit. However, since the mid-1980s, the concept of values has become increasingly central to the study and practice of public administration in many countries around the world. In some countries (e.g. Australia, Canada), values discourse pervades the public service. There are several reasons for this increased concern about values.

First, the private sector's emphasis in the 1980s on the concept of corporate culture and the accompanying emphasis on values had a spillover effect on public organizations; many of these organizations developed a statement of values, sometimes as a stand-alone document but usually as an integral part of a strategic plan. Second, some public organizations have been successfully transformed by focusing on a change in their values rather than in their structures (Denhardt, 1993). Third, the increased emphasis of reformers on holding public servants relatively more accountable for results than for process led to a focus on values as a possible alternative to rules, directives and guidelines. Fourth, and more recent, has been the upsurge of concern about public service values, already noted, that has resulted from the perceived neglect or undermining of traditional public service values by certain proponents of public sector reform.

A fifth and final explanatory factor has been the steadily rising interest since the late 1960s in public service *ethics* – a concept so tightly intertwined with that of public service *values* that many commentators use the terms values and ethics interchangeably. As a result, many writings on public service ethics deal explicitly or implicitly with values issues, and many writings on public service values deal in part with ethics issues. It is important to distinguish between these two concepts. A value is defined here as 'an enduring belief that a specific mode of conduct or end-state of existence is personally or socially preferable to an opposite or converse mode of conduct or end-state of existence' (Rokeach, 1973: 5). Values are enduring beliefs that influence the choices we make from among available means and ends. Clearly, not all values are ethical values, that is, not all values relate to questions of right and wrong, good or evil. It is helpful, therefore, to distinguish ethical values from other types of values.

Public administration scholars have classified public service values in various ways. This paper utilizes a three-fold classification (Canada, 1996) in which *ethical* values (e.g. integrity, fairness) constitute a separate category; the other two categories are *democratic* values (e.g. impartiality, rule of law), and *professional* values (e.g. effectiveness, service). This classification provides a basis for taking account of the enduring importance of democratic and ethical values in public administration and of the emergence of new professional values. These categories of values are not watertight compartments; a few values fall into more than one category (e.g. accountability as both an ethical and a democratic value and excellence as both an ethical and a professional value).

A broad classification of public service values that cuts across all other classifications is a division into traditional or 'old' values and 'new' or 'emerging' values. For example, such values as integrity, efficiency, effectiveness, neutrality, responsiveness and accountability have in many countries been traditionally associated with the notion of public service (Gilbert, 1959; Kernaghan, 1978). While the relative significance of such traditional values has changed over time, their overall importance in the constellation of public service values has endured. However, during the past few decades and especially since the mid-1980s, new values (e.g. innovation, quality) have risen to prominence and certain traditional values (e.g. accountability) have become relatively more important. A 1994 study showed that the top dozen values espoused by public organizations across Canada were, in order of priority, integrity/ethics, accountability/responsibility, respect, service, fairness/equity, innovation, teamwork, excellence, honesty, commitment/dedication, quality and openness (Kernaghan, 1994: 620). While several traditional values (integrity, accountability, fairness) were found to be highly cherished, 'new' values such as service, innovation, teamwork and quality were also highly ranked.

In addition, the meaning of some traditional values has been altered; note, for example, the relatively greater focus on accountability for results than for process. Note also that the meaning of certain new values is very similar to that of certain old values. For example, in some governments, reference to the traditional value of representativeness has been substantially displaced by reference to equity. And the meaning of the traditional value of responsiveness is similar to that of the 'new' value of service. Thus, some of the so-called new values are not all that new – a fact that will facilitate the balancing and reconciliation of traditional and new values in public administration.

Several of the new public service values (e.g. service, innovation) are identical to prominent private sector values. This reflects the fact that many of the recent public sector reforms have been inspired by private sector experience. The post-bureaucratic model is heavily influenced by private sector thinking and practice and several of the major means of moving towards that model (e.g. re-engineering, customer/client orientation) are commonly viewed as private sector management techniques. It is notable also that the new values fall primarily into the category of professional values. In considering the desirability of moving along the various continua, public organizations need to keep in mind the impact of new approaches to organization and management on democratic and ethical values as well as on professional ones.

[. . .]

Preserving and diffusing values

The implications for ethical values and principles of the various reforms involved in moving toward the post-bureaucratic model have become a significant source of concern in countries around the world (Kamto, 1997; Hondeghem, 1998). This concern has reinforced the already high level of anxiety, noted earlier, about the state of public sector ethics.

Much of the recent concern has focused on the ethical consequences of increased business involvement in the conduct of government activities (e.g. contracting out, partnerships) and the application to the public sector of business values (e.g. risk taking) and business practices (e.g. empowerment). George Frederickson (1993: 250) has argued, in respect of the United States, that when 'previously governmental functions are shifted to the private sector or shared, it is a safe bet that corruption will increase'. Alan Doig has noted that in Britain 'the speed and direction of devolved managerial autonomy, together with the promotion of an entrepreneurial culture and of privatization . . . have raised questions about . . . the weakening of the public sector ethos [and] the impact of private sector perspectives within a public sector context . . .' (Doig, 1995:207). And Maurice Kamto has observed that public service values associated with western governments are gradually being introduced into the governments of central and eastern Europe, but 'these values are finding it hard to take root in the face of administrative corruption arising in substantial part from neoliberal ideology' (Kamto, 1997: 298). He also blames neoliberal measures for increasing the 'ethical deficit' in the developing countries of Asia, Africa and Latin America.

The application of business values and practices to the public sector impacts not only ethical values like integrity but democratic values like neutrality as well. For example, the appointment of business people to head public agencies and the increased mobility of employees between the public and private sectors threaten political neutrality by increasing the likelihood of partisanship and patronage. The Organization for Economic Cooperation and Development (OECD), in its *Principles for Managing Ethics in the Public Service*, notes that '[i]ncreasing interaction between the public and private sectors demands that more attention should be placed on public service values and requiring external partners to respect those same values' (OECD, 1998: Section 7). And in early 1998, the British government announced that it was planning new legislation to permit public servants to take legal action against ministers who threatened their political impartiality or asked them to do political work. This was a response to criticism of the increasing politicization of the public service and, in particular, the growing influence of political advisers appointed from outside the public service by ministers rather than by competition and promotion.

There is particular concern about the extent to which it is possible to infuse programme delivery agencies (e.g. state-owned enterprises in New Zealand and service delivery agencies in Canada) with core public service values, especially if the organizations are headed by persons brought in from the private sector to manage them on a more 'business-like' basis. While New Zealand's public sector reforms have been widely praised, they have also encountered some problems in applying a business model to the public sector. Following the enactment of the 1988 State Sector Act, the State Services Commission published a *Public Service Code of Conduct* in 1990 and the *Public Service Principles, Conventions and Practice* guidance series in 1995 (New Zealand, 1996: 42). Then, in mid-1997, in response to concern that chief executives were ignoring matters that were not specifically listed in their contract with the government, the head of the public service prescribed a broader set of obligations. These obligations included taking account of the political needs of the government as a whole, adhering to high personal ethical standards, and managing 'their departments with long-term "stewardship" in mind' (Larson, 1998). The recently established Canadian Food Inspection Agency worried about how it 'would be able to advance public sector values while moving to a more entrepreneurial style of organization and management' (Doering, 1998: 14). Its response was to set out its core values in its business plan. Democratic accountability is reinforced by the fact that the minister to whom the agency reports is responsible to Parliament for safeguarding these core values.[1] It is notable, however, that no democratic values (e.g. accountability, neutrality) are explicitly included among the agency's core values.

Some western democracies (e.g. New Zealand, 1995; United Kingdom, 1996) have responded to actual or anticipated problems arising from reforms by drafting or strengthening statements of values or codes of ethics. New Zealand's reforms raised concerns 'as to whether the traditional ethical concepts had at least partly gone by the board. There was a very clear need to reaffirm – and perhaps in some areas to reformulate – the ethical basis of the Public Service' (New Zealand, 1996: 41). A learning point to be drawn from the experience of several countries is that governments need to take careful account of the value and ethical implications of reforms *before* implementing them. The bureaucratic/post-bureaucratic framework (Table 15.1) provides a mechanism for doing this in a systematic and comprehensive manner. As argued here, use of the framework for this purpose by a public service as a whole or by individual public organizations will be facilitated by identifying a limited number of core values that should be fostered. These values are usually set out in a formal document referred to in this paper as a statement of values; in some jurisdictions it is called a code of conduct.

There is significant congruence in the core public service values identified by different countries. It is not surprising that this congruence is more evident among the Westminster-style democracies of Australia, New Zealand and the United Kingdom where ministerial responsibility is a central constitutional convention. The value statements of these three countries contain a mix of democratic, ethical and professional values. Foremost among the democratic values are accountability, responsiveness and impartiality while integrity, honesty and respect are the most prominent ethical values. New Zealand and the United Kingdom include such traditional professional values as efficiency and effectiveness whereas Australia, in the declaration of values in its 1999 Public Service Bill, includes the new professional values of achieving results and managing performance (Australia, 1999).

In Canada, another Westminster-style country, the federal government has no service-wide statement of values, but the values articulated formally by public service leaders are very similar to those of other Commonwealth countries. [. . .] One of Canada's provincial governments, the Government of Ontario, has formally adopted a *Statement of Values and Ethics* composed primarily of the top values identified in the cross-Canada study described earlier. The Ontario statement includes several of the new professional values (e.g. innovation, creativity and continuous improvement). The intention in Ontario is to diffuse the core values throughout the public service by integrating them into its planning and accountability processes and fostering open dialogue about their implementation in the day-to-day operations of the public service. This effort is integrally linked to the province's ongoing reform initiatives and is led by its Restructuring Secretariat.

Despite the similarities in the core values of these governments, there are still significant differences in the content and format of their value statements. The British *Civil Service Code*, for example, is notable for its provisions on expectations for political executives (ministers) as well as for public servants. It reminds ministers of their duty to uphold the political impartiality of the public service and to give fair consideration to informed and impartial advice from public servants. In most value statements, advice as to the proper behaviour of politicians has to be inferred from advice to public servants. For example, New Zealand's *Public Service Code of Conduct* requires public servants 'to alert Ministers to the possible consequences of following particular policies, whether or not such advice accords with Ministers' views' (New Zealand, 1995: 11). The implicit advice to ministers is that public servants should not be punished for speaking truth to power.

The emphasis in most current value statements is on *traditional* democratic, ethical and professional values. Few statements reflect the increased importance of new professional values such as innovation and creativity and little effort is made to reconcile traditional and new values. Part of the explanation for these apparent deficiencies is the view of some government officials that the 'so-called new values' are a passing fancy or are at best second-order values that are less central to successful governance than the traditional ones.

Another explanatory factor is the practical need to limit the number of values contained in a value statement and the length of the statement itself. Pressure to limit the number arises also from the fact, noted earlier, that individual organizations often supplement the service-wide values contained in the statement with values related to their particular functions. Some governments (e.g. Canada, Norway) leave the development of value statements to individual organizations rather than adopting a government-wide statement. This approach is less likely to foster shared values across the service as a whole, and individual organizations are less likely to include democratic values. In Canada, democratic values like loyalty and political neutrality are commonly identified as central public service values. Yet these values are rarely included in the value statements of individual organizations; neither value was ranked among the top 20 values in the Canadian study mentioned earlier.

Among the arguments for restricting the number of values is the need to ensure that they are easy to understand, remember, communicate, adapt and identify with (Canada, 1987: 11). Also, specifying a limited number of core values facilitates use of the bureaucratic/post-bureaucratic framework for assessing the value implications of public sector reforms. An additional argument, both for identifying core values and limiting their number, is that they can provide a source from which principles, rules and guidelines governing public service conduct can be derived. For example, impartiality, a democratic value, and fairness, an ethical value, underpin the principle that public servants should make decisions on a non-partisan basis. This principle, in turn, underpins rules and guidelines bearing on the political activities of public servants. Australia uses this approach in its 1999 Public Service Bill. The Bill's explanatory note asserts that the values contained in the Bill 'provide the philosophical underpinning' and 'articulate the culture and ethos' of the public service. Among the values listed are apolitical public service, high ethical standards, accountability and responsiveness. These and other values underpin a code of conduct which is also contained in the Bill and which sets out a number of official duties, including honesty, compliance with the law, confidentiality and avoidance of conflict of interest.

A major theme in recent public service reforms has been the reduction of rules so that empowered public servants, held more accountable for results and less accountable for process, can be more creative, even entrepreneurial. However, some reforms create pressure for more, not fewer, rules (for e.g. in such areas as conflict of interest and non-partisanship). The fostering of shared values across the public service and in individual organizations can help to reduce the overall need for rules and to increase the use of the less intrusive management instrument of guidelines. Public servants are more likely to comply with the rules that remain and to respect the intent of guidelines if they see the connection between the content of these rules and guidelines and fundamental public service values. For example, one approach to controlling conflict of interest is to provide lengthy and detailed rules against it. Another approach is to explain that the need to avoid conflict of interest is grounded in basic and enduring democratic and ethical values such as impartiality and fairness; to develop broad conflict-of-interest principles based on these values; and then to draw from these principles a limited number of rules and guidelines. 'The best accountability systems recognize . . . that "control is normative . . . rooted in values and beliefs"' (Mintzberg, 1996: 81).

It is unrealistic to expect that a written statement alone will be sufficient to foster shared values and high ethical standards in the public service. A statement of key values should be viewed as an essential component of a broad regime [. . . that] could include [. . .] such measures as ethics codes, rules and guidelines; ethics training and education; ethics counsellors or ombudsmen; and the evaluation of ethical performance as a basis for appointments and promotions, especially at the senior leadership level. While statements of values (or codes of conduct) can serve important purposes, they can be severely undermined by leaders who do not model the organization's values. Public servants are more effectively motivated by concrete examples of values-based leadership than by lofty declarations of values.

Nevertheless, a carefully crafted statement of values can provide a firm foundation on which a comprehensive ethics regime can be built. The core values contained in the statement indicate the key questions to be raised about the impact of the various reforms associated with movement toward the post-bureaucratic model of public organization. The other components of the regime (e.g. training) provide measures by which public organizations can manage the ethical challenges arising from these reforms.

Note

1   The Agency's core values and operating principles are as follows:
     Workplace and People Values: Professionalism, Respect, Commitment and a Positive Outlook; Employment Values: Merit, Employment Equity, Mobility and Performance Recognition; and Leadership and Management Values: Openness, Integrity, Trust and Teamwork (Doering, 1998: 14).

References

Australia (1999) 'Public Service Bill 1999', explanatory memorandum. Available at: http://www.psmpc.gov.au/psact/psbill99.htm

Canada, Committee on Governing Values (1987) *Governing Values*. Ottawa: Supply and Services.

Canada, Deputy Ministers' Task Force on Public Service Values and Ethics (1996) *A Strong Foundation: Discussion Paper on Values and Ethics in the Public Service*. Ottawa: Privy Council Office. Available at: http://www.ccmd-ccg.gc.ca/publications.html

Denhardt, Robert (1993) *The Pursuit of Significance: Strategies for Managerial Success in Public Organizations*. Belmont, CA: Wadsworth.

Doering, Ronald L. (1998) 'Alternative Service Delivery and the Public Interest: The Case of the Canadian Food Inspection Agency (CFIA)', paper presented at the International Congress of the International Institute of Administrative Sciences, Paris, September.

Doig, Alan (1995) 'Mixed Signals? Public Sector Change and the Proper Conduct of Public Business', *Public Administration* 73 (Summer): 191–212.

Frederickson, H. George (1993) 'Ethics and Public Administration: Some Assertions', in H. George Frederikson (ed.) *Ethics and Public Administration*. New York: M.E. Sharpe.

Gilbert, Charles E. (1959) 'The Framework of Administrative Responsibility', *Journal of Politics* 21: 373–407.

Hondeghem, Annie (ed.) (1998) *Ethics and Accountability in a Context of Governance and New Public Management*. IOS Press.

Kamto, Maurice (1997) 'Reaffirming Public-Service Values and Professionalism', *International Review of Administrative Sciences* 63 (Sept.): 295–308.

Kaufman, Herbert (1956) 'Emerging Conflicts in the Doctrines of Public Administration', *American Political Science Review* 50(1): 1059–73.

Kernaghan, Kenneth (1978) 'Changing Concepts of Power and Responsibility in the Canadian Public Service', *Canadian Public Administration* 21(3): 389–406.

Kernaghan, Kenneth (1994) 'The Emerging Public Service Culture: Values, Ethics and Reforms', *Canadian Public Administration* 37(4): 614–30.

Kernaghan, Kenneth, Marson, Brian and Borins, Sandford (2000) *The New Public Organization*. Toronto: Institute of Public Administration of Canada.

Larson, Peter (1998) 'Public Service Reform: The New Zealand Way', *The Ottawa Citizen*, 2 May.

Mintzberg, Henry (1996) 'Managing Government: Governing Management', *Harvard Business Review* (May/Jun.): 75–83.

New Zealand, State Services Commission (1995) *Public Service Code of Conduct*. Wellington: State Services Commission.

New Zealand, State Services Commission (1996) *New Zealand's State Sector Reform: A Decade of Change*. Wellington: State Services Commission.

OECD (1998) *Principles for Managing Ethics in the Public Service*. Paris: OECD.

Peters, B. Guy (1995) 'The Public Service, the Changing State, and Governance', in B. Guy Peters and Donald J. Savoie (eds) *Governance in a Changing Environment*, pp. 288–320. Montreal/Kingston: McGill-Queen's University Press.

Rokeach, Milton (1973) *The Nature of Human Values*. New York: Free Press.

United Kingdom (1996) *The Civil Service Code*. London: Cabinet Office (Office of the Public Service).

Janet Newman

JOINED-UP GOVERNMENT: THE POLITICS OF PARTNERSHIP

From: Newman, J. (2001) 'Joined-up government: the politics of partnership', *Modernising Governance. New Labour, Policy and Society*, Chapter 6, Sage

[...]

Governing through partnership: a paradigm shift?

[...]

NOTIONS OF HOLISTIC GOVERNMENT are emblematic of the 'new' governance based on coordination through networks rather than markets or hierarchy. It is viewed in terms of plural actors engaged in a reflexive process of dialogue and information exchange. It is based on the idea of horizontal self-organisation among mutually interdependent actors, rather than hierarchical relationships. Network forms of governance must, then, be viewed as conceptually separate from partnership as structure (Lowndes and Skelcher 1998). Networks are informal and fluid, with shifting membership and ambiguous relationships and accountabilities. They may become formalised into official partnerships, but may also operate loosely across organisational boundaries. They are characterised by compromise rather than confrontation, negotiation rather than administrative fiat (Stewart 2000). The role of government is to enable, steer and coordinate rather than to control.

[...]

There is an assumption that networks of actors will engage in finding solutions to problems and that organisations will develop strategies that incorporate the advantages and benefits of partnership working.

The limits of partnership

Labour's focus on delivering 'joined-up' or 'holistic' government led to a great deal of experiment and action. The government introduced new funding arrangements, common performance indicators, integrated ICT and other forms of infrastructural shifts to help overcome some of the barriers to collaboration that had impeded partnership working in the past. The policies directed towards fostering partnership working did, however, vary. Partnerships and joint working can have a number of objectives:

- to create an integrated, holistic approach to the development and delivery of public policy;
- to overcome departmental barriers and the problems of 'silo' management;
- to reduce the transaction costs resulting from overlapping policies and initiatives through coordination and integration;
- to deliver better policy outcomes by eliciting the contribution of multiple players at central, regional, local and community tiers of governance;
- to improve coordination and integration of service delivery among providers;
- to develop new, innovative approaches to policy development or service provision by bringing together the contributions and expertise of different partners; and
- to increase the financial resources available for investment by developing partnerships and joint ventures between the public, private and not for profit sectors.

It is difficult to generalise about how well the partnerships set up under Labour met these objectives because of the wide range of structures and relationships encompassed by the term. Partnerships range from loose networks to more stable groupings with defined structures and protocols. They involve relationships that range from a base of formal contracts to the more elusive processes of reciprocity and trust. Different issues are raised by attempts to overcome departmental boundaries in central government in order to develop a more integrated approach to policy (the usual meaning of joined-up government); the creation of partnerships between the public and private sectors; multi-agency partnerships between service delivery organisations (e.g. health and social services); and local partnerships involving voluntary and community sectors in, for example, regeneration initiatives. To add to the complexity, it may well be that formal bodies with well-defined structures and procedures are sustained by a loose network of key individuals who 'make it work'; or that a formal contract is underpinned by informal relationships of trust which help resolve conflict and reduce transaction costs.

Stoker (2000) notes a number of different steering techniques used by government: cultural persuasion, communication, finance, monitoring and structural reform. Cultural persuasion (promoting partnerships) is a relatively weak instrument but may create an enabling climate supporting local flexibility. Communication (facilitating learning and encouraging access) promotes capacity-building and can be used to support the development of local networks without threatening flexibility. New financial regimes or new structures may facilitate network modes of governance but may also create new rigidities: as one line of differentiation is overcome, new ones are delineated as boundaries are redrawn and interests regrouped.

My aim is not to distinguish between different types of partnership but to explore the ways in which they were overlaid on each other to produce a possible shift in the mode of governance. Labour's use of partnerships as a way of governing encompassed a range of approaches, only some of which facilitate the growth of network-based modes of coordination. Much of the early focus of the Social Exclusion Unit was on communication and persuasion in an attempt to build sustainable responses to the problems of deprived communities and social exclusion. The emphasis here and in the zonal initiatives was on new forms of funding, joint resourcing and the development of outcome-based evaluation linked to cross-cutting performance indicators. The initial aim was to promote flexible forms of collaboration, experimentation and innovation.

[. . .]

The dynamics of partnership working

The 1990s also saw an explosion of 'how to do it' manuals and guidelines for partnerships and a number of more academic analyses of the difficulties of partnership working. While the former tended to highlight the importance of shared values, joint goals and other normative features associated with an optimistic model of partnership, the latter drew attention to a number of difficulties based on lack of trust, problems of accountability, inequalities, differences of power and the problems of the sustainability of partnership working over time (Huxham 1996; Huxham and Vangen 1996). Such problems are experienced within partnerships themselves but their origin may lie elsewhere: in the interaction between the external and internal collaborative environment created by such factors as the policy approach of government, the impact of funding regimes, and the cultures of parent organisations. However well a group may work at building collaboration and trust, it may nevertheless come unstuck because of external shifts or ambiguities. Such shifts took place in government priorities and strategies, and the purpose of partnerships was influenced by changing priorities in mainstream programmes. For example, as the programme of the Social Exclusion Unit developed over time, it became linked to a series of specific government targets – for instance on school exclusion – and the use of more prescriptive policy instruments linked to narrower forms of output, rather than outcome, measures. The experience of Education and Health Action Zones was of a shift to much narrower targets, more tightly linked to ministerial agendas, in place of their initial diverse and multiple policy objectives.

The dynamics of partnership were also influenced by shifts in partner organisations as they adapted to changes in national policy, changed strategic direction or adopted new structures and roles. Some private sector partners underwent significant changes in direction as they reassessed the risks and costs of public–private partnerships. The requirement that local authorities adopt new political structures based on elected mayors or Cabinet government began to influence the dynamics of local partnerships. The picture was also influenced by the sheer number of partnership-based initiatives launched by government. Many organisations became enmeshed in multiple and often interlocking partnership relationships, with different life-cycles and funding mechanisms adding extra sets of complexity and uncertainty to the work of the agencies and individuals concerned.

The combined effect of these processes was to create a series of dilemmas or tensions for partnerships (Newman 2000). These were resolved in particular ways depending on the way in which external constraints or opportunities were interpreted by participants. [. . .] Four of the principal imperatives which influence partnership working are those of *accountability* (having proper structures, formalised roles and transparent procedures), *pragmatism* (getting things done, meeting targets), *flexibility* (adapting fast to changing conditions, expansion), and *sustainability* (fostering participation, building consensus and embedding networks to ensure long-term development). Each of these is likely to be present in any partnership, though the balance between them may be uneven and may shift over time. The model (see Figure 16.1) is intended as a way of capturing or mapping the balance between different imperatives within any particular partnership. The terminology (towards . . .) is deliberately meant to suggest pulls or trajectories of movement rather than static categories or ideal types.

The vertical axis of the model represents the way in which partnerships are positioned in or shaped by their external environment. The top quadrants suggest a focus on self-steering or co-governance, while the bottom quadrants are more directly influenced by policy directives and performance management systems. The horizontal axis of the model represents aspects of the internal dynamics of partnership. The left-hand end suggests a dominant focus on the internal structures and procedures which are needed to ensure accountability (lower left-hand quadrant) or to build long-term network capacity (upper left-hand quadrant). The right-hand end of the horizontal axis suggests a dominant focus on external adaptation, with much less regard to internal structures and processes. The focus may be on pragmatism in order to respond to government incentives or targets (bottom right-hand quadrant), or on developing flexible networks in order to survive in a competitive and fast-changing environment (upper right-hand quadrant).

The different imperatives, each linked to a particular model of governance, are not necessarily reconcilable. For example, the kind of structural arrangements put in place to deliver accountability or ensure fair conduct may limit flexibility. The setting-up of clear operating procedures and accountable structures tends to create barriers to fast action. A pragmatic focus on the delivery of short-term

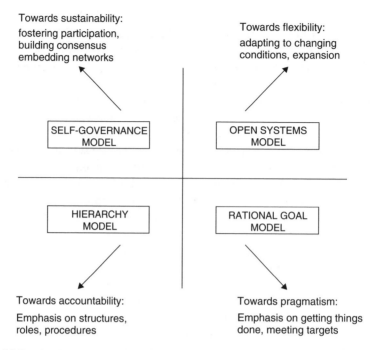

Figure 16.1 The dynamics of partnership working

goals may limit sustainability by inhibiting capacity-building within partner organisations or with local communities. The inclusive and participative activities which help build sustainability are precisely those which may be sidelined under pressure to deliver a bid or an outcome to a tight deadline.

Few partnerships fall neatly into a single quadrant: most are based on some form of compromise or equilibrium between the different models. The equilibrium may change over time, perhaps with a focus on openness at the beginning being constrained as the need for delivery against time-limited goals becomes pre-eminent. [. . .] But partnerships may also experience 'institutional drift', leading to inappropriate patterns becoming embedded and reproduced. For example, a fluid, initially responsive network may drift towards structure in an attempt to create institutional stability, a stability that is inappropriate to an uncertain and unstable environment. The internal dynamics of partnerships or networks may also be influenced as they adapt to new requirements or shifting external conditions. Each model produces specific problems whose resolution may require a re-balancing to accommodate other values, as illustrated below.

Towards accountability: here the focus is on partnership institutions (e.g. joint structures, joint planning mechanisms, joint governance arrangements) designed to formalise the interaction between organisations and regulate decision-making processes. The focus on formal accountability through the following of 'due process' does not, however, necessarily deliver *democratic* accountability: 'Accountability is couched in terms of managerial and technical project and programme management rather than in terms of political accountability to community and electorate' (Stewart 2000: 6). The mechanisms through which partnership boards are accountable to parent organisations or the wider public may be obscure. Many mandatory partnerships, or partnerships where there is low trust between organisations, are pulled towards a strong emphasis on structures and procedures (e.g. the now superseded joint planning structures between health and social services, or the newer crime and disorder partnerships). A focus on structures, systems and procedures may mean that decision-making is slow, leading to pressures to move towards pragmatism or flexibility. However, formal structures or procedures influence, rather than determine, internal partnership dynamics. Many such bodies do deliver productive collaboration, though often this takes place despite, rather than because of, formalised partnership arrangements. That is, the formalised institutions may be largely symbolic with emphasis being placed on one or more of the other models in day-to-day decision-making.

Towards pragmatism: the emphasis here is on joint activity around specific – and often short-term – objectives. Collaboration may be 'thin', driven by external requirements or obligations, rather than self-generated. This thinness is often a result of compliant responses to external demands (e.g. delivery against government performance targets for which collaboration is required) or more proactive responses to opportunities (e.g. bidding for government, European or other funding to a tight timescale). An emphasis on this model can be viewed as a product of short-term shifts in policy, or the use of incentive-based policy instruments. Adaptiveness is high but the capacity to deliver sustained outcomes may be low. The emphasis is on getting on with the job, not necessarily addressing process issues, and the partnership may not significantly affect the core strategies or cultures of mainstream organisations. However, the networks that develop may have a longer-term impact, and create movement towards longer-term responses represented in the values of flexibility and sustainability. Where the demand for pragmatism produces behaviour that transgresses the informal or formal decision-making rules of parent organisations, however, there may be a call for a tighter emphasis on accountability and transparency.

Towards flexibility: here collaboration tends to be driven by longer-term goals. It is 'thicker' in that collaboration is entered into on a voluntary basis in order to pursue particular strategies or set up initiatives to adapt a fast-changing environment more quickly than parent organisations can move. Networks are dynamic and fluid, held in place by network members rather than statutory requirements or incentives. Collaboration is entered into in order to deliver mutual goals (e.g. local economic development) rather than comply with government requirements or partnership demands, though the goals may result from shifts in government policy. Adaptiveness is high because of the emphasis on fluidity and flexibility: partnerships driven by this imperative are less vulnerable to short-term shifts in policy so may have the capacity to deliver longer-term change. However, there may be tensions between the partnership and the mainstream cultures of the parent organisation since the pace and nature of change in each will differ. Problems may occur when there is a distance between joint, network-based projects and parent organisations which may leave projects in a kind of organisational limbo (Hardy *et al.* 1992). This may create a pull within the network towards greater sustainability, or alternatively a pull back by parent organisations to ensure stronger structures of accountability.

Towards sustainability: here the focus is on setting up processes through which the capacity of partners – organisations, communities, user groups – can be developed over time. There is likely to be a focus on 'empowerment' and 'participation', bringing in and supporting users, community members and front-line staff to generate momentum and take responsibility for actions and outcomes. Culture change and learning in participating organisations may be emphasised in order to embed new forms of activity. New sources of leadership in community initiatives or collaborative projects may be sought to provide continued momentum. However, tensions between long-term, sustainable goals (overcoming inequality, building community capacity, preventing ill health) and mainstream policies requiring delivery against short-term targets may be particularly sharp. Coupled with this, the difficulties of achieving long-term change may lead to temporary pulls towards pragmatic responses, or the abandonment of the goal of sustainability altogether. Where it is pursued with some success, on the other hand, there may be calls from previously excluded or marginalised groups for new structures or protocols that devolve power and provide greater accountability.

[. . .]

References

Hardy, B., Turrell, A. and Wistow, G. (1992) *Innovations in Community Care Management*. Aldershot, Avebury.

Huxham, C. (ed.) *Creating Collaborative Advantage*. London, Sage.

Huxham, C. and Vangen, S. (1996) 'Working together: key themes in the management of relationships between public and non profit organisations', *International Journal of Public Sector Management*, 9, pp. 5–17.

Newman, J. (2000) 'The dynamics of partnership'. Paper presented to the seventh *International Conference on Multi-organizational Partnerships and Strategic Collaboration*, Leuven, July.

Stewart, M. (2000) 'Collaboration and conflict in the governance of the city region'. Paper presented to the seventh *International Conference on Multi-organizational Partnerships and Strategic Collaboration*, Leuven, July.

Stoker, G. (2000) 'Urban political science and the challenge of urban governance' in J. Pierre (ed.), *Debating Governance: Authority, Steering and Democracy*. Oxford, Oxford University Press.

Jane Broadbent and Richard Laughlin

PUBLIC PRIVATE PARTNERSHIPS: AN INTRODUCTION

From: Broadbent, J. and Laughlin, R. (2003) 'Public private partnerships: an introduction', *Accounting, Auditing and Accountability Journal*, 16:3, 332–341

Introduction

AS THE INSTITUTE OF Public Policy Research (IPPR) made clear in its, admittedly UK-biased, but still internationally relevant, report, *Building Better Partnerships* (IPPR, 2001, p. 15):

> ... people ... demand better public services ... However, ... to win this fight the case for public services needs to be made in terms of values and outcomes rather than particular forms of service delivery.

Public private partnerships (PPPs) are one form of this policy of liberalisation in the way public services are produced and delivered to the public. PPPs open up the possibilities for the provision of public services, not only to come exclusively from organisations owned and controlled by the public sector, but also from both public and private sectors in partnership. To accept that public services could be supplied by PPPs inevitably requires liberalisation in thought, since, as IPPR are at pains to point out, the "public good, private bad" (IPPR, 2001, p. 23) argument in the provision of public services is still very close to the surface. Like the IPPR, we too are of the view that PPPs cannot be ruled out on the basis of prejudice but need to be analysed with an open mind as to whether they do provide a "better", however defined, way of providing public services.

[. . .] The development of PPPs across the world has been less than uniform or unitary in nature (as is the case with most of the new public management reforms (Olson *et al.*, 1998)).

[. . .] Broadbent and Laughlin (1999, pp. 106–12) posed a research agenda a few years ago specifically in relation to PFIs. If we read this agenda as not totally applying just to either PFIs or the UK then it is surprising how many of the themes still stand: "what is the nature of PFI (PPP) and who is regulating its application?" and "how are definitions of PFI (PPP) in terms of value for money and risk transfer derived and operationalised?" In addition Edwards and Shaoul (2003) and Broadbent *et al.* (2003) start to address the vexed question of "what is the merit and worth of PFI (PPP)?"

It is important to provide a few building blocks, starting with trying to be clear about what constitutes "public services". This is because a private sector supplier arguably becomes a PPP, rather than remaining a private supplier, when it supplies "public services". This, in turn, requires definition of the borderline that distinguishes public from private services. One neat, but unfortunately incomplete, way to do this would be on the basis of whether charges need to be made to secure the respective services. However, whilst some public services are free at the point of delivery, many, even in those countries with a longstanding and extensive welfare state, are increasingly making charges for the services that are supplied to the public. A key element in differentiating the two sectors, we will argue, is the existence of a regime of state price regulation.

Broadbent and Guthrie (1992, p. 8) struggled with this same dilemma of demarcation when they were trying to define what constituted the "public sector". Their solution, which makes some important distinctions between ownership and control, provides a useful pragmatic vehicle for resolving this borderline problem. Their view is that if certain organisations, even though formally owned by private shareholders, are still the focus of "ownership" claims (over the outputs provided since they are in the "public interest") and control intentions (over input provision) by central and local governments, then these are still *de facto* part of the public sector and are delivering public services. Thus the provision of say utilities (gas, electricity, water) are public services, whether the organisations providing these services are now owned by private shareholders (as in the UK), having originally been part of the public sector, or are, and always have been, owned by private shareholders (as in the USA). A PPP is an approach to delivering public services that involves the private sector, but one that provides for a more direct control relationship between the public and private sector than would be achieved by a simple (legally-protected) market-based and arm's-length purchase. [. . .] Beyond privately owned public service suppliers (such as utilities) are the PPPs that have been developed in a more proactive or collaborative mode and which, from the start, have been recognised and labelled as such. It is the development of these latter PPPs in the traditional public sectors throughout the world that have been the subject of considerable research interest. These PPPs are the most recent development of "new public management" (NPM) (Hood, 1991, 1995) – the overall nature of which has become well-established in many countries.

In the UK, New Zealand and Australia particularly, as well as in other nations around the world, large parts of the public sector were subject to aggressive privatisation in the 1970s and 1980s. Because of its existing tradition, the USA never had to engage in such an extensive privatisation programme – a point Baker (2003) makes clear. Instead, the rest of the world simply caught up with the US model of provision of some key public services by turning to privatisation. Baker's consideration of the utilities companies in the USA argues these newly, or never privatised, organisations were the original PPPs. This argument rests on our earlier proposition that the nature of regulation and control is a crucial element in decisions about what might be seen as a PPP. In moving to provide public services, using private sector companies, it was essential that the various governments around the world could exercise some ownership rights and control over the nature, and, particularly, pricing, of the public services offered by these privatised companies. Hence, regulative regimes such as that described by Baker were developed.

The early 1990s provides a turning point in the UK, Australia and New Zealand. At that point, in all three of these countries, the regulated privatisation of major parts of the public sector, that provided the basis for the nascent PPPs, ceased. In the UK and Australia this was probably because there was little else that could legitimately be sold off. In New Zealand, on the other hand, as Newberry and Pallot (2003) demonstrate, this cessation was probably due to the political and economic problems engendered by the privatisation programme that had been pursued. The move away from large-scale privatisations in the UK led to an explicit attempt to engage with the private sector in a different way. This became known as the Private Finance Initiative (PFI). PFI was launched in 1992. This was followed by something similar in Australia under the generic titles of "privately financed projects" as English and Guthrie (2003) indicate. The generic term PPP has, however, increasingly been adopted in the UK even though PFI still predominates. New Zealand, on the other hand, so often the leader in NPM reforms, has yet to see a serious launch of PPPs due, it seems, to the political and economic repercussions of their privatisation programme and the association of PPPs with these disasters (Newberry and Pallot, 2003).

PFI as the exemplar PPP?

Given the significance of PFI in the development of PPPs worldwide it is important to provide some brief background into the history and nature of this, primarily, UK-based initiative. The UK's PFI was launched in Autumn 1992 by the Conservative Chancellor of the Exchequer, Norman Lamont. The longstanding ideological stance of the Conservative government that the private sector would supply better public services than if they were supplied solely through the public sector was a driver. It was in this context that PFI was launched. The use of PFI was limited before the general election of May 1997, when the Conservative government was finally defeated after 18 years in power. PFI, up to this time, was primarily used to finance transport projects – notably the Channel Tunnel joining the UK to mainland Europe. The stuttering progress of PFI could have stopped altogether had the incoming Labour government not had an about-turn on their original negative stance towards PFI. By bringing it in as a special case under the umbrella of their chosen "third way" approach – and arguing that PFIs were only one form of PPPs – the Labour government became ardent believers in its worth. They were determined to make PFI/PPP a success and also to expand its area of influence into all departments of central and local government. Now the driving force for PFI is HM Treasury in the heart of the government. As a result PFI is actively pursued with some 450 contracts worth over £50 billion underway or completed. The Labour government has taken PFI to new levels, both in terms of how and when to make PFI decisions as well as into areas where the Conservative government would have liked to go but were unsuccessful – notably in hospitals, schools and universities.

PFI, in its purest form, is a design build finance and operate (DBFO) system. It usually involves the provision, by a private sector consortium, of property-based services for a period of a minimum 30, and, more usually, 60 years, to a public sector "purchaser". In exchange for these services over this 30/60 year time horizon the public sector pays a monthly, in effect, lease cost to the private sector supplier. This monthly cost is revised periodically as the contract progresses. The central characteristics of a DBFO system is that the private sector supplier is deemed to be the provider of a "service package" involving the design of any building and the accompanying operational management of the building and its aligned services (following an output specification from the public sector purchaser). The private sector partner also has to manage the overall financing of the entire project, particularly at the outset where high capital costs have to be incurred.

PFI is clearly a PPP and is in marked contrast to how this "service package" would be supplied, if this supply came only from those employed by the public sector. To be fair the latter provision has rarely occurred. Even under normal public sector procurement the private sector may well be involved through definable sub-contracts where particular expertise may not be in the employment of the public sector. The real difference in the two forms of procurement lies in overall control of the service provision. There are various aspects to this. First, with PFI, the building is technically not owned by the public sector – although who has the "asset" of the building is a major disagreement in PFI. Second, the design of this building, along with the accompanying services, is the responsibility of the private sector. The public sector should not be actively involved in this specification – all it specifies is the outputs it requires in terms of services. Third, the public sector is locked into a long-term relationship, specified as best as possible through a legal contract, with a private sector supplier who might have different values and interests. A genuine concern to many is that this private sector supplier, with its profit emphasis and necessity to give priority to its shareholders, may or may not share the same public service values that might be the case if provision was exclusively made by those in the employment of the public sector. In fact, some have gone further to suggest that the profit motive, which inevitably must drive the private sector supplier, is fundamentally different to, and likely to clash with, the values and ethos of the public sector.

[. . .]

Some concluding thoughts

[. . .] Our task as researchers [. . .] is to probe and expose these contexts and their connection to our technical accounting-related systems and raise questions and make suggestions about their redesign. But any redesign will also inevitably be context-dependent since that is the fundamental nature of accounting. The papers in this special issue demonstrate, in different ways, this fundamental contextual nature and role of accounting.

Finally, with this more general point in mind, we need to end with some thoughts on [. . .] research on PFIs and PPPs and what a future research agenda might include. As indicated in the introduction, Broadbent and Laughlin (1999) posed a research agenda for the UK's PFI in five questions. This agenda provides a useful pragmatic framework for exploring the contribution of the papers in this special issue of *AAAJ* as well as providing a starting point for clarifying a research agenda for the future.

[. . .] This important evaluation research question cannot be comprehensively answered in the immediate future and neither can the remaining questions as to "how are PFI (PPP) decisions made in different areas of the public sector and what are the effects of these decisions?" and "is PFI (PPP) a form of privatisation?" These questions, like the one on the "merit and worth" of PPPs, require detailed and, we would argue, theoretically-informed, empirical studies in specific areas over a period of time before meaningful insights will be forthcoming. This is the challenge for the future and one which will probably need to be undertaken in "partnership" with the National Audit Offices around the world, as Edwards and Shaoul (2003) and Broadbent *et al.* (2003) suggest.

The other research question [. . .] is the importance of exploring the development of PPPs internationally. The move to PPPs is now a worldwide movement where there are marked differences in terms of levels of development and overall emphasis, all of which are in need of analysis and comparison. [. . .] More research clearly needs to be done, since PPPs are likely to be the major vehicle for developments in the provision of public services for many years to come. Understanding how different countries adopt and adapt PPPs to their needs will be important to understand.

References

Baker, C.R. (2003), "Investigating Enron as a public private partnership", *Accounting, Auditing & Accountability Journal*, Vol. 16 No. 3, pp. 446–66.

Broadbent, J. and Guthrie, J. (1992), "Changes in the public sector: a review of recent 'alternative' accounting research", *Accounting, Auditing & Accountability Journal*, Vol. 5 No. 2, pp. 3–31.

Broadbent, J. and Laughlin, R. (1999), "The Private Finance Initiative: clarification of a future research agenda", *Financial Accountability and Management*, Vol. 15 No. 2, pp. 95–114.

Broadbent, J., Gill, J. and Laughlin, R. (2003), "Evaluating the Private Finance Initiative in the National Health Service in the UK", *Accounting, Auditing & Accountability Journal*, Vol 16 No. 3, pp. 422–45.

Edwards, P. and Shaoul, J. (2003), "Partnerships: for better, for worse?", *Accounting, Auditing & Accountability Journal*, Vol. 16 No. 3, pp. 397–421.

English, L. and Guthrie, J. (2003), "Driving privately financed projects in Australia: what makes them tick?", *Accounting, Auditing & Accountability Journal*, Vol. 16 No. 3, pp. 493–511.

Hood, C. (1991), "A public management for all seasons", *Public Administration*, Vol. 69, Spring, pp. 3–19.

Hood, C. (1995), "The 'new public management' in the 1980s: variations on a theme", *Accounting, Organizations and Society*, Vol. 20 No. 2/3, pp. 93–119.

IPPR (2001), *Building Better Partnerships: The Final Report of the Commission on Public Private Partnerships*, Institute of Public Policy Research, London.

Newberry, S. and Pallot, J. (2003), "Fiscal (ir)responsibility: privileging PPPs in New Zealand", *Accounting, Auditing & Accountability Journal*, Vol. 16 No. 3, pp. 467–92.

Olson, O., Guthrie, J. and Humphrey, C. (Eds) (1998), *Global Warning! Debating International Developments in New Public Financial Management*, Cappelen Akademisk Forlag, Oslo.

John Clarke

SCRUTINY THROUGH INSPECTION AND AUDIT: POLICIES, STRUCTURES AND PROCESSES

Clarke, J. (2003) 'Scrutiny through inspection and audit: policies, structures and processes' in T. Bovaird and E. Loffler (eds) *Public Management and Governance*, Routledge

Introduction

ALTHOUGH PUBLICLY PROVIDED SERVICES have always been subject to forms of scrutiny, the emergence of new organizational forms and structures of service provision in recent years has made scrutiny an increasingly significant feature of their governance and management. In particular, the move towards more fragmented, dispersed and 'arm's-length' structures of provision has led governments to enlarge and enhance their repertoire of forms and practices of scrutiny.

Since the 1980s, we have experienced a period of innovation and reform in the organizational systems of providing public services. Such changes have been uneven internationally, and have been most heavily concentrated in Anglophone countries (Australia, Canada, New Zealand, UK and the USA) where neo-liberal politics have had most impact to date. Nevertheless, the model of reform (towards the de-monopolization of public sector organizations; the move towards marketization and privatization of service provision and an enthusiasm for the model of new public management) has attained international currency (Flynn, 2000).

In this chapter, I explore the view that the reform of public services has driven an expansion of forms of scrutiny (particularly those of inspection and audit) and has simultaneously led to a blurring of boundaries between audit, inspection, organizational design and consultancy. The purposes and processes of scrutiny have become complicated in the effort to govern a dispersed system of public provision at a distance. Expanded scrutiny – what Power has called the 'audit explosion' (1993, 1997) – emerges in this process of reform, and its continued spread has been driven by the problems of managing the organizational forms and relationships created by the reform process.

This chapter will explore the development of scrutiny, the changing forms and meanings of scrutiny, and the arguments about the necessity, desirability and effectiveness of such processes.

Levels and new forms of scrutiny

Until the 1980s, the archetypal organizational form of public service provision was that of professional bureaucracy, in which hierarchical administration of policies and resources left spaces for professional autonomy, judgement and practice (Clarke and Newman, 1997). Combined with the governmental processes of representative democracy, such systems contained particular models of accountability and scrutiny.

These centred on vertical chains of accountability through the levels of bureaucracy to senior officials and upward to elected politicians (at local, regional or national level). They were supplemented by norms of administration and professional practice, often embodied within ethical codes of conduct which were supervised by professional disciplinary bodies such as the medical model of professional self-regulation. In some cases they were also subject to professional inspection to evaluate and advise upon standards of practice (e.g. in teaching, social work and policing). Finally, the professional bureaucracies were typically subject to the practice of audit (in its traditional accounting meaning) to ensure that financial probity and good practice were being pursued in the handling of public funds.

The late twentieth-century reforms of public service organization disrupted these systems of accountability and scrutiny in two main ways. First, they fragmented and dispersed the organizations of service provision through the multiple strategies of decentralization, marketization and privatization, thus dislocating the possibilities of internal, vertical and hierarchical systems of control and scrutiny. The resulting complexity of organizational forms of public service provision – decentralized, semi-autonomous organizations linked in shifting webs of competitive and collaborative relationships, and subject to mixes of vertical and horizontal pressures for responsiveness and accountability – posed new problems of how to scrutinize service providers.

Second, however, neo-liberal advocates wove a compelling story out of the inadequacies, problems and frustrations of professional bureaucracies around the issue of trust. The combination of representative democracy and professional bureaucracy rested on assumptions about the effective articulation of the public interest through political representation, administrative neutrality and professional disinterest (Dunleavy, 1991; Clarke and Newman, 1997). Neo-liberal critics (especially public choice theorists) argued that none of these assumptions held – and that politicians, bureaucrats and professionals were better viewed as fundamentally venal, self-interested and seeking to maximize their own power, resources and status. Although neo-liberals certainly did not invent mistrust of, and challenge to, the practices of public service organizations, they did organize them into a coherent case for the dismantling of such institutions. In particular, this story of mistrust demanded new forms of discipline and scrutiny to supplement the introduction of market forces.

New practices of audit

Audit historically has meant the practice of scrutinizing financial control processes and financial decision making, as in the work of the National Audit Office in the UK and national and regional audit courts in other OECD countries. The practice of fiscal scrutiny – the role of audit in its accountancy meaning – is concerned to verify the accuracy of financial statements and to check whether money has been spent for the purposes declared. In this narrow sense, audit is an effort to ensure sound financial management and to stop fraud and corruption. The need for such financial scrutiny was reinforced in the 1980s by rising anxiety about public spending and, from a different perspective, by a drive towards 'businesslike' methods in public agencies, with the attendant dangers of financial malpractice. The establishment of organizations and procedures of financial scrutiny is still high on the agenda in other European countries such as Spain, and is currently regarded as a crucial issue in Central and Eastern European countries.

However, in more recent years the practice of audit in relation to public services has come to include a much wider range of evaluative and normative functions, most evidently in the work of the Audit Commission in the UK.

Cutler and Waine (1997, pp. 30–31) have argued that the Commission has developed

> a major extension of the role of audit, which traditionally has been mainly concerned with the accuracy of accounts and ensuring that public bodies were acting within their legal remit. Value for money (VFM) audit, however, involves an assessment of service performance, an area which, of course, intersects with professional judgements that were of limited or no relevance to the narrower financial and legal concerns of traditional audit practice.

The expansion of the meanings and practices of audit is a significant process in the context of UK governance and is echoed in some other national settings. In the UK, the Audit Commission's VFM studies have linked questions of accounting, evaluation, the identification of 'best practice', issues of organizational design, and management consultancy (Clarke et al., 2000). That is, the

Commission became an agency of policy and organizational innovation, prescribing best practice, identifying dangerous deviations and divergences, advising on the most effective organizational systems, structures and cultures, and propounding the need for better management of public services. In many other countries, the audit function of government has also expanded its role. One of the most active (and widely published) Audit Courts is the Canadian Office of the Auditor General.

Although not the focus of this chapter, a parallel blurring of boundaries may be observed in the large private sector accounting firms which developed policy and management consultancy practices alongside (and sometimes interleaved with) their audit work.

New roles of scrutiny agencies

This development of audit means displacing or coopting professional knowledge bases. *Displacement* implies that they are subordinated to the specification of 'quality' by politicians or managers. *Cooption* implies that the professional knowledge base is integrated into the VFM audit or policy evaluation model (e.g. through processes of peer review).

The achievement of improved organizational performance has been increasingly viewed as the province of 'good management' rather than professional standards. The pursuit of 'quality', 'excellence' or 'standards' means that evaluative agencies have come to colonize organizational terrain that was previously the province of professional expertise. Different public services have seen different accommodations between professional expertise and evaluative agencies. Hughes and his colleagues (1996) have suggested that the emergent audit-and-inspection regimes that operate in different welfare fields vary partly as a result of the relative power of the different professional groups.

Case Example

The New Roles of the Auditor General of Canada

The Auditor General's responsibilities were clarified and expanded in the 1977 Auditor General Act. The Auditor General was given a broader mandate to examine how well the government managed its affairs, in addition to its continuing role of scrutinizing the accuracy of financial statements. However, the important principle was maintained that the Auditor General does not comment on policy choices, examining only how those policies are implemented.

The Act directs the Auditor General to address three main questions:

1   Is the government keeping proper accounts and records and presenting its financial information accurately? This is called 'attest' auditing. The auditor attests to, or verifies, the accuracy of financial statements.

---

2   Did the government collect or spend the authorized amount of money and for the purposes intended by Parliament? This is called 'compliance' auditing. The auditor asks if the government has complied with Parliament's wishes.

3   Were programmes run economically and efficiently? And does the government have the means to measure their effectiveness? This is called 'value-for-money' or performance auditing. The auditor asks whether or not taxpayers got value for their tax dollars.

In December 1995 the position of Commissioner of the Environment and Sustainable Development was established within the Office of the Auditor General and an obligation was placed on government departments to publish annual sustainable development strategies.

Source: Office of the Auditor General of Canada (2002. *What we do*, http:// www.oag-bvg.gc.ca/domino/other.nsf/html/bodye.html). Reproduced with the permission of the Minister of Public Works and Government Services, 2003.

The development of evaluation has been marked partly by a *shift from compliance to competition*. The evaluation of performance has centred on producing comparative information ('league tables' and the like) through which organizations are judged in terms of their relative success in achieving desired results.

The proliferation of types and agencies of scrutiny suggests that governments continue to have problems coordinating public provision. In particular, the fragmented and dispersed organizational systems developed during the past twenty years pose distinctive problems of control. There are also continuing arguments about whether scrutiny agencies are the most effective or appropriate method of coordination. The 'high cost/low trust' mix of external scrutiny poses questions about value and efficacy; while the competitive, intrusive and interventionist mode of scrutiny creates potentially antagonistic relationships (between provider organizations; between providers and scrutiny agencies, and between provider organizations and government). 'Audit', in its most general sense, has become the focus of controversy about whether it promotes better public services, and whether it is the best way to promote better public services. Some of these issues are discussed further in the following section.

Challenges to scrutiny

In this section, I explore three areas of challenge to the regime of expanded scrutiny of public service provision. The first deals with problems about the methods of scrutiny and evaluation; the second with problems of representing the 'public interest' in scrutiny processes; and the third examines challenges about the necessity and desirability of scrutiny as a means of controlling public services.

Methodological problems of evaluation

There is a growing literature that explores the political, organizational and methodological problems associated with evaluation. The methodological problems concern the reliability and replicability of the knowledge that 'audit' produces. The technical notion of audit (in its accounting sense) aimed to produce reliable knowledge of organizations' financial performance and financial systems. Other forms of evaluative scrutiny have been criticized for using less robust methodologies. [. . .] Scrutiny organizations have tended to accept that there have been methodological problems, but that they will be overcome in the next, methodologically improved, round of evaluation. Other methodological problems concern the difficulty of identifying the causal variables associated with performance change (Pollitt, 1995).

The organizational consequences of the 'audit explosion' form a second focus of concern. Systems of evaluation, it is suggested, distort organizational performance, making it focus on what is being measured: 'what is counted is what gets done'. It is argued that public service organizations are typically multiple stakeholder and multi-objective organizations, but audit processes tend to focus on a limited number of objectives, usually those currently highly valued by central government (Newman, 2001a). In a different way, audit and inspection have had consequences for audited organizations in that they require them to divert scarce resources into the process of being evaluated (Power, 1993). Data have to be collected (often in new formats for different scrutiny agencies). Documentation and systems have to be made to conform to auditing requirements. On-site 'visits' have to be prepared for, stage-managed and performed. The outcomes of inspections, audits and evaluations have to be managed (particularly in relation to valued stakeholders). The 'audit explosion' has multiple costs – both in the creation and maintenance of the audit agencies, and in the organizations being audited.

Third, it has been a consistent point of criticism that public services were poorly documented, producing little reliable information about their performance other than accounting for 'inputs'. As a result, organizations have been required to produce auditable information about their activities, with a steadily increasing emphasis on outputs and outcomes (the effects produced by the organization's activities). Such information would allow the organization to be evaluated both intrinsically and comparatively (i.e. is it efficient, and is it more or less efficient than similar organizations?). These demands for auditable organizations have been framed by discourses of accountability and transparency – against the suspicion of 'producer domination' of organizational choices.

This concern with producing evaluative information creates a number of subsidiary dilemmas (at the intersection of the organization and the auditing agency):

- To what extent can the objectives of the organization be clearly and simply specified? (e.g. What is a school for?)
- To what extent is the performance of the organization measurable? (e.g. Do exam results measure school success?)

- To what extent is organizational performance a closed system in which outcomes reflect the effect of organizational activity? (e.g. Who or what else contributes to 'results'?)
- To what extent can comparability be guaranteed between organizations? (e.g. What unmeasured or unmeasurable factors within or outside organizations may differentiate organizational performance?)

Each stage of evaluation involves potentially contested processes of social construction. There are potential conflicts over the definition of objectives; over the choice of indicators; over the attribution of causal effects; and over how comparison is effected. More substantively, however, the construction of these evaluative processes requires an organization that produces auditable information.

The representation of public interest in scrutiny agencies and practices

There have been many political controversies surrounding the rise of scrutiny, which involve questions of social and political 'independence'. A different way of putting this is to ask what biases may enter into the systems of 'independent' evaluation. There are at least three possibilities that have been raised by critics. The first concerns social biases about the public interest: whom do 'auditors' have in mind when they see themselves as *representing the public*? Given the arguments over 'representation' in political life and public services (about the composition of organizational bodies in relation to the social composition of the nation), this is likely to become an increasingly significant question. Like the judiciary and magistracy, scrutineers may be scrutinized in terms of their ability to represent the diversity of the public's social composition and interests.

There are other controversies about the social biases of scrutiny that centre on the 'enthusiasms' of auditors within the sphere of organizational and occupational controversies. Can auditors or inspectors lay claim to know the 'one best way' in the face of contested choices that may be rooted in organizational, occupational or local-political knowledges and imperatives? Much of the controversy that surrounded OFSTED's role in schooling in the UK centred on its dogmatic insistence on one approach to teaching. Such partisan enthusiasms call the supposed independence of evaluation into question.

Finally, there are questions about the 'political' independence of scrutiny agencies. They typically occupy an ambiguous constitutional space, created by government but 'at arm's length' from it. The precise arrangements vary between countries and between different sorts of agency. However, the increasing involvement in performance (rather than merely financial) evaluation aligns the agencies more directly with assessing organizations against current government policies and targets. Similarly, the blurring of boundaries between evaluation, consultancy and prescription narrows the distance between evaluation and government, creating possibilities for critics to challenge the claimed independence of scrutiny agencies. The shift away from the traditional audit function to being one of the key elements of the new governance implicates scrutiny agencies more directly in the business of government politics, policy and control.

None of these challenges has halted the rise of scrutiny processes. Indeed, they are typically dismissed as the defensive complaints of 'producer interests' unwilling to make themselves 'transparent' and 'accountable'. Nevertheless, they represent important political issues for the future development of governance relationships.

The necessity, desirability and effectiveness of scrutiny processes

Scrutiny processes are inherently 'low-trust/high-cost' models for controlling public services and they tend to be shaped by centralist assumptions and orientations. As a result, they accentuate some tendencies in the new governance, but restrict or even repress others. They fit less readily with diversification, innovation and participatory models of local governing of services. They are also more difficult to adapt to forms of network and partnership working: producing problems of overlap, integration and multiple 'ownership' (Newman, 2001b).

However, they seem likely to remain a favoured tool of central governments in the context of fragmented and dispersed systems of service provision. It may be that the most severe challenge to them emerges not from the public service sector, but from the misfortunes of audit in the private/corporate sector. The recent (2002) spectacular failures of audit to uncover or report fraud and malpractice in major corporate enterprises, and the blurring of lines between audit, consultancy and management in the activities of large accounting firms, have called 'audit' into question as an effective governance mechanism. Arguments have raged about the causes of such failures (weaknesses of the US model; bad management; overly 'cosy' relationships between auditors and auditees and so on). Similarly, arguments about how audit might be put right proliferate – including the inevitable suggestion that 'auditors need to be audited' *(Financial Times*, 3 July 2002). Whether such problems will have implications for the organization of scrutiny in its various forms in the public sector remains to be seen.

Summary

In this chapter I have tried to outline the development of scrutiny systems as part of the new governance of public services. I have emphasized the appeal of processes of audit, inspection and evaluation as a means of government's exercising 'control at a distance' in dispersed and fragmented systems of service provision. I have suggested some of the instabilities and sites of potential challenge associated with the 'audit explosion', particularly those associated with the expansive blurring of roles towards organizational or management consultancy on the one hand and towards prescriptions of organizational practice on the other. As such, scrutiny processes are likely to remain a site of potential tension in the relationships between governments, public service organizations and the public. Much of this is likely to be concentrated in increasingly fractious relationships between central governments (committed to the reform of public services) and service providers (trying to lessen the 'burden' of scrutiny and concentrate limited resources on service provision). The balance of scrutiny – whether it intensifies or moves to what is sometimes called 'light touch' – is likely to depend on whether relationships of trust can be reconstructed around the triangle of public, government and public services. In the absence of such trust relationships, the 'audit explosion' is likely to continue.

References

Clarke, J. and Newman, J. (1997) *The Managerial State: Power, Politics and Ideology in the Remaking of Social Welfare*. London: Sage.

Clarke, J., Gewirtz, S., Hughes, G. and Humphrey, J. (2000) 'Guarding the public interest: auditing public services' in J. Clarke, S. Gewirtz and E. McLaughlin (eds) *New Managerialism, New Welfare?* London: Sage/Open University.

Cutler, T. and Waine, B. (1997) *Managing the Welfare State*. Oxford: Berg.

Dunleavy, P. (1991) *Democracy, Bureaucracy and Public Choice*. London: Harvester Wheatsheaf.

Flynn, N. (2000) 'Managerialism and public services: some international trends', in J. Clarke, S. Gewirtz and E. McLaughlin (eds) *New Managerialism, New Welfare?* London: Sage/Open University.

Hughes, G., Mears, R. and Winch, C. (1996) 'An inspector calls? Regulation and accountability in three public services', *Policy and Politics*, 25:3, pp. 299–313.

Newman, J. (2001a) 'What counts is what works? Constructing evaluations of market mechanisms', *Public Administration*, 79:1, pp. 89–103.

Newman, J (2001b) *Modernising Governance: New Labour, Policy and Society*. London: Sage.

Pollitt, C. (1995) 'Justification by works or by faith? Evaluating the new public management', *Evaluation*, 1:2, pp. 133–154.

Power, M. (1993) *The Audit Explosion*. London: Demos.

Power, M. (1997) *The Audit Society*. Oxford: Oxford University Press.

Rob Paton

MEASUREMENT AND ITS PITFALLS

From: Paton, R. (2003) 'Taking measures – lessons from the literature', *Managing and Measuring Social Enterprises*, Chapter 3, Sage

Introduction

NONPROFITS NOW OPERATE IN an environment permeated by expectations of measurement. The reasons usually offered for preferring measurement-based performance management are:

- Defining performance explicitly, and specifying the level expected, demands greater focus and clarity – it reduces the scope for obfuscation, ambiguity and misunderstanding.
- Measures can summarise the important aspects of a complex situation making it easier to spot where and when expectations are not being realised
- Measurement expresses and encourages an approach to decision-making (including recognition and reward) based on facts and analysis, rather than anecdotes and opinion, not to mention wishful thinking and self-serving claims.
- Measurement can assist learning by allowing greater comparability – over time and between units – and by helping identify 'what works'.

To the extent that these claims are sound in particular circumstances, measurement offers some or all of the following benefits – enhanced supervisory control, greater day-to-day autonomy of-operating units, steady performance improvement, and reduced supervision costs. But how sound are these claims?

[. . .]

An explosion of research

The last 10 years have seen an explosion of interest in and research on the measurement of organisational performance inspired by three trends:

- the reduction in data handling and processing costs as a result of ICT developments;
- the vastly increased measurement efforts in the private sector, particularly in pursuit of non-financial measures of performance;
- the impact of the new managerialism in government and nonprofits.

So what does this literature suggest is likely to happen as social enterprises give increased attention to performance measurement?

[. . .]

The discussion aims to highlight some of the common themes from diverse contexts with a view to clarifying:

1   what is known about the different ways performance information can be used and the issues that arise; but also
2   what may be different about measurement in social enterprises (and why).

As Kendall and Knapp (1995) have pointed out, the main divide in discussions of effectiveness and performance is between those with a rationalist/positivist approach and those with a social constructivist perspective.

[. . .]

The limits to rationalisation

Technical desiderata and flawed realities

The attributes of performance measures that are needed if systems of performance measurement are to assist motivation, feedback control and learning are now well understood. The lists vary as authors express the ideas in slightly different ways, but the same issues and requirements recur, whether with reference to commercial or public organisations, namely:

- they should be *valid* and *reliable* (and 'non-manipulible') and hence provide an appropriate motivational focus;

- they should be *parsimonious*, that is, relatively few in number – lest the 'cognitive limits' of those wanting to understand the performance in question are exceeded;
- they should be *comprehensive*, in the sense of covering all significant dimensions of performance, including the strategic;
- they should be *acceptable, meaningful* and *credible* to a wide range of constituencies;
- they should be *pervasive* and *integrative* allowing the aggregation of results and comparisons both externally and internal;
- they should be *relatively stable*, allowing the tracking of performance over time;
- they should be constructed to have *explanatory* power, aiding diagnosis of low performance, assisting learning and giving insight about future prospects not just reporting past results (sometimes referred to in terms of 'attributability' and 'drill down');
- they should be *practicable* – capable of being quite promptly reported and without adding unduly to administrative costs.

Nevertheless, it is now quite clear that in practice, measurement systems never manage to combine all these attributes.

[. . .]

Many of the difficulties are hidden in the concept of performance itself, which sounds like a unitary attribute but is always multi-dimensional and hard to operationalise. [. . .] Partly this is because of the time dimension of performance – which may refer to past achievements, current functioning, or future prospects. Thus desired outcomes (including profits in the case of companies), which may be very useful as *incentives*, are of limited value as indicators of continuing and future performance (Carter, Klein *et al.* 1992, p174; Bruns 1998). Hence, the enormous effort devoted to finding other, non-financial measures (such as quality, customer satisfaction and loyalty, intellectual capital) that may be leading indicators of profit. Unfortunately, however, most of these are extremely hard to measure – which is to say, they subsume many dimensions requiring multiple indicators of uncertain reliability – as the continuing business and academic research effort testifies. As a result, it is commonplace for senior managers to be faced with 50, 60 or more 'top level' measures.

[. . .]

These issues are likely to be even more acute in nonprofit contexts where concepts of effectiveness and performance are often broad (Herman and Renz 1997, 1999; Forbes 1998); and where one important dimension is often a degree of social or community impact – for which 'the flows of information involved are often remarkably high' as Bovaird (1998) puts it.

[. . .]

Such overload can easily lead to a pattern of oscillation as first noted in Blau's classic study of the employment office (Blau 1963). The use of a limited set of indicators encourages staff to neglect unmeasured dimensions of performance, so new measures are added; but in due course the resulting set exceeds cognitive limits, so there are calls for sharper focus and greater selectivity. This leads to a 'cull' of measures and a much more limited set – and so on.

[...]

The pursuit of control

Measurement-based performance management assumes that measures of performance provide a basis for organisational control. If a system of performance measurement does not provide an appropriate focus for managerial effort and a sound basis for recognition, then there is something wrong with it. Measures, it is said, should have 'bite'. At the same time, however, the dysfunctional consequences of using performance measurement for control are well understood, not least in the private sector.

[...]

A key issue, therefore, is how serious these known and predictable dysfunctions are likely to be. Measurement optimists blame major difficulties on poor design and/or implementation failures, and accept minor difficulties as a price worth paying for the demonstrable benefits. Moreover, the difficulties do sometimes subside. Carter, Klein *et al.* (1992) report cases of initial resistance, denigration and perfunctory compliance (including the 'mass baptism' of existing data) being followed by pragmatic engagement with measurement and the discovery of uses, culminating in constructive dialogue.

[...]

Partial measurement

The pessimists argue that the *measurability* of performance is critical. Austin (1996) usefully distinguishes between situations in which measurement sets encompassing all the aspects that make a significant contribution to overall performance can be implemented; and those in which, for whatever reasons, only partial measurement is practicable. Where 'full measurement' exists performance indicators *do* provide an effective and economical basis for control – because the only way to improve performance-as-measured is to improve overall performance as intended. By contrast, in situations of 'partial measurement' the use of performance information directly or indirectly for control (eg as part of gauging the performance of sub-unit managers) quickly introduces 'incentive distortion'. Managers and staff have an incentive (indeed, they may come under pressure) to improve performance-as-measured at the expense of intended overall performance.

Hence the importance of a comprehensiveness measurement set. In fact, however, full measurement or even anything approaching it is rarely practicable (even if possible from a social research point of view). Partial measurement is the norm.

[...]

The problem of incomplete measurement has long been recognised but is usually judged – e.g. through appeals to 'managerial' judgement in respect of the important unmeasured dimensions.

[. . .]

Hence, even if some dimensions of performance are measurable, judgements of overall performance may still be and appear arbitrary. Again, there are clear parallels with what has been reported in nonprofit contexts. In particular, Tassie, Murray *et al.*'s important study of the evaluation of a nonprofit highlighted the way that decision-makers, even when using an extensive set of formal criteria (and considerable information pertaining to them), still made use of additional informal considerations:

> As a result, the [Voluntary Social Service Organization] developed a somewhat cynical view of the [Federal Funding Organization's] funding decision process. As one said, 'It's all politics.' In this context, the term 'politics' meant for them a process that was not clear, was subject to influences that the VSSO could not counter, and led to an evaluation process that was different from the formally pronounced one.
> (Tassie, Murray *et al.* 1996, p 359)

Performance measurement for learning?

Another solution to the difficulties facing measurement advocates in situations where only partial measurement is possible is to play down the control aspects and emphasise the informational uses of performance measurement – that is, its value for problem identification, process improvement, logistical coordination, mutual understanding and learning. There are two problems with this approach. The first is that it may not be believed – and for good reason. The temptation for managers to use such information, either explicitly or implicitly, in forming judgements of performance is too strong, and sooner or later they (or their successors) will breech earlier undertakings. Hence those subject to such a regime will be wary.

[. . .]

The second problem in emphasising the informational uses of measurement is that of attribution. If learning and improvement are to take place, performance has to be measured in ways that allow changes or differences in performance to be related to a particular contribution or to differential conditions. But often performance is co-produced through the joint action and interaction of several parties – some of whom may well be external to the organisation. So even if it can be established that an improvement in performance has occurred, the reasons for this are likely to be contested (though a shortage of claimants for the credit is unlikely). Likewise, if the situation is changing rapidly, learning by controlled repetition becomes very difficult. Both problems arise in the private sector – but they are also familiar in public and nonprofit contexts. Hence, although learning and improvement may be given as reasons for performance measurement, the contribution it makes for these purposes may be very limited compared to discussing the processes in detail with those directly involved.

The social construction of performance

Differentiated constructs, integrated systems

Much writing on performance measurement assumes the feasibility and desirability of close integration between different reporting levels. That is, the performance measures set by the top level should also provide the basis for performance analysis at lower levels, and the information used at lower levels can be combined to inform higher level measures. When it is then observed that the information used to measure the performance of sub-units and the information actually used to manage performance within them are rather different, and moreover, that the organisations' performance measures do not help managers improve the performance of their sub-units, this is seen as a weakness of the system.

In fact, what performance *means* is different at different levels and in different domains, and its measurement and management changes accordingly. Hence, it is generally appropriate for levels to be loosely coupled, rather than closely integrated. In the case of companies, external reporting to shareholders (financial accounting) has provided such a poor basis for internal performance measurement and management that a whole profession grew up around management accounting, in order to remedy the problem. More recently, popular guidance for corporate managers on performance measurement takes it for granted that measures of performance at different levels and in different spheres will be expressed in quite different terms. [. .] The relationship between levels in terms of performance information then becomes an important and difficult issue. Establishing connections between the information given by centrally designed systems and the local operating context as understood much more intuitively by local managers requires much talking through – it does not happen simply by driving abstracted measures down through the organisation (Ahrens and Chapman 1998).

In nonprofit contexts, the three main levels were usefully described by Kanter and Summers (1987) as the *institutional* (concerned with legitimacy in the eyes of major external stakeholders), the *managerial* (concerned with resource use) and the *technical or professional* (concerned with service quality and outcomes). Characteristically, institutional performance measures create a framework for governance – what needs to be achieved in order to maintain legitimacy and a licence to operate. These are given by regulatory bodies, major funders and contractors. Within this framework, an organisation's leaders create their own more elaborate system of performance measurement – to feed institutional reporting requirements, but also to inform their own decision making and to set a performance framework for professional ('street level') activities. In their turn, the team leaders or first line managers may have their own performance-related information, partly explicit in records and partly tacit (in memory). Some of this practice knowledge may be context specific but it is also likely to be more detailed and elaborate, combining much current and background information in complex mental models about how to pursue a range of goals and maintain a web of relationships. This formal and informal information is, likewise, drawn on to provide or embellish accounts of their sub-unit's performance, to inform their own performance improvement efforts and as a basis for dialogue with staff.

The point is that although these conceptions of performance are related, they cannot just be aggregated and dis-aggregated. They are rooted in different concerns and experiences; they involve very different constructs, values and levels of abstraction; they reflect the discourses of different policy, managerial and professional communities and evolve accordingly; their alignment is always problematic (Sanderson 1998).

Competing frameworks

The literature contains three responses to the existence of competing conceptions of performance. The first is to promote some version of one's own conception as fundamental and an adequate foundation for other users as well. This is what is happening when institutional performance frameworks are imposed on nonprofits, as with the promotion of outcome funding, or the definition of nonprofit effectiveness in terms of their programme effectiveness. The mirror image – which might be termed 'educate our masters' – is implicit in the views of many leaders in the nonprofit sector.

[. . .]

A second approach is to try to incorporate all the competing goals and rationales of nonprofits into one master framework. This is the approach of Kendall and Knapp (2000) whose framework has eight measurement domains and 22 separate indicator sets. As the authors acknowledge, the cost and feasibility of creating worthwhile indicators in relation to some of the 22 concepts are considerable. How this approach might be used outside of lavishly resourced research contexts remains unclear.

The third approach is to abandon the 'realist' position and accept that performance is and will remain an evolving and contested concept, with particular measurement sets being the expression either of the thinking of a dominant group, or of a negotiated compromise among a wider group, at some point in time. Such a position (described as the emergent approach) has been summarised in the following terms in relation to nonprofit effectiveness:

> Accordingly, in the emergent approach to organizational effectiveness, assessments of effectiveness are not regarded as objective facts but neither are they regarded as arbitrary or irrelevant. Rather, the emergent approach holds that definitions and assessments of effectiveness have meaning but that the meaning is (a) created by the individual or organizational actors involved (b) specific to the context in which it was created (c) capable of evolving as the actors continue to interact.
>
> (Forbes 1998, p 195)

From this point of view, measures are not the means of estimating some underlying reality; rather, they construct and imbue with authority the notions of performance associated with particular points of view. The performance constructed by particular measures is bound to be partial, contextual and contingent, constituted partly by the social processes of its selection and gathering, but also by the lenses of those who interpret it. On this basis, plurality, contingency and contestation are signs of organisational life; not failure. Stable, coherent, consensual systems of measurement are probably an indication of domination by some one or some group (Greene 1999).

Implementation issues

Performance measurement systems do not spring into existence fully elaborated and the idea that they may involve an on-going process of social negotiation is helpful in understanding the issues that arise. Designing and operating them requires managerial time, expertise and effort, which is always in limited supply. In particular, those introducing performance management face a dilemma over their approach to those who will be subject to the arrangements. Do they spell out detailed definitions and reporting procedures, and perhaps even police them through audit – and risk generating resistance, introducing dysfunctional rigidities (because they lack information about operating circumstances), and generating additional costs for both parties? Or do they set out general principles and invite cooperation in a shared endeavour – thereby risking the dilution and diversion of the original aims? Up to a point, directive and accommodating elements can be tactically intertwined according to the relative power of the parties, but in general, limited resources are best used in ways that engage cooperation rather than provoke resistance.

[. . .]

Even in cases where measurement regimes are largely imposed, some scope for interpretation is likely to remain. If the detailed and highly institutionalised rules of accounting standards still leave scope for creative accounting, it is hardly surprising that operational definitions of performance indicators do so as well. Hence, how a performance measurement system operates in practice will depend not just on the intentions of those who commission it, but on the resources, commitment and approach of those that design and operate it. Its enactment will also depend on the responses chosen by the organisations or sub-units who are subject to it. They may have to adjust their operating policies (in ways that may or may not be dysfunctional) in order to achieve satisfactory performance as measured. But this may not be necessary. The other options are to try to influence the design of the scheme; to engage in creative accounting; and to concentrate on promoting favourable interpretations of what will usually be ambiguous results, eg by building relationships with the performance managers, and presenting strong and favourable narratives ('spin') around the performance data. And obviously, in each case these can only be countered by additional managerial effort on the part of the performance manager.

Hence, even if the intention is integrated control, one can confidently predict that this will be diluted in its enactment. Significant weaknesses in implementation are virtually inevitable – and they will often be benign, in the sense of making dysfunction less likely or pronounced. These considerations have three implications.

First, because such difficulties are actually well understood by performance managers – if not publicly acknowledged – they moderate their ambitions for performance measurement, adopting instead what can be called a strategy of *selective control*. The performance measures become in effect a screening device through which (apparent) low performance can be identified. Such cases are then investigated with the measures being used alongside other, non-quantitative information, to make more considered judgements about performance, to understand it, and to seek improvements.

Second, faced with 'the same' measurement regime, different sub-units or agencies can and do respond in a wide variety of ways. Depending on local circumstances and leadership, a range of accommodations and adaptations are possible – from dutiful compliance to creative improvisation (Jackson 1998). Again, since the enactment of measurement-based performance management is non-deterministic, dysfunction is far from inevitable.

Third, given the difficulties of carrying through measurement-based performance management, those tasked to do so may (not unreasonably) choose the option of *collusive implementation*. A sympathetic approach to design and operation of the measures, limited if any scrutiny, accepting optimistic interpretations of the results, highlighting 'progress' and overlooking failings – all these make supervision easier, and also allow success to be reported to those who originally commissioned the scheme, rather than difficulties.

The symbolic dimension

This last point introduces the possibility that in some circumstances – especially those where measurement is difficult and cause–effect relations obscure – the contribution of performance measurement may be more symbolic than instrumental, which does not mean it is unimportant. The existence of the system may satisfy institutional level requirements for evidence of purposeful and proper management, thereby sustaining legitimacy and ensuring continued access to resources (Meyer and Scott 1983).

[. . .]

Moreover, within the organisation, the development and introduction of performance measurement may be useful, by expressing and reinforcing the organisation's commitments, by stimulating dialogue and greater clarity over what the organisation is really trying to do – as is often claimed. This could be true even if the measures were of limited value in informational terms.

[. . .]

The dynamics of measurement

One implication of the constructivist perspective is that, despite stability being one of the desirable features of measurement systems, one would not expect measurement systems to be stable. Rather, they would be expected to change and evolve over time – which is, in fact, what is increasingly reported. Some patterns have already been referred to, including 'gradual acceptance' (resistance giving way to creative accommodation), 'oscillation' (between completeness and parsimony), and 'over-use' (initial benefits leading senior managers to expect too much). Another trend is a steady, underlying increase in the number of performance measures in use by organisations – hardly surprising, given falling relative costs of information handling. But more importantly, there is the phenomenon of 'measurement churn', that is, the continuous replacement of old measures with new, and the redesign of measurement systems.

[. . .]

Whatever the reasons, in the private sector, at least, reported dissatisfaction with performance measurement systems is increasing, and the life expectancy of measurement systems is falling (Meyer 1998; Frigo 2000).

Performance measurement in social enterprises

What is different about social enterprises?

The preceding discussion suggests that where conceptions of performance are largely shared, where measurability is high, cause-effect relations well understood, attribution possible, and the scale of operations large enough to spread the costs of designing and operating measurement systems, the situation can be considered favourable for measurement. Likewise, where performance is a contested concept, the measurability of important dimensions impractical, cause-effect relations poorly understood, attribution problematic, and the scale of operations modest, then the situation is unfavourable for measurement. Such situations are certainly not uncommon in private and public organisations. However, it is likely they arise even more often in social enterprises, where, as we have seen, performance is often a contested concept, measurability of important dimensions is in question, cause-effect relations obscure, co-production through partnerships and collaboration common, and organisations usually small or medium-sized. Indeed, it can be argued on theoretical grounds that the very reasons why activities are undertaken in the nonprofit sector are also the reasons why performance measurement will be deeply problematic.

Against all this, it may also be the case that social enterprises also provide a more favourable context for measurement in one respect: to the extent that they are smaller organisations with strong shared missions, they may be less prone to certain measurement dysfunction (eg sub-optimisation, myopia) than others. [. . .] Nevertheless, overall, high expectations from performance measurement in such contexts – for example, that it can be a substitute for more discursive modes of management – look decidedly unrealistic.

Assessing performance measurement systems

One theme of this discussion has been the need for modest expectations regarding the contribution of performance measurement – more or less wherever it is undertaken. The technocratic fantasies of control that haunt discussions of performance management imply success criteria against which any actual system will be seen to fail. But what is the alternative – how, for example, might one distinguish a crude and imperfect but 'good enough' system of measurement from one that was more trouble than it was worth? And would the difference between such systems lie in its technical features or in the manner of its use? How do we know if performance measurement 'works'?

The obvious answer – through a systematic study of the costs and benefits – is problematic: how are the benefits to be measured? If the increases in performance-as-measured are taken as benefits, then one has already assumed much of what is at issue. But if other independent measures of performance are used, then on what basis are they assumed to be better indicators, rather than merely different (Meyer and Gupta 1994)? The costs of measurement, being diffuse, will also be challenging to measure. Moreover, without some kind of control or comparison, one cannot know the counter-factual. These problems may not be insuperable, but it is ironic that we still await the first rigorous quantitative evaluation of performance measurement.

One success criterion is simply that the system continues to have the confidence of senior managers – it is seen by them as worthwhile. Another test would be that, to an independent observer, the system appears to deliver a number of benefits whose value outweighs the negative effects of any dysfunctional behaviour also triggered or accentuated by the system; and that the administrative burden of measurement is not excessive in relation to the benefits. Clearly, any such judgement would need to be based on the views of a range of participants from the different levels or domains involved and not just 'product champions'. It would need to take into account both specific instances of benefit (eg the use of information in forming a decision) and possible diffuse benefits concerning the communication of priorities, the negotiation of commitments and values, or the increased confidence of external stakeholders. It would have to explore, as far as was practicable, whether the different sorts of dysfunction commonly associated with measurement were significantly present. Clearly, the outcome of such an appraisal might well be equivocal.

Some initial research questions

The preceding discussion suggests some of the concepts and issues that will be relevant in understanding what is happening in social enterprises as they give more attention to measurement in situations highly unfavourable to measurement.

First, we need to understand how managers view these issues and the different approaches to the challenge that are being adopted. Do they 'believe' in measurement? Is more measurement seen as a threat or an opportunity? What strategies are they pursuing?

Secondly, how are measurement changes being implemented? For example, are there efforts to use the new systems as a basis for greater control either of, or within, the organisation – or is implementation much more gentle and exploratory (eg selective control, collusion)? And how are managers dealing with the issues of 'domain alignment' – are institutional reporting requirements driving the development of the information systems of nonprofits at the expense of managerial and operational needs – or are these being loosely and creatively linked?

Thirdly, what sorts of benefits, both direct and indirect, are being claimed, and are the usual dysfunctions becoming apparent (and at what levels)? What about costs (and timescales)?

Fourth, are any longer-term patterns becoming apparent? These include aspects of measurement behaviour such as loss of variation, and measurement churn, but also possible impacts on the organisational culture: are the managers of social enterprises now displaying a greater commitment to measurement? How do they combine this with their awareness and experience of behavioural responses to measurement?

[. . .]

Bibliography

Ahrens, T. and C. Chapman (1998). *Sustaining Antagonistic Harmony – food margin control in a UK restaurant chain*. Performance measurement – theory and practice; the first international conference on performance measurement, Cambridge, England, Centre for Business Performance, Cambridge University.

Austin, R. D. (1996). *Measuring and Managing Performance in Organisations*. NY, Dorset House.

Blau, P. M. (1963). *The Dynamics of Bureaucracy*. Chicago, University of Chicago Press.

Bovaird, T. (1999). Achieving Best Value through competition, benchmarking and performance networks. Warwick and London, University of Warwick and the Department of Environment Transport and the Regions.

Bruns, W. (1998). *Keynote address: Profit as a performance measure*. Performance Measurement – theory and practice; the first international conference on performance measurement, Cambridge, England.

Carter, N., R. Klein, *et al.* (1992). *How Organisations Measure Success*. London, Routledge.

Forbes, D. P. (1998). "Measuring the Unmeasurable." *Nonprofit and Voluntary Sector Quarterly* 27(2).

Frigo, M. (2000). *Current trends in performance measurement systems*. Performance Measurement 2000 – *Past, Present and Future*, University of Cambridge, Centre for Business Performance, Cambridge University.

Greene, J. C. (1999). "The Inequality of Performance Measurements." *Evaluation* 5(2): 160–172.

Herman, R. D. and D. O. Renz (1997). "Multiple Constituencies and the Social Construction of Nonprofit Effectiveness." *Nonprofit and Voluntary Sector Quarterly* 26(2): 185–207.

Herman, R. D. and D. O. Renz (1999). "Theses on Nonprofit Effectiveness." *Nonprofit and Voluntary Sector Quarterly* 28(2).

Jackson, A. (1998). *The ambiguity of performance indicators*. First International Conference on Performance Measurement, Cambridge, Centre for Business Performance, Cambridge University.

Kanter, R. M. and D. V. Summers (1987). Doing Well by Doing Good: dilemmas of performance measurement in nonprofit organizations, and the need for a multiple constituency approach. *The Nonprofit Sector: A Research Handbook*. W. W. Powell. New Haven, Yale University Press.

Kendall, J. and M. Knapp (1995). A Loose and Baggy Monster: Boundaries, definitions and typologies. *Introduction to the Voluntary Sector*. London, Routledge.

Kendall, J. and M. Knapp (2000). "Measuring the Performance of Voluntary Organizations." *Public Management* 2(1): 105–132.

Meyer, J. W. and W. R. Scott (1983). *Organizational Environments: Ritual and Rationalilty*. Beverly Hills, CA, Sage Publications.

Meyer, M. (1998). *Keynote address. Finding performance – the new discipline in management.* Performance Measurement – theory and practice; the first international conference on performance measurement, Cambridge, England, Centre for Business Performance, Cambridge University.

Meyer, W. and V. Gupta (1994). "The Performance Paradox." *Research in Organisational Behaviour* 16: 309–369.

Sanderson, I. (1998). "Beyond Performance Measurement? Assessing 'Value' in Local Government." *Local Government Studies* 24(4): pp 1–25.

Tassie, B., V. Murray, *et al.* (1996). "Rationality and Politics: what really goes on when funders evaluate the performance of fundees?" *Nonprofit and Voluntary Sector Quarterly* 25(3): 347–363.

PART FOUR

Leadership in policy work

INTRODUCTION

AS EXPLORED IN THE preceding parts, the complexity of policy work is generated both by the unprecedented difficulty of public issues and by the divergent troop of players expecting a voice in the drama. Not surprisingly, this complexity gives rise, often, either to *stasis* – policy work that fails to progress – or to mere policy *displays* – announcements and initiatives that lack substance, support and staying-power, and that leave street-level services unaffected.

So we come to the 'L' word. After decades in which management was the answer, management is now widely seen as insufficient. Yes, as a bundle of purposeful, rationalising, systematic approaches and practices, it provides a valuable, indeed necessary, toolkit. But management brings its own risks, distortions and pitfalls; it, too, can become another absorbing set of processes, another way of re-producing bureaucratic dysfunction. The 'leadership turn' has been a way of directing attention both to the subtler personal dimensions of organizing (concerning, e.g., personal initiative, influencing skills, risk-taking, creativity, personal values and commitments) and to the centrality of being able to bring about substantive change or innovation, in complex settings and when subject to many conflicting expectations.

This has stimulated a huge amount of writing and research, exploring the nature of leadership in new, post-bureaucratic, organizational and inter-organizational settings. One useful recurring theme in this work has been a shift of focus from 'leaders' to 'leadership', with the latter often distributed, or revealed in *horizontal influencing* as much as vertical uses of the resources of one's position. Another important line of work has been contributed by adult developmental psychologists, notably Robert Kegan (1994), who has provided a compelling and highly readable account of what work in post-bureaucratic organizations can mean for us psychologically. This developmental perspective is now beginning to bear fruit in terms of new and deeper conceptions of leadership, and more discriminating approaches to leadership development (see, for example, Torbert and associates, 2004; Rooke and Torbert, 2005).

However, as far as leadership in relation to public policy issues is concerned, the work of Ronald Heifetz stands head and shoulders above other writings. His book *Leadership Without Easy Answers* (from which Reading 20 is extracted) develops an original theory of leadership that is remarkable for three reasons. First, it provides a boldly normative perspective, within which leadership is not just about being influential or attracting supporters: it is about tackling, and stimulating others to tackle, the adaptive challenges that really matter for a community, organization or society. Success, however acclaimed, in tackling side issues does *not* amount to leadership. This is a demanding precept but it is developed with wisdom and humanity. It follows that this is a theory of leadership that has been developed from and for the public domain – at all levels and in its various manifestations. It 'fits' for politicians as for public managers, and also captures particularly well the leadership contributions that have often been provided from civil society and third sector organizations. Finally, it embraces the non-rational dimensions of our behaviour in groups, especially in relation to authority and when conflict arises.

Heifetz's theory has two foundations: one is the idea of adaptive challenges, and how they differ from more familiar problems. The second is the distinction between leadership with authority and leadership without authority – a distinction which, at a stroke, cuts through libraries of confusions. While the extracts chosen explain these central ideas, a short chapter cannot do justice to the richness of the book, which also contains detailed illustrations of the concepts in relation to the success and failures of various holders of public office and community representatives. These are eminently workable ideas, and ones that still manage to avoid the idealization and grandiosity that haunts so much of the leadership literature.

Like leadership, strategy is a term much used and abused. It, too, carries a whiff of grandiosity and derring-do. And as with leadership theories, the prevailing ideas of strategic management emerged in the corporate world, in response to a primarily competitive *problematique*, and were then urged upon public managers. In Reading 21, Mark Moore provides an elegant review of the development of strategic thinking in the private sector before going on to offer his own formulation of the central strategic issue for those in senior positions in public organizations.

On both counts, the analysis is invaluable. He shows how one can usefully adopt and adapt ideas from private sector management, but that on their own these will not be enough. In doing so he avoids *both* a facile genericism ('organizations are organizations, and management is management...') and sectoral preciousness, the simplistic and over-stated claims of difference. Moore's simple device of a strategic triangle highlights the central task of senior managers in public agencies: defining a purpose and approach (in terms of the substantive public value to be created) that is sustainable in the institutional arena *and* that is operationally feasible at street-level. Riding either one of these 'horses' may not be easy, but it is relatively straightforward; for those who move on quickly, it may even lead to career success. But what the public sector needs is people capable of riding both horses simultaneously (and as the Scot Jimmy Maxton famously remarked, 'if you can't ride two horses you don't deserve to be in the bloody circus').

What is involved in bringing about operational change in service organizations is graphically described by John Seddon in Reading 22. Seddon is a consultant and iconoclast who has been building a formidable reputation for his application of the principles of lean manufacturing to service operations. His approach falls in a long tradition of applied social science – it is redolent of the re-design of work around the primary task that the Tavistock Institute pioneered in the 60s, for example. As such, his perspective and experience is important for several reasons. For one thing the scale of the savings and productivity improvements realized undermine attempts to deny the scope for improved results in public services. He also shows how important it is for those who want to change things to engage with the *underlife* of organizations, how things really work. In doing so he highlights the dysfunctions of so much managerial practice and procedure once it takes on a life of its own, disconnected from the overall purpose. Never underestimate human creativity when it comes to inventing new forms of well-intentioned goal displacement. And as Seddon emphasizes, it makes no sense then to blame the workforce for difficulties and misconduct, when such behaviour is simply adaptive in its context. Responsibility lies with those who are responsible for the system as a whole.

At this point we had hoped to include a further reading or two on other approaches to renewal and innovation in public services – something on entrepreneurship and *intra*preneurship, perhaps, or on the experience of reconstructing services through partnerships or collaboration with service users. Perhaps we were looking in the wrong places. But the reporting and analysis to date still tends to be embedded in particular contexts (thus for example the writing on social enterprise, though it contains important experience, tends to reflect parallel conversations in the US, UK and continental Europe). This, along with its frequently gushing tone, makes it hard to identify the broadly applicable concepts (in an era of performance rhetoric even modest improvements are presented as mould-breaking innovations). It would seem that theory with the clarity, analytic purchase and generality of the other readings in this section remains to be developed.

The last reading draws again on Mark Moore's seminal 'Creating Public Value'. His discussion of the ethical and role dilemmas of public managers deftly cuts down a string of excuses for playing safe (with the attendant paralysis) – while also firmly eschewing ego-centric, macho and manipulative versions of 'strong leadership'. In effect, he shows what integrity means in the draining environment of high-level public management.

One common theme runs through all these chapters: Heifetz, Moore and Seddon all highlight the importance of how we *think* about the challenges we face. Change begins with how we *read* situations. Thinking in more systemic terms – seeing the bigger picture, understanding the dynamics of the whole not just the parts, building up an integral view that avoids false dichotomies – is both a recurring motif in these readings and a key capability for leadership in policy work.

REFERENCES

Kegan, R. (1994) *In Over Our Heads: the mental demands of modern life*, Cambridge, Mass.: Harvard University Press.

Rooke, D. and W. Torbert (April 2005) Seven Transformations of Leadership, *Harvard Business Review*, Cambridge, Mass.: Harvard Business School Press.

Torbert, W and associates (2004) *Action Inquiry: The secret of timely and transforming leadership*, San Francisco: Berrett-Koehler.

Ronald A. Heifetz

MOBILIZING FOR ADAPTIVE WORK

From: Heifetz, R. A. (1944) 'Leadership as adaptive work', *Leadership Without Easy Answers*, pps from which extract taken 22–24, 31–32, 36–39, 71–74, 87–88, 125–128, 184–188, 207–208, Belknap Press

THIS STUDY EXAMINES THE usefulness of viewing leadership in terms of adaptive work. Adaptive work consists of the learning required to address conflicts in the values people hold, or to diminish the gap between the values people stand for and the reality they face. Adaptive work requires a change in values, beliefs, or behaviour. In this view, getting people to clarify what matters most, in what balance, with what trade-offs, becomes a central task. In the case of a local industry that pollutes the river, people want clean water, but they also want jobs. Community and company interests frequently overlap and clash, with conflicts taking place not only among factions but also within the lives of individual citizens who themselves may have competing needs. Leadership requires orchestrating these conflicts among and within the interested parties, and not just between members and formal shareholders of the organization. Who should play a part in the deliberations is not given, but is itself a critical strategic question. Strategy begins with asking: Which stakeholders have to adjust their ways to make progress on this problem? How can one sequence the issues or strengthen the bonds that join the community of interests so that they withstand the stresses of problem-solving?

To clarify a complex situation such as this requires multiple vantage points, each of which adds a piece to the puzzle. Values are shaped and refined by rubbing against real problems, and people interpret their problems according to the values they hold. Different values shed light on different opportunities and facets of a situation. The implication is important: *the inclusion of competing value perspectives may be essential to adaptive success*. In the long run, an industrial polluter will fail if it neglects the interests of its community. Given the spread of environmental values, it may not always be able to move across borders. Conversely, the community may lose its economic base if it neglects the interests of its industry.

Viewing leadership in terms of adaptive work points to the pivotal importance of reality testing in producing socially useful outcomes – the process of weighing one interpretation of a problem and its sources of evidence against others. Conceptions of leadership that do not value reality testing encourage people to realize their vision, however faulty their sight. Assessing circumstances is made complex because we cannot always define problems objectively. The methods of science make major contribution to reality testing, yet they cannot reliably define our problems both because the scientific method has limited capacity to make predictions and because our problems can only be diagnosed in light of our values. With different values, we screen reality for different information and put the facts together into a different picture. If a society values individual freedom, it will tend to highlight those aspects of reality that challenge freedom. And as a corollary, it will also be inclined to neglect those elements of reality upon which another society with another central value, like shared responsibility, will focus. The aspect of truth each sees depends significantly on who cares about what.

Typically, a social system will honor some mix of values, and the competition within this mix largely explains why adaptive work so often involves conflict. People with competing values engage one another as they confront a shared situation from their own points of view.

Failures to adapt

Our organizations and societies face many kinds of adaptive work that we cannot afford to avoid. The renewal of ethnic strife in the destabilized post-cold war international system requires the invention of new methods for dealing with festering problems of racial enmity. The simultaneous increases in crime, prison population, and prevalence of drugs in the streets require serious differentiation of fact from fiction and close reasoning about causes and effects. Why is this so?

People fail to adapt for several reasons. In some cases they may misperceive the nature of the threat. Based on their experience and science, the people of Pompeii made a reasonable but tragic estimate of the risk that Vesuvius might erupt. In our age, we are fortunate to have discovered already our dependence on the ozone layer.

In some other cases the society may perceive the threat, but the challenge may exceed the culture's adaptive capability. Innumerable human tribes and organizations have disappeared with the onslaught of disease, environmental challenge, invasion, or competition because they could not develop the ability or find the means to adjust appropriately.

Finally, people fail to adapt because of the distress provoked by the problem and the changes it demands. They resist the pain, anxiety, or conflict that accompanies a sustained interaction with the situation. Holding onto past assumptions, blaming authority, scapegoating, externalizing the enemy, denying the problem, jumping to conclusions, or finding a distracting issue may restore stability and feel less stressful than facing and taking responsibility for a complex challenge. These patterns of response to disequilibrium are called *work avoidance mechanisms* in this study, and they are similar to the defensive routines that operate in individuals, small groups, and organizations.

Diagnostically, an organization or community may experience any one of these difficulties in adapting. But when one takes action, the final cause of adaptive failure – the tendency to avoid distress – holds the key to setting strategy. It frequently provides the ultimate impediment to adaptive change because the learning associated with identifying blind spots and options that others cannot see, or strengthening a community's problem-solving capacity, will generate conflict and distress. Thus, a key question for leadership becomes: How can one counteract the expected work avoidances and help people learn despite resistance?

Though differing in form depending on the culture and complexity of the social system, work avoidance mechanisms seem to operate in any social context. In a small group, less powerful members will sit back and "watch the gladiators fight" as the chairperson and a colleague who represents a challenging perspective engage in an angry exchange that diverts attention from the issues on the table and diminishes a sense of shared responsibility. In an organization, people will follow standard operating procedures even when they know the procedures do not fit the situation. In a community or nation, voters will choose "good news" candidates even when they suspect that progress on pressing problems will require hard adjustments on their part.

Yet though we frequently avoid adaptive work, we seldom do so deliberately. Work avoidance mechanisms are often unconscious, or at least disguised from the self. Sometimes they reflect comforting misdiagnoses of the situation – a social system may scapegoat one of its factions because of a dominant perception that the faction is indeed responsible for the problem. A mob that burns a man in effigy may believe that its problem would be solved if it could burn the man himself. Yet even killing an accused heretic like Salman Rushdie would do little to integrate the traditional and modern strains within Islamic societies.

Reality testing – the effort to grasp the problem fully – is often an early victim of disequilibrium. Initially, people will apply routine practices for realistically assessing and addressing problems. But if these do not pay early dividends, restoring equilibrium may take precedence over the prolonged uncertainty associated with weighing divergent views and facing the need for changing attitudes and beliefs.

Distinguishing work from work avoidance is no science. Each culture will have its own typical patterns of response to stress – work-producing as well as work-avoiding. While more research should clarify the distinction between productive and avoidance behaviors in different social systems, some rules of thumb are useful. One might detect work avoidance when the subject of discussion is suddenly taken off the table (as with diversions); when the level of stress associated with an issue suddenly drops (often following an apparent technical fix); when the focus shifts from attending to the problem itself to alleviating the symptoms of stress; or when responsibility for the problem is displaced to an easy target (as with scapegoating). One ought to take a skeptical stance, at least momentarily, when some action suddenly makes everybody feel good.

Of course, what looks like momentary periods of work avoidance from one vantage point may be part of someone else's strategy. Leadership often requires pacing the work in an effort to prepare people to undertake a hard task at a rate they can stand.

Authority in social systems

Consider the hospital personnel that staff the emergency room. Without an explicit hierarchy of authority to provide a swift and coordinated response, chaos would ensue. Someone takes charge, usually a physician, and all eyes turn to her for cues and instructions. Information flows from all the members of the staff toward her. She provides a focus of attention that orients members of the team to their place and role; she provides direction; she stops any disruptive conflict that arises on the team.

The staff of an emergency room face a kind of problem similar to many everyday situations. These problems are *technical* in the sense that we know already how to respond to them. Often, they can only be accomplished with mastery and ingenuity. They are not easy, nor are they unimportant. These problems are technical because the necessary knowledge about them already has been digested and put in the form of a legitimized set of known organizational procedures guiding what to do and role authorizations guiding who should do it.

For these situations, we turn to authority with reasonable expectations. In our various social systems, our authority structures and the norms they maintain govern thousands of problem-solving processes. Meeting a host of vital and everyday problems, they are the product of previously accomplished adaptive work.

Over the course of history, we have successfully faced an array of adaptive challenges by developing new knowledge and organizations with new norms. Now that we have them, many of our problems have become routine. Our authority systems already "know" how to respond. And because we know how to respond, the stresses generated by these problems are temporary.

For many problems, however, no adequate response has yet been developed. Examples abound: poverty at home and abroad, industrial competitiveness, failing schools, drug abuse, the national debt, racial prejudice, ethnic strife, AIDS, environmental pollution. No organizational response can be called into play that will clearly resolve these kinds of problems. No clear expertise can be found, no single sage has general credibility, no established procedure will suffice. Stresses build up and produce a sense of urgency among certain groups within society and sometimes throughout society. In these situations, our inclination to look to authority may generate inappropriate dependencies.

These are the times for leadership. Problems that cause persistent distress do so because the system of accepted dependencies being applied to them cannot do the job. We look to our authorities for answers they cannot provide. What happens, then? Authorities, under pressure to be decisive, sometimes fake the remedy or take action that avoids the issue by skirting it. We instigate drug wars across our border instead of facing the ills of our cities. In the short term, of course, this may quell some of the distress at home. If the administration succeeds in shifting the public's attention to a substitute problem in a foreign nation, then the problem at home may cause less discontent. Attention is deflected from the issue, which *appears* to be taken care of. But in the long term, some problems get worse, and then frustration arises both with the problem situation and with those people in authority who were supposed to resolve it. In response to our frustration, we are likely to perpetuate the vicious cycle by looking *even more earnestly* to authority, but this time we look for someone new offering more certainty and better promises.

Habitually seeking solutions from people in authority is maladaptive. Indeed, it is perhaps the essence of maladaptive behavior: the use of a response appropriate to one situation in another where it does not apply. Authority relationships are critical to doing work in many routine situations and, applied properly, can be used invaluably in more challenging times; yet misapplied, they serve to avoid work.

The flight to authority is particularly dangerous for at least two reasons: first, because the work avoidance often occurs in response to our biggest problems and, second, because it disables some of our most important personal and collective resources for accomplishing adaptive work.

Distinguishing adaptive from technical work

The practice of medicine illustrates the distinction between technical and adaptive problems, and the dynamics these problems generate. Patients come to physicians with symptoms and signs of illness. They hope that their doctor will be able to "fix" the problem, but they do not know if their hopes are well-founded. Often, the physician can indeed cure the illness. If a person has an infection, there are many times when the physician can say, "I have an antibiotic medication that will almost definitely cure you. The medication is virtually harmless." For the purpose of our discussion, we can call these technical situations Type I – situations in which the patient's expectations are realistic: the doctor can provide a solution and the problem can be defined, treated, and cured on the basis of (1) using the doctor's expertise, and (2) shifting the patient's burden primarily onto the doctor's shoulders.

In Type II situations, the problem is definable but no clear-cut solution is available. The doctor may have a solution in mind, but she cannot implement it. And a solution that cannot be implemented is not really a solution; it is simply an idea, a proposal. Heart disease sometimes presents a Type II problem. The patient can be restored to more or less full operating capacity, but only if he takes responsibility for his health by making appropriate life adjustments. In particular, he will have to consider the doctor's prescriptions for long-term medication, exercise, diet program and stress reduction. He will have to choose among these.

In these situations, the doctor's technical expertise allows her to define the problem and suggest solutions that may work. But merely giving the patient a technical answer does not help the patient. Her prescribing must actively involve the patient if she is to be effective. The patient needs to confront the choices and changes that face him. The doctor's technical answers mean nothing if the patient does not implement them. Only he can reset the priorities of his life. He has to learn new ways. And the doctor has to manage the learning process in order to help the patient help himself. The dependency on authority appropriate to technical situations becomes inappropriate in adaptive ones. The doctor's authority still provides a resource to help the patient respond, but beyond her substantive knowledge, she needs a different kind of expertise – the ability to help the patient do the work that only he can do.

Type III situations are even more difficult. The problem definition is not clear-cut, and technical fixes are not available. Chronic illness and impending death from any cause often fit this category. In these situations, the doctor can continue to operate in a mechanical mode by diagnosing and prescribing remedies (and a "remedy" of some sort can usually be found). Yet doing so avoids the problem-defining and problem-solving work of both doctor and patient.

In Type II and III situations, *treating the illness* is too narrow a way for the patient and the physician to define the task. It applies a technical formulation to a nontechnical problem. When critical aspects of the situation are probably unchangeable, the problem becomes more than the medical condition. For example, if the patient's diagnosis is an advanced stage of cancer in which the likelihood of cure is remote, it may be useless – indeed, a denial of reality – to define the primary problem as cancer. Cancer, in this case, is a *condition*. To the limited extent it can be treated at all, it is only part of the problem. To define cancer as the primary problem leads everyone involved to concentrate on finding solutions to the cancer, thus diverting their attention from the real work at hand. The patient's real work consists of facing and making adjustments to harsh realities that go beyond his health condition and that include several possible problems: making the most out of his life; considering what his children may need after he is gone; preparing his wife, parents, loved ones, and friends; and completing valued professional tasks.

Table 20.1 summarizes the characteristics of the three types of situations.

Table 20.1 Situational types

Situation	Problem definition	Solution and implementation	Primary locus of responsibility for the work	Kind of work
Type I	Clear	Clear	Physician	Technical
Type II	Clear	Requires learning	Physician and patient	Technical and adaptive
Type III	Requires learning	Requires learning	Patient> physician	Adaptive

Unfortunately, neither doctors nor patients are inclined to differentiate between technical and adaptive work. Indeed, the harsher the reality, the harder we look to authority for a remedy that saves us from adjustment. By and large, we want answers, not questions. Even the toughest individual tends to avoid realities that require adaptive work, searching instead for an authority, a physician, to provide the way out. And doctors, wanting deeply to fulfill the yearning for remedy, too often respond willingly to the pressures we place on them to focus narrowly on technical answers.

An authority figure exercising leadership has to tell the difference between technical and adaptive situations because they require different responses. She must ask the key differentiating questions: *Does making progress on this problem require changes in people's values, attitudes, or habits of behavior?* If people recognize the problem and can repeat a well-worked solution, then she can engage an authoritative response with practical efficiency and effect. In situations that call for adaptive work, however, social systems must learn their way forward. Even when an authority has some clear ideas about what needs to be done, implementing change often requires adjustments in people's lives.

Hence, with adaptive problems, authority must look beyond authoritative solutions. Authoritative action may usefully provoke debate, rethinking, and other processes of social learning, but then it becomes a tool in a strategy to mobilize adaptive work *toward* a solution, rather than a direct means to institute one.

As suggested, this requires a shift in mindset. When using authoritative provocation as part of a strategy, one must be prepared for an eruption of distress in response to the provocation and to consider the next step early on. One has to take the heat in stride, seeing it as part of the process of engaging people in the issue. In contrast, the mindset which views authoritative action *as a solution* to an adaptive problem would logically view an aggravated community as an extraneous complication to making headway, rather than an inherent part of making progress. Operating with that mindset, an authority figure would likely respond defensively and inappropriately when the community retaliates.

Leading with authority

Having an authority relationship with people is both a resource for leadership and a constraint. Authority is a resource because it can provide the instruments and power to hold together and harness the distressing process of doing adaptive work. Authority is a constraint because it is contingent on meeting the expectations of constituents. Deviating from those expectations is perilous.

Authority is also a straitjacket. Constituents confer resources in exchange for services. Power is received in the promise of fulfilling expectations – people in authority, we insist, must provide direction, protection, and order. These expectations often make good sense. In technical situations, adequate preparations for the current problem have been made already. Procedures, lines of authority, role placements, and norms of operation have been established. People have a sufficiently clear idea about what needs to be done and how to go about doing it. Creativity and ingenuity may be needed, but only to devise variations on known themes, not new themes altogether.

Our expectations of authority figures become counterproductive when our organizations and communities face an adaptive challenge – when the application of known methods and procedures will not suffice. We continue to expect our authorities to restore equilibrium with dispatch. If they do not act quickly to reduce our feelings of urgency, we bring them down. Sometimes, we kill them.

That we sometimes call these situations "crises in leadership" is symptomatic of the problem of habitually blaming authority. Stymied by our expectation that authorities should provide in adaptive situations what they can and do provide routinely, we blame them for the persistence of frustrating problems that demand our own adaptive work. And so, predictably, our authorities supply us with fake remedies and diversions. We ask for it. If they want to maintain the authorization we give them, they have to deliver, or provide *promises* of deliverance. When we discover that our authorities have failed, too frequently we expiate our failures by scapegoating them and looking for someone with fresh promises.

Exercising leadership from a position of authority in adaptive situations means going against the grain. Rather than fulfilling the expectation for answers, one provides questions; rather than protecting people from outside threat, one lets people feel the threat in order to stimulate adaptation; instead of orienting people to their current roles, one disorients people so that new role relationships develop; rather than quelling conflict, one generates it; instead of maintaining norms, one challenges them.

Of course, real life is fluid. An authority figure, even in adaptive situations, will have to act differently to fulfill each of these social functions depending on several factors, as just mentioned: the severity of the problem, the resilience of the social system, the ripeness of the issue, and time. For example, in an organization one may have to act firmly to maintain norms and restore clear role assignments, while challenging people with questions and raising conflict about direction. But to make tactical decisions to move between technical and adaptive modes along each of these five dimensions, one first needs a clear conception of the differences. Table 20.2 outlines the shifts that adaptive situations require of authorities.

In adaptive situations, fulfilling the social functions of authority requires walking a razor's edge. Challenge people too fast, and they will push the authority figure over for failing their expectations for stability. But challenge people too slowly, and they will throw him down when they discover that no progress has been made. Ultimately, they will blame him for lack of progress. To stay balanced on the edge, one needs a strategic understanding of the specific tools and constraints that come with one's authority.

Yet in either case, an authority figure cuts his feet. When he is the focus of hopes and pains that are beyond his magic, or any magic, some people are bound to attack, at least in words. Even the most agile cannot dodge these attacks completely, nor shield himself, mentally and physically, from an assortment of wounds.

Table 20.2 Leadership with authority in adaptive situations

Social function	Situational type	
	Technical	Adaptive
Direction	Authority provides problem definition and solution	Authority identifies the adaptive challenge, provides diagnosis of condition, and produces questions about problem definitions and solutions
Protection	Authority protects from external threat	Authority discloses external threat
Role orientation	Authority orients	Authority disorients current roles, or resists pressure to orient people in new roles too quickly
Controlling conflict	Authority restores order	Authority exposes conflict, or lets it emerge
Norm maintenance	Authority maintains norms	Authority challenges norms, or allows them to bechallenged

We have begun to explore the resources that authority brings to directing this process. These tools can be organized according to five strategic principles of leadership:

1   *Identify the adaptive challenge.* Diagnose the situation in light of the values at stake, and unbundle the issues that come with it.
2   *Keep the level of distress within a tolerable range for doing adaptive work.* To use the pressure cooker analogy, keep the heat up without blowing up the vessel.
3   *Focus attention on ripening issues and not on stress-reducing distractions.* Identify which issues can currently engage attention; and while directing attention to them, counteract work avoidance mechanisms like denial, scapegoating, externalizing the enemy, pretending the problem is technical, or attacking individuals rather than issues.
4   *Give the work back to people, but at a rate they can stand.* Place and develop responsibility by putting the pressure on the people with the problem.
5   *Protect voices of leadership without authority.* Give cover to those who raise hard questions and generate distress – people who point to the internal contradictions of the society. These individuals often will have latitude to provoke rethinking that authorities do not have.

Leading without authority

We see leadership too rarely exercised from high office, and the constraints that come with authority go far to explain why. In public life, people generally look to their authorities to solve problems with a minimum of pain, and where pain must be endured, they often expect their officials to find somebody else to bear the costs. In the 1990s, we hear across the country, "Cut the deficit – but don't raise my taxes, raise his." "Cut military spending, but don't close my factory or my army base". Many of us want change, "but not in my back yard," a syndrome so common that it has a name: NIMBY. Our politicians find it very hard to raise tough questions at election time because their constituents insist on protection. When we do elect activists, we want them to change the thinking and behavior of other people, rarely our own. We can hardly blame our public officials for giving us what we ask for.

The scarcity of leadership from people in authority, however, makes it all the more critical to the adaptive successes of a polity that leadership be exercised by people without authority. These people – perceived as entrepreneurs and deviants, organizers, and troublemakers – provide the capacity within the system to see through the blind spots of the dominant viewpoint. Often they remain relatively unknown.

Analysts have generally neglected the distinctive problems and opportunities of mobilizing work from positions of little or no authority. Thus, nearly all studies of leadership, in addition to many histories, focus primarily on figures of authority. Just as social systems organize themselves in relation to a structure of authority, focusing attention at the head of the table, our social commentators do so as well. Leadership may more often emerge from the foot of the table, but that is not where we spend most of our time looking. We study the lives and characteristics of heads of state and CEOs of corporations, assuming all the while that we are studying leaders and not simply authority figures who serve the social functions of direction, protection, and order, sometimes in adaptive situations that demand their leadership, and sometimes in routine situations that do not.

That I use the metaphor of the table, with the head traditionally a man and the foot characteristically a woman, is no accident. Leadership without authority has been the domain to which women have been restricted for ages. Even today, Congress remains over 90 percent men, and we are only beginning to imagine seriously the election of a woman President in our time. Having been denied formal authority roles in most societies, some women have learned strategies for leading without authority, and some have learned not to try leading at all. The same can be said of many disempowered groups.

Women who have managed to carve out roles of authority were likely to be ignored by traditional historical and social science scholarship, which focused on the activities of men. In the United States, for example, women have headed social reform movements dating back more than 150 years, but only recently, with the emergence of women's history as an established academic field, have their accomplishments been chronicled.

The question, however, remains, "Can someone exercise leadership from the foot of the table, or even from outside the family – without any authority, formal or informal?" I think the answer is yes, and in several ways. Some people, like Gandhi, lead societies without holding formal office of any kind. More frequently, people have a base of formal authority within their own subgroup, like Lech Walesa as head of Solidarity in Communist Poland, Martin Luther King Jr. as founder of the Southern Christian Leadership Conference, or Margaret Sanger as head of what became Planned Parenthood. In addition, they have a wide network of informal authority in the community at large, as did Gandhi. But these people lead not only within the boundaries of the communities that authorize them, formally and informally, but also across those boundaries, reaching to communities where their words and actions have influence despite having no authorization. In segments of the larger community that these leaders influence, they lack both kinds of authority. In a sense, they lead across two boundaries: the boundary of their formal organization, if they have one, and the boundary defined by the wider network of people with whom they have gained informal authority (trust, respect, moral persuasion).

In fact, many people daily go beyond both their job description and the informal expectations they carry within their organization and do what they are not authorized to do. At a minimum, these people exercise leadership momentarily by impressing upon a group, sometimes by powerfully articulating an idea that strikes a resonant chord, the need to pay attention to a missing point of view. A staff assistant will speak up at a meeting even though she has no authority to do so. Or someone will run an unauthorized experiment and later announce the results. Or in the early hours of a disaster, some people will step forward and mobilize others to face and respond to the crisis.

Furthermore, many people have engaged in various forms of civil disobedience to mobilize adaptive work among communities that were indifferent or hostile. Those they led across formal and informal boundaries gave them no authority whatsoever, certainly not in the early stages of their efforts.

Thus, when we speak of leadership without authority, we are referring to a very large set of stances, from the person operating from the margins of society even to the senior authority figure who leads beyond his pale of authority, challenging either his own constituents' expectations or engaging people across the boundary of his organization who would ordinarily or preferably pay him no mind.

Over time, a person who begins without authority or who leads beyond whatever authority she has may have to construct, strengthen, and sometimes broaden her base of informal authority in order to get more leverage. She may find that an initial, rebellious leadership action puts her in an informal authority position that requires trust, respect, and moral force in order to sustain progress. Such were the beginnings of King, Gandhi, and Sanger. An emerging leader may need a base from which to speak to hard issues without being ignored or cast out altogether. Furthermore, to involve the relevant factions in the community, she may need people across boundaries to believe that she represents something significant, that she embodies a perspective that merits attention. When that happens, she has to respect both the resources and constraints that come with authority, formally from her own group, and informally from beyond. Just as leading with authority requires protecting voices of dissent, a leader without authority will have to "take counsel" from her adversaries, incorporating in her strategy whatever wisdom of theirs connects to her central thesis.

As she seeks informal authority from those across organizational or factional boundaries, she has to place her cause in the context of the values of her opposition. In addition, she may have to learn from her antagonists in order to correct for the possible narrowness of her own views. She is not just teaching; she is being taught.

The benefits of leading without authority

Leadership, as used here, means engaging people to make progress on the adaptive problems they face. Because making progress on adaptive problems requires learning, the task of leadership consists of choreographing and directing learning processes in an organization or community. Progress often demands new ideas and innovation. As well, it often demands changes in people's attitudes and behaviors. Adaptive work consists of the process of discovering and making those changes. Leadership, with or without authority, requires an educative strategy.

Senior authority generally includes the power to manage the holding environment, direct attention, gather and influence the flow of information, frame the terms of debate, distribute responsibility, regulate conflict and distress, and structure decision processes. Yet the constraints of authority suggest that there may also be advantages to leading without it. First, the absence of authority enables one to deviate from the norms of authoritative decision-making. Instead of providing answers that soothe, one can more readily raise questions that disturb. One does not have to keep the ship on an even keel. One has more *latitude for creative deviance*.

Second, leading without or beyond one's authority permits focusing hard on a single issue. One does not have to contend so fully with meeting the multiple expectations of multiple constituencies and providing the holding environment for everybody. One can have an *issue focus*.

Third, operating with little or no authority places one closer to the detailed experiences of some of the stakeholders in the situation. One may lose the larger perspective but gain the fine grain of people's hopes, pains, values, habits, and history. One has *frontline information*.

However, because the benefits and constraints differ, those who lead without authority must adopt strategies and tactics that are at once more bold and subtle. First, without authority, one has very little control over the holding environment. One can shape the stimulus, but one cannot manage the response: one cannot institute an organizing structure, pick a temporizing side issue, secure a new norm, or provide a calming presence. A leader without authority can spark debate, but he cannot orchestrate it. Without authority, a leader must regulate distress by modulating the provocation. Furthermore, without authority one may have a frontline feel for a single issue in depth, but not as broad a sense of the multiplicity of challenges facing the community which affect its stance on any particular issue. This may render the leader without authority less aware of the other crucial problems confronting the society and the ripeness of his issue in relation to other pressing issues that may need to take priority.

In monitoring levels of distress, any leader has to find indicators for knowing both when to promote an unripe issue and whether the stress generated by an intervention falls within the productive range for that social system at that time.

Different organizations and societies will have different sources and levels of resilience, and each social system requires serious analysis. But as a general rule, the leader operating without authority can read the authority figure as a barometer of issue ripeness and systemic stress because social systems generally charge authority figures with the particular job of resolving ripe issues.

Second, in attracting and directing attention to an issue, a leader without authority has to take into account the special vulnerability of becoming a lightning rod. Rather than orchestrating the debate among competing factions, one becomes a faction readily targeted for attack. Of course, authority figures frequently get attacked as well, but the resources at their disposal for deflecting attention and letting others take the heat are often unavailable to leaders without authority.

Third, just as people look to authority to solve problems, leaders without authority commonly make the mistake of assuming that only authority figures have the power to affect change. As a result, there is a strong temptation to identify the authority figure as the audience for action: "If only we could bring *him* around, everyone else would move in the right direction." In general, however, people in power change their ways when the sources of their authority change the expectations. Their behavior is an expression of the community that authorizes them. Thus, a strategy that mobilizes the stakeholders in the community may be quite a bit more likely to get work done than the strategy of "challenging authority."

But without authority, a leader stands relatively naked before the people, often appearing to be not only the identifier of a distressing problem but also the source of the distress itself. All eyes turn to the person who raises disturbing questions, and some of those eyes are hostile. Groups can avoid problems, at least temporarily, by shooting the messenger. Thus, although attention is a major tool of leadership, it also makes one a likely target of attack. If a person lacks authority, people take issue not only with the substance of his point of view but with his right to raise it. Indeed, they often attack the right and ignore the substance.

The mechanisms for killing the messenger are varied and subtle depending on the culture, the organization, and the problem. Yet attacks often follow a general pattern: first, a person or faction raises a difficult question that generates some distress by pointing to a potential conflict over values and purpose, norms and organizational relationships, power, or strategy. Second, in response, the disquieted members of the system will turn their gaze to a senior authority figure, expecting him to restore equilibrium. Finally, the authority figure pressed by these expectations to reduce distress, feeling emotionally compelled to act, neutralizes or silences the "problem" faction, directly or indirectly. These moves happen fast. The authority figure may not even be aware of the way others have gotten him to perform the role of executioner on their behalf.

A major challenge of leadership, therefore, is to draw attention and then deflect it to the questions and issues that need to be faced. To do so, *one has to provide a context for action*. The audience needs to readily comprehend the purpose of unusual or deviant behavior so that it focuses less on the behavior itself, or the person, and more on its meaning.

Mark H. Moore

ORGANIZATIONAL STRATEGY IN THE PUBLIC SECTOR

From: Moore, M. H. (1995) 'Organizational strategy in the public sector', edited from *Creating Public Value*, Harvard University Press

PUBLIC MANAGERS CREATE PUBLIC value. The problem is that they cannot know for sure what that is. Even if they could be sure today, they would have to doubt tomorrow, for by then the political aspirations and public needs that give point to their efforts might well have changed.

Despite the ambiguity, managers need an account of the value their organizations produce. Each day, their organizations' operations consume public resources. Each day, these operations produce real consequences for society — intended or not. If the managers cannot account for the value of these efforts with both a story and demonstrated accomplishments, then the legitimacy of their enterprise is undermined and, with that, their capacity to lead.

Nor are their responsibilities limited to current operations. Some resources used today will not be valuable until tomorrow. Investments in new equipment, new knowledge, and new human capabilities, for example, are necessitated by the prospect of change and justified by the expectation that they will improve future performance. Even if no *explicit* investments are made, current operations will affect future performance, for today's experiences shape the culture and capabilities of tomorrow's organization. Public managers, then, are obliged to hold a vision of public value, good for today and into the future.

[. . .]

Managerial discretion and leadership in the public sector

With the ambiguity about purposes and means comes some degree of discretion and, with that, an opportunity for leadership. Society *needs* leadership from these managers to help it learn what is both desirable and possible to do in public domains for which these managers are temporarily responsible.

Of course, it is easy to exaggerate the degree of discretion that public managers possess. Close, continuing oversight by elected executives, legislatures, the media, and interest groups sharply limits their discretion. The managers are also held in check by the limited capabilities of the organizations they lead and the restricted opportunities to innovate and experiment. Taken together, these political and organizational constraints often leave relatively little room for manoeuver.

Still, in most cases, there is more discretion than most public managers (and their overseers) acknowledge. Nearly always, the politics surrounding a public enterprise are sufficiently contentious to suggest several different plausible and sustainable conceptions of public value. Similarly, there are usually enough criticisms of the efficacy of current operations and enough proposals for improvement that enterprising public sector executives can find some room for innovation and experimentation.

On occasion, public executives are given very wide latitude, indeed. This often occurs when a new problem has arisen or past approaches to a problem have become widely discredited. At such times society becomes far more willing to accept leadership from its managers and to entertain a broader set of possible actions.

[. . .]

The managerial task facing [public managers is] to chart a path for their enterprises and to make the most of their respective opportunities.

Defining mission and goals in the private sector

Private sector executives face the same challenge. They, too, must chart the course of their enterprises. [. . . S]ociety looks to them for this kind of leadership with much less reluctance than it looks to public executives. Private sector executives commonly respond by setting out strategic goals and developing operational plans for their organizations.

[. . .]

Initially, such techniques might seem to have limited applicability to public sector contexts. After all, there is widespread agreement about the goal of private sector enterprises: to maximize the long-term wealth of their shareholders. No such consensus exists about the goals of libraries, municipal sanitation departments, environmental protection agencies, and juvenile correctional facilities.

Private sector executives also gain enormously from measurement systems that tell them relatively promptly and accurately whether their planned course of action has succeeded or not. If they make money, they have a strong indication that they have created value. That is the message the bottom line conveys.

For their part, public sector executives may have to wait longer for program evaluations or benefit–cost analyses to be completed. Moreover, even when completed, such efforts produce much less compelling information about the ultimate value of public sector efforts, for the debate continues about the proper goals of the enterprise.

These features of private sector management clearly *do* ease the difficulty of setting and maintaining the direction of private sector organizations. They *may* make the techniques of private sector executives less relevant to public sector executives. But it is easy to exaggerate the significance of these differences.

After all, the concept of "maximizing long-term shareholder wealth" is, fundamentally, an abstraction. It is as abstract as the concept of "public value." By itself, it cannot resolve the complex, concrete issue of what particular products a private sector company should seek to produce and what particular investments in new plant and equipment should be made now to ready the organization to achieve the abstract goal of maximizing shareholder wealth.

To guide a company's efforts, business plans must be reasonably concrete. They must set out particular products, particular marketing plans, and particular financial arrangements. Inevitably, such plans are shot through with uncertainties. No one can be sure about consumer tastes, new technological possibilities, or the future price of capital. The uncertainties leave plenty of room for debate about whether a particular plan offered by management is the best plan to maximize long-term shareholder wealth.

[. . .]

All important business planning decisions are about the future, not the past. Somewhat surprisingly, then, when private and public sector managers confront the future, they often find themselves in the same leaky boat: their conceptions of value must be grounded in a *theory* of value rather than in demonstrated performance.

The concept of corporate strategy

To deal with the uncertainty about what path to take to produce value for shareholders, private sector executives and those academics who work with them have developed and relied on the concept of "corporate strategy." Initially, no small degree of mysticism surrounded this concept. It was much easier to describe a corporate strategy in operation and explain why it seemed to be successful than to set out the methodology to create one for the future. Later, analysts made some progress in developing more rigorous methods for investigating the strategic opportunities of particular firms in particular industries.

[. . .]

Perhaps the single most valuable feature of this concept is that it encourages chief executives to see their organization in a wider, longer-term, and more abstract context than is possible without its aid. Specifically, use of the concept directs the attention of chief executives away from the problem of producing today's products. Instead, it focuses their attention on the external market environments in which their organizations operate, especially on customers and competitors, and on the future.

Customers are important for an obvious reason: in the end, if a private sector enterprise is to be successful, it must produce something that customers want. It is all very well for entrepreneurs to have a hunch about what customers want; it is far better to know from the customers themselves what they desire. It is also important to recognize that consumers could change their minds about what they consider valuable not only through the provision of abstract information about products but also through experience. Thus, marketing, understood as both a search for what consumers value and a device for building ongoing relationships with customers, became a key element of any well-conceived corporate strategy.

Competitors are important for an equally obvious reason: it does little good to have a desirable product if one's competitors have a better one. Moreover, even if a manager had a breakthrough in a product or a production technology that gave her a competitive advantage, she must assume that her competitors will eventually be able to do the same. Consequently, in assessing their competitive advantage, managers must ask not just how large it is but also how long it will last.

Once private sector executives began thinking about their market environments and how advantages within that environment tended to erode over time, they naturally looked at change and uncertainty as well, for if anything seemed clear in that environment, it was that the environment would change. Consumer tastes would change. So would technology. And so would the price of capital. These changes could improve or weaken a firm's competitive position.

In addition to great uncertainty about these factors, there was plenty of room for strategic interaction among the competing firms. If a competitor moved one way, the best moves for one's own firm would be quite different than if the competitor had moved a different way. And everyone's moves would be influenced by what one did with one's own firm.

Faced with such uncertainties, private sector executives were encouraged to think in terms of "positioning" their firms in their environment rather than advancing down some determinant path toward wealth maximization. Their task was not simply to continue to refine their specialized capabilities for producing their current products; it was also to become diversified for the future and agile in adapting to new opportunities. Current production only answered yesterday's problem and provided a base for the future. It did not guarantee a successful future.

Thus, the concept of corporate strategy impelled executives not only to look outside their organization at the external market environment but also to think dynamically and strategically: they had to think about how their market environments were likely to change; how their organizations were then positioned to exploit predictable opportunities or respond to predictable threats; and what investments, undertaken then, would strengthen their position in the future.

Distinctive competence

The challenge of positioning their firms in dynamic competitive markets also caused private sector executives to analyze their own organizations in somewhat different terms. They looked for their own "distinctive competence."

Initially, the concept of "distinctive competence" seemed to return executive attention to the present and the firm's current operations. It did not seem to concern the market environment or the future. It focused on what the organization currently knew how to do. In application, however, identifying the distinctive competence of an organization required the manager to identify an abstraction — a set of *general* capabilities the organization possessed that might indicate what position the firm could occupy in its current product markets or, indeed, in other product markets it might begin operating in.

Thus, for example, one electronic appliance firm identified its distinctive competence as "putting motors in folded metal boxes." On the one hand, this phrase described a manufacturing capability rather than a product and thus seemed concrete. On the other hand, it was an abstraction that not only covered many different products produced by the firm but also suggested some new products. Furthermore, it identified the distinctive competencies of the firm compared to others in the same industry. Thus, it became possible for a manager to think: "This is what we know how to do in general. I wonder how many valuable products we could create with this set of general capabilities."

By thinking about organizations in terms of customers, competitors, and distinctive competence, private sector executives found it possible to draw back from the compelling day-to-day tasks of producing and delivering their current products and to think about their enterprises both in a wider context and in somewhat more abstract terms. That stance turned out to be helpful because it allowed managers to identify threats and opportunities in their environments that would otherwise have been missed. It also helped them become more imaginative and more accurate in analyzing the varied routes they could take to maximizing shareholder wealth in the complex competitive environments in which they found themselves.

Strategy in diversified conglomerates

These original concepts were most appropriate for single product firms or for firms whose product lines clustered within a particular industry. As firms changed into multiproduct conglomerates, and as the financial profiles of enterprises began to contribute to high rates of return as much as desirable new products or low-cost technologies, the concept of strategy underwent important adaptations.

First, many different things within an enterprise began to acquire strategic significance. A strategic asset did not have to be a product or a technology. It could be key personnel, a strong relationship with suppliers, or a particularly valuable manufacturing location offering both transportation and tax advantages.

Even a license from a regulatory agency could qualify. In short, as strategic analyses became more sophisticated, they revealed the strategic value of many different features of a given enterprise.

Second, instead of viewing the firm as a single business, managers came to see the firm as a portfolio of different businesses. The portfolio of businesses might turn out to produce some cost or marketing advantages to particular businesses within the family as a result of complementarities in financial transactions, production, distribution, or marketing.

But even if the portfolio did not really have any of these technological possibilities, it would still have an advantage insofar as diversification of products and industries spread a particular firm's risk. If an enterprise had products in several different industries, it was less vulnerable to occasional downturns in a particular industry and better able to take advantage of rapid growth in new sectors. Diversification had its price in that the central focus of the organization might be lost and, with that, some of its productive capacity. But for many firms, the financial advantages of a diverse portfolio of products more than compensated for the loss of focus and expertise.

Thus, strategy shifted its focus to the relative strength of a firm's different products in different markets and analyzed how returns from one product would finance the development and inevitable risks of a newer product. It emphasized the problems of distributing risks and managing transitions from one portfolio of products to another, rather than finding a particular market niche in which to hole up.

Strategy as a sustainable deal

More recently still, the concept of corporate strategy seems to be going through another revision – this time to deal with powerful challenges to corporate governance and management. One of these challenges has come from the increasing power of outside agents other than the shareholders and the customers to make effective claims on the corporation's assets and activities.

In the past the principal group with whom management had to contend in defining the overall purposes of the firm was labor. Indeed, until recently, labor has been quite effective in making claims on organizations for such things as increased pay, safer working conditions, more reliable pensions, and so on.

More recently, others have joined labor in making effective claims on private enterprise. Government, for example, now wants more from corporations than mere tax revenues. It seeks to use corporations as agents for social objectives ranging from environmental protection to affirmative action. Even more recently, local communities have managed to make some claims on corporations sensitive to their image as a good corporate citizen. The cumulative pressure from these various groups has gradually shifted the effective focus of a corporation from maximizing shareholder wealth to accomplishing that goal subject to an increasing number of social constraints – constraints that on occasion seem more important than the original goal itself.

Predictably, these changes have stimulated another important change. Increasingly, companies find themselves vulnerable to hostile takeover attempts by entrepreneurs who claim to see some unexploited economic value in the enterprise and offer to buy control of the firm at prices far above market values. Their willingness to pay the higher price testifies to their confidence that the assets of the firm could be used more intensively, or more productively, or with greater loyalty to the shareholders' interests. The shareholders are inclined to go along. Consequently, management has become concerned about warding off such takeover attempts.

These challenges to corporate governance have forced private sector managers to abandon the illusion that the authority to set the course of the company's future development has been delegated irrevocably to them. Their purposes and plans, once routinely approved in annual shareholder meetings, are now often contested by truculent shareholders, aggressive corporate raiders, determined government regulators, and angry local communities. As one business school professor put it, "We used to think that setting the strategy of the firm was the prerogative of the chief executive officer. Now we see that a successful strategy is simply a sustainable deal among a variety of stakeholders that includes the shareholders, the creditors, the customers, the employees, the suppliers, the government, and the local community."

In sum, the concept of strategy in the private sector has helped private sector executives analyze opportunities for positioning and using their enterprises in an increasingly complex and dynamic world. By focusing attention on environmental threats and opportunities, and by encouraging them to see their organizations in terms of their particular distinctive competencies and the strategically important assets they control, the concept has aided private sector executives in formulating concrete business plans. Increasingly, they are also encouraged to negotiate their plans with all those who have a stake in the enterprise.

Defining mission and goals in the public sector

Our question is whether these concepts can be usefully adapted for use by public sector executives. At the outset, the differences between the two sectors may seem crippling. For example, the focus on competitors seems out of place, since many government organizations consider themselves monopolies. Similarly, the notion that government agencies might offer a portfolio of products with each one supporting another in financial terms also seems a little bizarre.

Yet the concept of corporate strategy applies meaningfully to public sector executives. For example, the notion that the organization might have a distinctive competence wider than its current use is consistent with [innovations in public service]. The proposition that public sector executives should connect their performance to the aspirations of citizens, overseers, and clients fits [the notion of] public value [used here]. And finally, the idea that organizations need to be positioned in an uncertain, dynamic market, and that a successful organizational strategy must embody a sustainable deal among stakeholders, captures the dilemma of [public managers] far more clearly than the idea that they have a well-defined mandate to achieve. Corporate strategy may even help public sector executives accommodate themselves to a reality they have long fought – namely, that their mandate for action is both ambiguous and vulnerable to change, and that an efficient response to that reality may require organizations to be adaptive and flexible rather than rigidly focused on achieving a clearly defined objective.

The strategic triangle

For the last several years the public management faculty of the Kennedy School of Government has worked with a rudimentary concept of organizational strategy adapted for the public sector. In this conception, an organizational strategy is a concept that simultaneously: (1) declares the overall mission or purpose of an organization (cast in terms of important public values); (2) offers an account of the sources of support and legitimacy that will be tapped to sustain society's commitment to the enterprise; and (3) explains how the enterprise will have to be organized and operated to achieve the declared objectives.

In developing a strategy for a public sector organization, a manager must bring these elements into coherent alignment by meeting three broad tests. First, the strategy must be *substantively valuable* in the sense that the organization produces things of value to overseers, clients, and beneficiaries at low cost in terms of money and authority.

Second, it must be *legitimate and politically sustainable*. That is, the enterprise must be able to continually attract both authority and money from the political authorizing environment to which it is ultimately accountable.

Third, it must be *operationally and administratively feasible* in that the authorized, valuable activities can actually be accomplished by the existing organization with help from others who can be induced to contribute to the organization's goal.

These tests are powerful because they identify the necessary conditions for the production of value in the public sector. To verify their necessity, imagine what happens to managers and their organizations if any one of these three conditions is missing.

If managers have an attractive purpose broadly supported by the political environment but lack the operational capacity to achieve it, the strategic vision must fail. Either the goal will be rejected as unfeasible or the political world will find a different institutional vehicle for accomplishing it.

If managers have a substantively valuable goal that is administratively and operationally feasible but cannot attract political support, then that enterprise, too, will fail. The want of capital and resources will doom it.

If managers conceive of some organizational activities that can command political support and are administratively feasible but lack any substantive significance, then, over the long run, that strategy will fail – not necessarily because the organization will be diminished, but simply because its operations will be wasteful and someone will eventually get around to blowing the whistle.

Finally and most painfully, if managers have substantively valuable ideas but are unable to attract political support or administer them feasibly, then those ideas must fail as strategic conceptions. Such ideas are "academic" in the worst sense of the word.

The utility of the framework

This framework, like the concepts of corporate strategy in the private sector, helps public sector executives draw back from the task of presiding over and maintaining their organizations, while refocusing their attention on the question of whether their political or task environments now either require or allow them to change their organizational purposes in the interest of creating additional public value. It helps them maintain a sense of purposefulness that allows them to challenge and lead their organizations toward the production of greater public value. (It is important to keep in mind that a manager might increase public value by downsizing the organizations's operations and returning money to private consumption. In the public sector as in the private, *growth* is not always desirable. Indeed, one of the persistent values in our political environment is the desire to keep the public sector as small as possible.)

More particularly, use of the concept encourages public sector managers to: scan their authorizing environments for potential changes in the collective, political aspirations that guide their operations; search their substantive task environments for emergent problems to which their organizations might contribute some part of the solution; and review the operations of their own and other organizations in search of new programs or technologies that their organizations could use to improve performance in existing (or conceivably new) missions.

Taken together, analysis of the external demands and of the internal capabilities helps managers understand why their organizations function as they do and the extent to which managers can count on smooth sailing in the future. If citizens and their representatives are demanding what the organizations are happily producing, managers might well rest easy. If, however, important inconsistencies exist between what citizens and their overseers desire and what the organizations supply, then the executives have to realign their mandates and their organizations.

Even the absence of trouble between mandates and operational capabilities does not necessarily imply that all is well. Managers, guided by the strategic triangle, have to consider the possibility that while citizens and overseers seem happy, somehow the organization still fails to produce anything of value. They have to check intermittently to find out if the assumptions they and citizens make about the ultimate effectiveness of their enterprises are, in fact, true. That is the challenge implied by defining the concept of public value somewhat independently of the political support and legitimacy of the organization, and by suggesting that analytic techniques such as program evaluation and benefit-cost analysis have an important role to play in helping managers locate and recognize the creation of public value.

They also have to consider the possibility that things change – that new political demands will emerge, or that new technological possibilities will appear. To the extent that these changes redefine what is valuable for their organizations to do, managers have to be alert and respond with suitable adjustments.

In short, the concept focuses managerial attention *outward*, to the value of the organization's production, *upward*, toward the political definition of value, and *downward* and *inward*, to the organization's current performance. To the extent that this review reveals important incongruities in the position of the organization, then the manager of that organization would be encouraged to rethink his or her basic strategy until it was once more properly aligned.

Analytic techniques for strategic planning

Each point of the triangle provides a different vantage point for considering the question of what would be valuable (and feasible) to do. More important, each point engages a different set of analytic methodologies for answering the basic question symbolized by that point on the triangle.

For example, in asking whether a particular organizational goal is substantively valuable, managers are encouraged to raise normative questions about the value of their efforts and to bring to bear the analytic apparatus that can help them answer those questions. The technical apparatus of program evaluation and benefit-cost analysis can be wheeled out to help make this important determination. Managers can also apply philosophical and legal analyses of social justice, fundamental fairness, and any individual rights that might be affected by an organization's operations.

In asking whether a goal is politically sustainable, one invites an analysis of the politics surrounding the organization. This could include an analysis of the important values that are at stake in the organization's operations, the interests of those legislators who oversee the organization's operations, the claims pressed by interest groups, or the bits of conventional wisdom that now justify and guide the organization's activities.

In asking whether a particular goal is organizationally doable, one can rely on the techniques of feasibility assessment and implementation analysis. These techniques draw on what is known about the ways in which, and the rates at which, organizations can change their activities.

In sum, thinking strategically in the public sector requires managers to assign equal importance to substance, politics, and organizational implementation. Currently, these elements remain disconnected. Some, such as academic experts and policy analysts, specialize in substance. Others, such as political appointees or the directors of legislative affairs offices, specialize in politics. Still others, such as those who direct offices of administration and management, specialize in administrative feasibility. Thus, thinking strategically means integrating these diverse perspectives. If any perspective is left out, some important consideration in choosing a value-creating path will be lost.

A contrast to classic traditions of public administration

The strategic triangle is designed to influence how managers distribute their attention, thought, and action across their operational environments. It can be particularly helpful to them in performing the crucially important task of defining their organization's overall mission and goals. To deepen understanding of the strategic concept and further evaluate its utility, compare its recommended focus to the orientation commonly associated with the classic tradition of public administration.

Perhaps the most notable difference is that the classic tradition of public administration does not focus a manager's attention on questions of purpose and value or on the development of legitimacy and support. The classic tradition assumes that these questions have been answered in the development of the organization's legislative or policy mandate. The policy mandate simultaneously defines the organization's purpose and creates a normative presumption that such a purpose would be publicly valuable to pursue. The mandate also explicitly provides the organization with the resources – the money and public authority – it needs to achieve its purpose. Finally, it authorizes the managers to deploy those resources to achieve the mandated goals.

Given that the questions of resources, authorization, and value have all been resolved in the establishment of a policy mandate, managers must pursue the downward- and inward-looking tasks of deploying available resources to achieve the mandated objectives as efficiently and effectively as possible. In accomplishing this goal, managers rely on their administrative expertise in wielding the instruments of internal managerial influence: organizational design, budgeting, human resource development, and management control. To the extent that managers look upward and outward, they do so primarily to ensure that they operate within the framework of mandated objectives, that is, to ensure that they are properly accountable. The definition (and redefinition) of purpose is left to policymakers.

In contrast, the strategic triangle rests on the assumption that public managers should define an organization's overall purpose and mission. It also reminds them to develop conceptions of valuable purposes from sources beyond the boundaries of their own administrative expertise. They are encouraged to use analytic techniques to scan their task environments and evaluate their own performance as the basis for forming independent views of the value of planned or past activities.

Managers should interact with the political system not simply through the medium of their mandated purposes but instead through more continuous and interactive dialogue. They should look behind the mandate to see how different political aspirations have been reflected in the mandate that seeks to guide them, and how the balance of political forces seems to be changing over time. They should engage political overseers in deliberation to improve their judgment about what the political system would regard as valuable. Moreover, they should adopt this stance toward politics not only at those rare times when legislation affecting their organization is being considered but routinely.

Even more radical is the idea that managers' knowledge of the distinctive competence of their organization – combined with what they are learning through their current operations about the needs of their clients and potential users – might suggest potentially valuable new activities for them to initiate. [. . .] Like private sector managers who seek niches in their environments that they are well positioned to fill, so strategically oriented public sector managers might spot new opportunities for their organizations to meet emergent political demands or to respond to new needs that were not previously recognized.

Thus, this strategic conception seeks to incorporate the techniques of political analysis and policy analysis as well as administrative and organizational analysis in the required repertoires of public sector managers. In doing so, the concept of strategic management in the public sector seems to elevate public sector executives from the role of technicians, choosing from well-known administrative methods to accomplish purposes defined elsewhere, to the role of strategists, scanning their political and task environments for opportunities to use their organizations to create public value. It also changes their administrative job from assuring continuity and efficiency in current tasks to one of improvising the transition from current to future performance. Like private sector executives, public sector executives serve to position the organization they lead to create public value, not simply to deploy resources to accomplish mandated purposes.

Now, such a broad invitation may pose hazards for democratic governance. It may be dangerous to encourage public sector executives to use their imaginations to search for public value. In gauging this risk, however, we must keep in mind that the primary change being recommended is *in the thoughts and actions of managers*, not in the existing institutional arrangements that hold them accountable. In action, managers will still be bound by the tight process of oversight that now constrains them and by the rigidities of the bureaucracies that they seek to lead. The only new action I propose is that managers feel authorized to search their environments with purposeful, value-seeking imaginations and then to act on any opportunity they see through interactions with their political authorizing environments and innovations within their own organizations. If they succeed in finding and exploiting opportunities to create value, it will be because they earn their success in the tough institutional environments in which they find themselves, not because their world has become less demanding.

[. . .]

John Seddon

BEYOND COMMAND AND CONTROL: REDESIGNING SERVICES FROM THE BOTTOM UP

From: Seddon, J. (2003) 'Beyond command and control', extracted from *Freedom From Command and Control. A Better Way to Make the Work Work*, Vanguard Publishing

OUR ORGANISATIONAL NORMS ARE based on command and control thinking. We think of our organisations as top-down hierarchies, we separate decision-making from work, we expect managers to make decisions with measures like budgets, standards, targets, activity and so on. We teach managers that their job is to manage people and manage budgets. These are the principles and practices that constitute command and control management.

Doubts about the command and control philosophy of management are now common. People discuss the problems caused by the top-down imposition of targets in our public services. But problems such as these cannot be solved or answered within the prevailing view. To do so leads us to find better ways to do the 'wrong thing righter'. We need to determine what is the right thing to do, to treat the causes rather than the symptoms. We should be realising that these problems must be treated as signals for us to call into question some quite fundamental beliefs.

The customer service centre as a system

I am going to unpick the current philosophy and introduce the systems alternative – the better way. I shall start with planning for a service centre.

There are two broad types of demand on any service centre – value demand, the calls we want, and failure demand, the calls we don't want. Value demand is what the service centre exists to serve; it represents the demands customers make for things they want, things that are of value to them. Failure demand is created by the organisation not working properly. I define it as follows:

> Failure demand is demand caused by a failure to do something or do something right for the customer.

It is a fundamental mistake in call centre design and management to treat all demand as units of production. Failure demand represents a significant cost. Removing it has an enormous impact on the economics of a system. Consider the following statistics: In the financial services sector I have found failure demand to run from 20 to 45% of demand; in police forces, telecommunications, and local authorities I have found failure demand to run as high as 50 to 80%. Consider the cost associated with such levels of waste – for that is what it is. In service organisations failure demand is often the greatest source of waste.

The first step in working with failure demand is to establish whether it is predictable. To do this you need to understand the 'type and frequency' of demand. How many of each type do we have and do these recur over time? This helps us understand predictability, which is crucial. If failure demand is predictable, you can and should act to remove the causes. If it is unpredictable the best thing to do may be nothing. Things will always go wrong; you need to sort out what is going wrong predictably.

I have been writing about this simple phenomenon for many years. I hear from many managers who have become aware of the enormous potential for working on removing failure demand. But the causes of failure demand lie well outside their control. In the short term the action that needs to be taken would require the leadership of a senior manager, someone whom the hierarchy would 'look up' to. In the longer term what is required is a change to the whole system. Roles and measures have to change from managing through the hierarchy to managing flow, managing the work end-to-end.

In some service centres I find managers do try to determine the reasons for a customer call, but most often they do so with an 'internal' – 'what we do with it' – perspective. When I look at 'call coding', as it is often described, I find the codes make no distinction between value and failure demand. Worse, call coding is often 'compulsory' – it is a forced part of the 'wrap' procedure (the work an agent has to do following a call). This only encourages agents to put in any code that will move them on – they don't want to get 'bad wrap' data, as too much time in wrap will mean the agent will get paid attention to. In short, I have yet to find good information about the nature of demand in our service centres.

With value demand you need to deliver what the customer wants efficiently. To do this means working on the work flow, from the customer demand through to its completion. The traditional service centre manager has no information about flow. Instead he will be using data about activities, standards and costs. It leads the manager to put the 'best' people in the places where customers will find it hard to get to them. The 'production' logic is 'I can't have my most able people taking the easy calls', so managers create levels and specialist functions to receive calls from those who filter at the 'front end'. The manager will have no idea how much re-work, duplication, errors and time is built in to the system and, in turn, how much failure demand this creates.

In the case of failure demand you act to remove the causes. The impact can be seen immediately on measures of productivity and customer service. With value demand you act by designing to meet it in the most efficient way. You want customers to experience 'pulling value' from the organisation. If you design the work to do the 'value work' – what matters to the customer – and only the value work, costs will fall as service improves, something that most call centre managers find counter-intuitive, for their whole world is based on production assumptions, equating service with cost.

In the mid-nineties I worked with an IT company's help desk. It was a traditional design. Managers measured the volume of demand and the workers' activity ('production') to do resource planning. Agents were monitored for their call activity, experts were right at the back of the flow. The engineers – the people who do the work – studied the nature of demand on the system. They discovered they treated a wide variety of demands by the same process. By tracking each of the major types of demand through the system they could see waste and its causes. For the first time they established a true measure of end-to-end fix time from the customers' point of view. It was stable and averaged six days.

They took action. The experts moved to the front of the flow. They had learned from meeting customers to find out what mattered to them that the customers were experts too. They realised the fastest way to establish the value work in any call was to have the two experts talk to each other.

Many managers will now be thinking 'but what about the cost?' Remember cost is end-to-end. They found much duplication and re-work in the functional design.

The experts either closed the call by solving the problem or passed it to someone who had the best skill set for resolution. It was a one stop or one pass philosophy. Their capacity (productivity) quadrupled, end-to-end time went down to an average of less than a day. Morale was up to boot. The engineers worked to solve problems like how best to pass work and who to, how to track the type and frequency of demand and work with it intelligently. Being clever people they developed IT tools to aid their efforts.

I should warn you against interpreting this case by drawing the general conclusion that we should always 'put experts at the front'. The point is that the nature of demand will tell you about the requirements for expertise. The customer demand dictates the value work, the value work dictates the expertise required. In this case the complexity of demand dictated an 'expert' response.

Acting on demand creates the greatest leverage on a service centre. Performance improves enormously. Perhaps the greater priority is to restore morale. Happy people make better workers. In service centres people are unhappy because they are monitored to death and the way measures are used destroys their morale. These people are best placed to understand and act on demand – it would give meaning to their work and is a cornerstone in destroying the sweat shop culture. The nature of demand is just one thing managers of service centres cannot 'see'. Let's step back and build a picture of the typical service centre organisation to learn more about what managers **do** see.

Acting on the work not the workers

The sweat shop culture has been created by the production logic where the focus of management is on how to 'get them to do it' – take the requisite number of calls. It is to act on the worker not the work.

Managers monitor their measures to manage resource against demand volumes. Top management will often be heard to say things like 'if only we could reduce our average call length by 30 seconds, we could improve our bottom line by . . .' This is to focus on entirely the wrong thing. Of course, top management has no other view than cost data. They could be experiencing seventy per cent failure demand, but management is focused on 'taking the calls', not improving the system.

The service centre manager sees his or her job as setting and monitoring work standards, productivity and procedures. It is an uncritically inherited assumption of traditional management thinking that people are the primary causes of poor or good performance rather than the system in which they work. As a consequence, management becomes concerned with working on the people. Paradoxically, managing productivity in this way undermines productivity because the major causes of variation in performance are in the system – the work and the way the work works. As the manager is preoccupied with meeting his service standards, team leaders become preoccupied with making sure people do 'as they should' – according to the plan. People are set targets or work standards. They are derived from the plan, not the work.

Let us suppose I work for you in a service centre and you have set a work standard of one hundred calls per day. Yesterday, I did one hundred and twenty calls, today I did eighty. What happens to me?

In most service centres this means I'd get paid attention to. In harsh cultures this can mean bullying. In many service centres there are now policies about treating staff well, so the manager would turn up and 'coach' rather than bully. But is this of any real difference? It is, most often, a mistake to even turn up. If you look at my performance over time you might find I could do as few as seventy-five and as many as one hundred and twenty-five calls in a day – the variation is in the system.

Figure 22.1 shows my capability – what I am achieving and how predictable my performance is. My capability is measured by taking time-series data: the calls I can handle every day, plotted over time. The statistical variation in my daily measures sets the upper and lower limits – what can be expected as 'just as likely' results.

There is always variation, in anything that we do. In a call centre, variation will be caused by the nature of the call, customers, products, procedures, availability of information, knowledge of the service agent and so on. There will be many causes. To improve performance we need to understand and act on the causes. This is an easy exercise to run in any service centre. Put the current performance

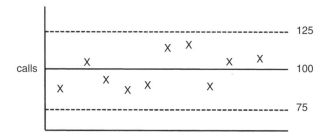

Figure 22.1 John's capability

measures in a capability chart, explain to people that the chart shows variation and ask what they think, from their experience, the causes of variation might be. Then having brainstormed the causes, return to the list and ask: which of these are attributable to the system – the way the work works – and which are attributable to agents? It is as Deming and others taught: 95% or more of variation in performance is in the system. By working on the agents, service centre managers are working on the 5%. It is an extraordinary waste of management resource.

If service centre workers' behaviour is subject to variation, the extent and nature of that variation must be established before any action can be contemplated, otherwise managers will make the situation worse. Managers (and service agents) need to know whether variation in performance is attributable to agents or the system. Current approaches to people management in call centres ignore this important question.

To hold the worker accountable for their performance when in fact their performance is governed by the system causes stress. Because their managers hold them accountable for the work they do, service centre workers often believe, as their managers do, that they are accountable for performance. When they have a bad day they leave work feeling guilty, ashamed, responsible.

When, as will be inevitable, they risk becoming losers, agents 'cheat' – they do anything they need to do to make their numbers. People's ingenuity is engaged in surviving rather than improving performance: it is a tragic waste of human talent. Agents close a call before the customer is finished, and sometimes before the customer has started; they tell customers to call back, they re-route difficult calls, in short they do all they can to avoid missing work targets or standards. Knowing that they do these things to survive exacerbates their feelings of demoralisation. These are not bad people; they work in a bad system. The human costs of demoralisation are incalculable. The obvious costs are recruitment and training as these conditions create high turnover of staff. But the real costs are higher – poor service and high costs are associated with customer dissatisfaction and staff dissatisfaction.

The better way to think about managing people is to lead them in understanding and acting on the system. It harnesses service agents' ingenuity towards contributing, learning and improving, rather than engaging their ingenuity against the system. Just as service agents are best placed to understand and work against demand, they are best placed to address the question: what are the causes of variation? Causes of variation identified as within the team's control can and should be acted on by the team. Causes of variation identified as beyond the team's control can and should be acted on by the manager. The measures help both managers and agents learn to 'see' the waste and causes of waste in their work.

Management's focus changes from managing people – ensuring that people do as they 'should' – to managing the system – understanding and improving how well the work flows, end to end, to fulfil the customers' demands. It is a step that managers are only prepared to take when they have first learned that their organisation's performance is governed by the system and not the people. Once managers make this conceptual leap, they stop wasting time doing people management ('one-to-ones'); the impact on productivity is enormous.

By seeing the purpose as 'serve customers' a completely different set of measures can be developed that help managers and agents understand and improve performance. To change the nature of measurement in our organisations is a major shift. It cannot be achieved by announcement; people who believe in the current measures need to learn for themselves what is wrong with them and then need to learn how to work with the better alternative. Managing with functional measures always causes sub-optimisation, because parts achieve their ends at the expense of the whole.

Only by managing costs end-to-end, associating costs with flow, can you reduce costs in a sustainable manner. Capability measures are measures of the work that tell you about the predictability of performance. In the service centre this means knowing about the predictability of demand, the predictability of agent performance, the predictability of work flows that go beyond the agent and so on. The point is simple: using these measures to understand and improve performance will improve the bottom line. In the current management philosophy it is assumed the bottom line can be influenced by using functional measures, targets, standards, etc., to direct performance. In fact the only thing that one can reliably predict is that managing in this way could make things worse. How can I be so sure? Service organisations, by their very nature, have high levels of variety in the work demands. To tackle the variety with a command and control philosophy is to stifle the organisation's ability to handle variety. The better able an organisation is to absorb variety, the better the flow, hence the lower the costs and the better the service. Capability measurement is essential in understanding about how well the system absorbs variety.

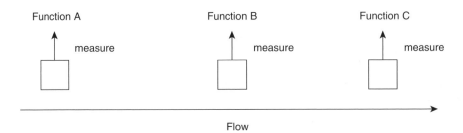

Figure 22.2 Managing functions damages flow

Housing repairs: a break-fix system

Local Authorities and Housing Associations manage large stocks of housing. Inevitably houses need repairing. The majority of housing organisations manage repairs with two measures, budget and time to repair. The latter has been mandated by government as a 'Best Value Performance Indicator' (BVPI). The BVPIs have to be reported as percentages of repairs completed in certain times: the percentage of emergency repairs competed in 24 hours; urgent repairs completed in 7 days and 'non-urgent' repairs completed in 28 days.

In most housing repair organisations the repair work is controlled through something called the 'Schedule of Rates'. This is a comprehensive listing of repair types and their associated costs. These 'rates' are used either to pay sub-contractors or pay bonuses to employees.

The purpose from the customer's (tenant's) point of view is to do the repair properly and quickly. So the first thing to do in taking a system view is to establish the organisation's capability versus purpose, measuring end-to-end time from the tenant's point of view. Figure 22.3 shows the results from one example:

The capability chart showed the average end-to-end time to be about 31 days, the lower limit 0 days and the upper limit about 85 days. The chart also showed a number of 'special causes' or 'signals' – data points well above the upper control limit. These events were investigated to find out if they were different from other events and were found to be no different. It showed the system was unstable. It is clear from the chart that the system was becoming more unstable as time went on. I shall return to this.

The team that built this chart could not use the data available in the organisation, as the reported data were percentages of achievement of the BVPIs. As a matter of interest all the BVPIs were being achieved. Yet the chart shows a different picture. To establish end-to-end time from the tenant's point of view, the team had to laboriously take each and every request for a repair and track it

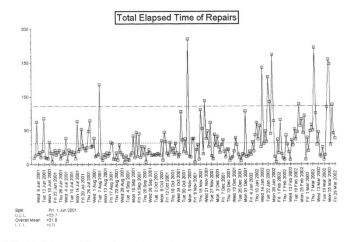

Figure 22.3 End-to-end time for all repairs

through to completion. What they learned in doing this was alarming; however, it was not unusual – these things are to be found in all similar systems.

Firstly, targets were being achieved through 'cheating'. Jobs were closed and re-opened even though they had not been completed, sometimes with 'justification' – 'if tenants are out the measure should not count'. Secondly, 'cheating' occurs with changing job classifications to meet times – is this 'an emergency', 'urgent' and so on? Thirdly, one repair from a customer's point of view may be four jobs in this system. To repair a window may require four trades, each would have a job sheet and each of these would be subject to the BVPI regime. The purpose of the system is to comply with targets, thus the 'de-facto' purpose is 'open and close jobs' not repair properties. People's ingenuity is focused on the wrong things.

The capability chart also shows that things were getting worse. If you go back to Figure 22.3 and study the chart, you will see that the overall picture is worsening – variation is increasing. The analysis team re-calculated the control limits on the chart, choosing two places where they thought from visual inspection that the chart appeared to be changing for the worse. The results are shown in Figure 22.4.

The chart shows that the capability in March 2002 was an average of 51.4 and an upper limit of 146.7 – things were clearly getting worse. The chart led the team to ask the question: What happened at the two occasions when things clearly took a step change for the worse?

In October 2001 a new management structure was put in place. New supervisors, keen to be the best in terms of achieving BVPIs, actually de-stabilised the system (yet they were unaware). In November 2001 a call centre was introduced, something mandated by government policy. This caused further de-stabilisation. Again, no one knew until the 85 measure invited the question.

So how well was the system achieving purpose? Not well, it was becoming more and more unstable and from the tenants' point of view it was taking a long time to complete repairs. At this point managers might be seeking someone to

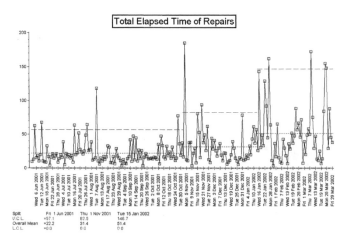

Figure 22.4 End-to-end time for all repairs, re-calculating limits

blame. Yet the blame lies in the design and management of work. It is of no value to blame the supervisors and workers for 'cheating'; the measurement system drives that behaviour – the hierarchy will judge the workers and supervisors alike on achievement of arbitrary measures. The call centre workers cannot be blamed for they are only doing as directed by their managers. Of course the blame lies with management, but is it reasonable to blame managers for following the guidance of government and not knowing what they do not know? They may be guilty but it is hardly their fault.

The team now knew about the 'what' of performance – how well the system achieved its purpose. The next step was to find out the 'why'. Figure 22.5 shows the basic flow of work in housing repairs.

You might ask what could go wrong? It seems quite logical: a tenant would call the call centre to report a problem, the call centre worker would complete a works order, detailing the work to be done using the Schedule of Rates, and pass it to the supervisor who would allocate it to a tradesman. The tradesman would get the necessary materials and complete the repair. To find out what is going on you have to ask questions about demand and flow. As we saw with service centres, the best place to start is with demand – what is the nature of customer demands on the repairs process?

Approximately forty percent of demands into the call centre were 'failure demands' – for example, tenants progress-chasing their repair or complaining that the repair had not been completed to their satisfaction. The remainder were 'value demands' – people requesting repairs to their properties. The failure demands clogged the system – the call centre workers would have to problem-solve these and get back to the customer with an answer. It often took time to locate tradesmen or supervisors to get an answer for the tenant.

The call centre worker is effectively responsible for diagnosing the reported problem and determining its solution – that is to say determining the work to be done, deciding a specification from the Schedule of Rates; this in turn will determine how the tradesman is paid. Tradesmen would dispute the work specified on the Schedule of Rates most of the time (in fact in excess of 90% of the time). Because of this an administrative function, a cottage industry, had been established to deal with these matters. The administrators would take returned works orders from the tradesmen upon which the tradesmen had altered the Schedule

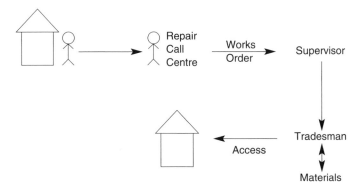

Figure 22.5 Housing repairs – basic flow

of Rates code and pass the same to the tradesmen's supervisors who would make a judgement as to what was correct. Subsequent changes would need to be returned for further administration. None of this adds any value to doing the work – it is all waste.

Arranging access is also done in the call centre. Yet supervisors would allocate work according to value (earnings) to the tradesmen – and favouritism could play a part in allocating work. Tradesmen would schedule their work to maximise their earnings. As a consequence tradesmen often had problems with gaining access and performing the repair. In addition the tradesmen would have to wait for up to an hour each morning, queuing to get their materials. In summary, the system picture looked as in Figure 22.6.

All of these problems had been created by design. Managers may believe that this organisation would work just fine if everybody did as they should. But such thinking ignores the fact of variety. To design a service that works one needs to learn how to design against demand, to understand the nature and extent of variety in demand and thus optimise the way the system works in response to that.

Diagnosing a repair could never be satisfactorily achieved by two parties – the tenant and the call centre worker – who know little about the expertise of the tradesmen. Turning this diagnosis into a specification and linking that to pay are the conditions that lie at the heart of the system's failure. The waste in this system included: re-visiting the properties, re-working the Schedule of Rates paperwork, disputes with respect to pay, doing more than was required in the repair hence wastage of materials and labour, and so on.

Having gained knowledge about the 'what and why' of current performance, the people who did this work re-designed it. The first step in re-design is to clarify the value work. In this case it can be described as diagnosis, access and repair. The re-design was as follows. The customer called the call centre who routed the call directly to a tradesman who was working on the estate (they had learned that demand was predictable by geography and thus had determined where to be

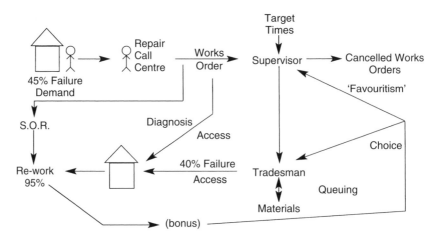

Figure 22.6 Housing repairs as a system

located). The tradesman would arrange to visit the tenant by mutual agreement. The tradesman would then arrive and, if possible, complete the repair (understanding demand led them to learn what materials to carry). If it were not possible to complete the repair, for reasons of materials or trade skills, the tradesman would arrange for a repair at an agreed date. Within weeks the end-to-end time for repairs fell. All repairs were being completed in eight days. As well as transforming performance, the change transformed morale because the people who did the work re-designed the system.

Alongside the reduction in repair times there was less wastage of materials. Jobs used materials as required, not according to the Schedule of Rates; there was no incentive to use extra materials. Beyond those consequences managers set about further reducing the costs of materials by working on the predictability of demand for materials by type and reducing the time materials spent in their system.

The tradesmen elected to be paid a salary rather than a bonus based on the schedule of rates as they could see that the schedule of rates bonus was one of the system conditions causing sub-optimisation. And this is an important point about intervention. If this exercise had begun with managers suggesting to workers their payment system should change, it would never have got off the ground.

One way into a break-fix system is to study how often it actually works in respect of purpose: how often breaks are fixed at the point of transaction. This cannot be learned from management reports; it needs to be learned by being in the places of transaction. When you spend your time in those places you find out how well the service works for customers. You will also start to appreciate the waste: re-work, doing too much work, duplicating work and so on. The extent, nature and costs of this waste are hidden from managers; they cannot be seen in the current measures. Instead the current measures are another cause of sub-optimisation. These are the things you learn when you study your organisation as a system. It is not something that can be delegated; it is the defining mark of a good leader.

Learning to see

All organisations are systems; they are simply not understood and managed as such. When you learn to look at any traditionally managed organisation as a system you find a multitude of forces working against purpose. For managers this comes as a shock. Some of what you discover seems perverse – people 'do their jobs' but create enormous harm to the system. They are unable to change the system: it is a shackle imposed and controlled by those who are remote from the work. People do perverse things sometimes without knowledge of the consequences, for these things cannot be seen on management's radar. Sometimes they are aware of dysfunctional consequences and are frustrated at their inability to do something about it. Sometimes managers, in particular, are aware and seek to avoid exposing the problems or acting on them for fear of retribution. If there are big problems exposed, someone has to be to blame. It can be far safer to behave as normal and turn a blind eye. Hierarchies don't like bad news.

Studying the organisation as a system is going to reveal bad news. Be clear about the fact that you are expecting bad news and you want to know. Many leaders I have worked with use the words 'at least you know' as a refrain. It is a useful leadership tactic, making the exposing of bad news good news.

Studying the organisation as a system creates urgency. It gives you knowledge about the 'what and why' of current performance and it enables you to see the leverage for change. When you can see for yourself, for example, the waste and causes of waste in work, you are stimulated to address the problems. When you can see how simple the flow ought to be for a customer, you have an enthusiasm for fundamentally re-designing it.

You start by considering the purpose of the system from the customers' point of view. Then you study customer demand; you need to know the type and frequency of demands customers make on the system. For every high frequency predictable demand you then need to know the system's capability in responding and how predictably the system responds. Then and only then do you study the work flow. In every work flow there are two kinds of work: value work, the activity required to deliver what matters to the customer, and waste. Having identified the waste you then look for the causes of waste. These are system conditions: structure, measures, process design, procedures, information technology, management roles and so on. Last but not least you can now see how the current thinking about the design and management of work is the root cause of sub-optimal performance.

You might think it quite straightforward. We should simply teach this material to people in classrooms. But systems thinking is learned by doing; it is only by doing things that most managers can unlearn, can find out for themselves that their current beliefs about the design and management of work are flawed. It is something that cannot easily happen in a classroom. In presentations managers often hear things they think they understand. They recognise words like process, flow, demand and will think of things they already do that fit their idea of those words. More than that it is difficult to persuade managers of the folly of their current measurement and/or inspection methods without any data to prove it from their own system; they 'know' the logic of their current methods, it is not easy to dissuade them of their merits. In the detached environment of a classroom, distinctions in understanding and action cannot be easily explored. Presentations of a systems perspective on a managers' organisation leads managers to argue, defend, rationalise and do anything to preserve the status quo. It is a natural human response.

Rather than have a dialogue in the detached environment of a classroom it is vital to have a dialogue where the work is done. How does the work work? How do current system conditions help or hinder the way the work works? It is only when one is with the work that one can assess the current methods in use and determine better systems and methods. It is only in this environment that one can take a reliable view of what is currently done and with what consequences.

Despite my advice, some clients have insisted that presentations on systems thinking are an important pre-requisite to making any change. Organisations espouse values like 'buy in' and 'inclusion'. People translate my advice not to make presentations as 'exclusion' whereas it is based on a firm view of when and how to involve people. As well intentioned as it is, making presentations sets hares running. Misunderstandings prevail and it makes the task of intervention only more difficult.

If you want to make the transition from command and control to systems thinking, you have to ask yourself some fundamental questions:

- Do you want to lead an organisation where the people who do the work control and improve the work? It means you will devolve decision-making. To do that is not simply to mouth the word 'empowerment', it is to give up your current conception of management. The people who do the work will manage and control the work with different measures from those you are used to. You yourself will do a different job.
- Are you prepared to change your own role? Could you conceptualise your work as 'working on the system'? Are you prepared to find out just how different this is from what you might currently do?
- Are you prepared to do these things when those above you might not understand it or condone it? When those in higher places choose to dictate the numbers to be obtained, they actually undermine the organisation's ability to achieve them. Are you prepared to take this tension on as you find out what would be the better measures for improving the economics of this system? Can you resist managing with these measures downwards?
- And would you want to be the carrier of the news when you find it?

If you can answer yes to all of the above, are prepared to learn by doing (start at check), and will talk about what you learn, no matter how painful it is, with those who do the work, then you'll make an excellent leader.

Mark H. Moore

ACTING FOR A DIVIDED, UNCERTAIN SOCIETY

From: Moore, M. H. (1995) 'Acting for a divided, uncertain society', edited from *Creating Public Value*, Harvard University Press

[W]HEN THEY ARE BEING successful,] managers exhibit a certain kind of consciousness: they are imaginative, purposeful, enterprising, and calculating. They focus on increasing the value of the organizations they lead to the broader society. In search of value, their minds range freely across the concrete circumstances of today seeking opportunities for tomorrow. Based on the potential they see, they calculate what to do: how to define their purposes, engage their political overseers and coproducers, and guide their organizations' operations. Then, most remarkably of all, they go ahead and do what their calculations suggest they should.

This sort of enterprise may be rare. Moreover, society may not much value such qualities among public executives. Indeed, some citizens may fear that if public executives commonly possessed such qualities, initiative in defining public purposes would shift to appointed rather than elected officials, with deleterious consequences for the quality of democracy. Yet, my purpose [. . .] is precisely to encourage imagination, purposefulness, enterprise, and calculation among public executives. Inevitably, then, I must confront the ethical and psychological challenges of exercising this kind of leadership. If the managerial orientation and techniques proposed herein threaten democracy, they should be rejected. If they cannot be embraced by the many ordinary people who will be asked to do these jobs, then they will be irrelevant.

Ethical challenges of public leadership

When we citizens imagine the virtues of public executives, two quite different images come to mind. One is the image of public servant. In this conception, managers act as faithful agents of their political masters. Their sole moral duty is to lend their substantive and administrative expertise to the achievement of whatever purposes have been sanctioned by laws, elections, or courts. The more neutral and responsive they become, the better public servants they make.

Note that in this conception the managers' own views of valuable public purposes are treated as irrelevant at best, and suspect at worst. Indeed, the managers are specifically obligated to suppress their own ideas of what would be in the public interest in favor of the (normatively superior) judgments of their political overseers.

A second, contrasting view casts the public executive as an independent moral actor. The Nuremberg trials following World War II most powerfully expressed this view. There, Nazi officials were executed for war crimes despite protestations that they had simply followed orders. The court judged that public officials could never entirely forsake their personal moral responsibility: even though they were bound by authority to their political masters, they remained independent, accountable, moral actors.

Note that this conception requires public officials to express their own views of what is right and good. Indeed, it obligates managers to use their moral views to resist commands by superiors that are illegal or immoral. Nor should they remain silent in such cases. Instead, their duty is to protest – loudly enough that others who care about the values that are being sacrificed may rally to their cause. The public executive as moral leader shows a "profile of courage" in the face of either injustice or venality, even when these are allied with intimidating political power.

Inconsistent images of virtue

That we citizens hold these two images of virtue is somewhat surprising, for, superficially at least, they seem inconsistent. Starkly put: in the first view, public officials are *discouraged* from having (let alone acting on) their own views of what is right; in the second, officials are morally *obligated* to have (and act on) their moral views.

Clearly, we are ambivalent: on the one hand, we fear the idea that public officials might have their own views of public value and pursue them at the expense of society's true interests and values. When we think this way, we implicitly put a great deal of trust in the capacity of our political institutions and processes to define and establish society's true interests and values, and we are quite concerned about the power of bureaucratic agencies to upset these deliberations.

On the other hand, we also fear a world in which our public officials have no moral responsibility. If they are not morally accountable for their actions, then one of the bulwarks against corruption or injustice in the political system might weaken. When we think this way, we remind ourselves that political institutions are often vulnerable to the corruption of short-term particular interests and may have to be resisted by conscientious officials who take the wide and long view of the public interest.

Reconciling inconsistent views

To some degree, of course, the views that I have presented as stark opposites can be reconciled. One could argue, for example, that managers' obligations to act on their own moral views depend on the importance and universality of the values they are defending. If the conflict between political overseers and managers concerns mere policy differences, then bureaucratic officials are obligated to keep their mouths shut. After all, gaining the right to have one's policy preferences count in the formation and execution of public policy is precisely what democratic elections are about, and that right should not be undermined by bureaucratic resistance.

But if the conflict concerns either fundamental injustice or corruption, then subordinate officials are obligated to shout their indignation from the rooftops, for no election gives public officials a right to do injustice or to steal. Often, this distinction between policy differences, on one hand, and fundamental injustice or corruption, on the other, is quite clear, and these simple rules will clearly indicate when managers should yield gracefully and when they should actively resist specific political pressures from overseers.

At times, however, the distinction blurs as human passions come into play. It is all too easy for public officials who disagree with one another to attribute their differences not to disagreements about policy but to either injustice or corruption among their opponents.

[. . .]

A different way to reconcile the apparently conflicting views of virtue is to say that public officials have the duty to act as advocates for their views *before* policy decisions are made. Once a decision is made, however, their obligation shifts to ensuring faithful implementation of the newly adopted policies.

[. . .]

This approach fails to account for the ongoing nature of decisions. In both the theory and practice of democracy, policy decisions remain open to review. This is not quite to say that nothing ever gets decided. There are moments when collective, authoritative judgments are made and codified in laws, executive orders, or policy agreements. In those moments, some public values are judged more important than others, and resources and organizational performance shift in response. Moreover, given the difficulty of bringing the complex political systems to these points of decision, once a decision has been made, a strong desire not to reopen the decision acts to hold decisions fairly constant.

Yet, even with these qualifications, it remains true that all decisions will come up for reconsideration sooner or later. Indeed, experience in implementing policies will often give new reasons for review. And, once there is a reason for review, the moral duty of the public executive will shift again to giving voice to the objections.

[. . .]

These approaches to reconciling conflicting ideas of virtue may work enough of the time to save the apparently inconsistent images of virtue among public officials. Viewed from the perspective of conscientious managers who would like to manage both effectively and democratically, however, these images remain quite unsatisfactory. On the crucial questions of how public managers should engage their overseers in valuable discussions about what is worth doing and what important innovations should be undertaken, the images (even with reconciliations) provide only a few alternatives: silent, dutiful obedience; aggressive advocacy followed by quiet obedience or resignation depending on the outcome of the decision; or noisy martyrdom. None of these particularly appeals to individuals who would like to make sustained, individual contributions to the public good.

Doubtful assumptions and unwarranted cynicism

Even worse, the images of virtue seem to be based on some dubious assumptions about how democratic governance really works. They seem contrived more to reassure citizens and overseers that public managers are effectively under control than to recognize the moral dilemmas of public managers and to give them useful guidance. Two false assumptions undergird and distort this discussion.

The first is the comfortable assumption that the actions of public managers are now guided by clear, coherent, and stable mandates, forged in the sustained heat of ongoing political debate. Of course, some such mandates do exist. And where they are present, there can be no doubt that the manager has the moral duty to implement them.

In the far more typical case, however, managers are guided by mandates in which political conflicts have been papered over rather than resolved. Even if resolved, the resolution is often temporary, and conflict will reopen at the first sign of difficulty in implementing the new policies.

Where conflict continues unresolved, it is by no means clear to whom government managers are accountable or for what particular purposes. Often, they have to decide for themselves how the competing forces in their political environments should be balanced. And they tend to do so in the ongoing course of implementation by adapting to criticisms rather than by reopening the policy debate to secure a clearer and more coherent mandate. Thus, decisions made by managers in implementation are often as important as policy choice in determining what the policy will be.

The second false assumption is that those who choose to work for the government are content with putting their own moral views about the public interest and public value in abeyance. In reality, many people work for the government precisely because they want to enact some particular view they have of the public interest. Indeed, that is one of the small compensations the government provides in what is otherwise an uncompetitive effort to recruit some of society's most talented individuals. Moreover, we citizens often join the managers in judging it a virtue for public managers to have causes. We like officials who have purposes they are willing to pursue at a financial sacrifice. Yet if we organize our governmental institutions to attract and compensate people who have specific causes they would like to pursue, we ask a great deal from such people in requiring them to abandon their cause when politics or policy fashion changes and to establish a different public purpose as paramount.

Because the traditional images of virtue among public sector managers are founded on sand, they not only fail to provide useful guidance but also foster cynicism and hypocrisy among practicing managers. Often, public managers will *claim* to represent the virtues they are supposed to possess. They may even think they are loyal to them. In reality, however, they will search covertly for ways to express their real values. Instead of trying to accommodate conflicting claims in new syntheses, they will decide instead to anchor their preferred vision of their purposes with that portion of their (divided) authorizing environment that agrees with them. Thus, the secret image of virtue among government managers becomes one of skilled advocates building powerful dikes protecting themselves, their organizations, and their causes from the political tides that sweep over the more gullible, dutiful bureaucrats.

[. . .]

In short, managers are judged by how skillfully they recruit a political constituency to support their preferred policy position, rather than by how creative they are in integrating or adapting to conflicting political forces.

Public managers as explorers

There is a different way of thinking about the proper role of public sector executives – one tied much more closely to the reality of modern governance but geared to preserving, even enhancing, the ideals of democratic accountability. In this image, public executives are neither clerks nor martyrs. Instead, they are *explorers* commissioned by society to search for public value. In undertaking the search, managers are expected to use their initiative and imagination. But they are also expected to be responsive to more or less constant political guidance and feedback. Their most important ethical responsibility is to undertake the search for public value conscientiously.

"Conscientiously" in this context means something quite simple: they have to be willing to openly state their views about what is valuable, and to subject those views both to political commentary and to operational tests of effectiveness. They should not hide their views or frustrate efforts to test the value of their operational or administrative theories. They must report honestly on what their organizations are seeking, doing, and accomplishing. Based on those reports, overseers of the organizations can offer a continuing commentary of praise and criticism – not all of it coherent or consistent. The managers' duty, then, is to use that commentary to revise their efforts to define and produce value as the technical and administrative possibilities present themselves.

[...]

"After-the-fact" accountability

Note that in this image of public sector management the nature of the dialogue that managers have with their overseers – the ways in which they are held accountable – diverges from the process envisioned by the classic paradigm. In the classic paradigm, authorization is supposed to occur "before the fact." If managers have new ideas, they are supposed to present them for approval before they initiate action. In the ideas suggested here, before-the-fact consultation remains an attractive and desirable option. In that mode, managers listen, consult, and respond to the varied concerns of their many overseers. They may even offer a vision to balance the competing interests at stake in their domains of responsibility. But the ideas presented here also give public managers greater leeway to consult with their authorizing environment after the fact, through evaluations of what they have accomplished.

Of course, after-the-fact evaluations have always been a part of the dialogue with overseers in the conventional paradigm. But once one sees managers as explorers searching for public value through effective action, then the relative importance of the after-the-fact discussion of results increases. Indeed, it may be easier for managers to learn what is both possible and desirable by producing it first and seeing how people respond rather than by trying to get them to say what they want in the first place.

Strategy as enhanced accountability

In this new paradigm public managers are duty bound to have and present ideas of public value. They even have the right and the responsibility to nominate new ideas for consideration as circumstances change. And these ideas will be their own in the sense that the managers will fashion them, articulate them, and be viewed as responsible for having suggested them.

But if the ideas are to succeed, they will have to incorporate much from the surrounding environment. They will have to fit with the political aspirations of overseers. They will have to engage the employees who will be asked to help achieve the new goals. And they will have to meet the test of plausibly representing a set of purposes that citizens and taxpayers would choose to support if they had deliberated carefully on the question.

Note that these are the same tests that must be met by the development of a sound corporate strategy in the public sector.

[...]

Substantive and operational risks

Of course, [. . .] there may be many possible strategic visions – many different paths to creating public value. In choosing among them, managers will inevitably face difficult moral choices. Often the difficult moral question will be how much substantive risk managers should impose on society in pursuing their adopted strategies. In committing to a particular strategic vision, public managers often have to bet on how political values will change or hope that some new programmatic capabilities can be developed in their organizations, rather than know these things for sure. In guessing, they expose society and their organizations to risk.

The greater the substantive and operational risks foisted on the society, the greater managers' personal responsibility.

[. . .]

But they perceive potential gains to be harvested by making the changes they do and assume that once society sees these other gains, it will judge that the value of their enterprises has increased.

Risking democratic accountability

At times the difficult moral question to be decided in committing to a particular strategy will focus not on substance and operations but on politics and accountability. The issue will be how aggressively, and on behalf of what values, public managers should engage and respond to their political environments.

[M]anagers can choose to be more or less aggressive and manipulative in advocating their views. Precisely because political conflict exists, managers can choose their allies and play one side against the other. Because they control information and have important relations with constituency and client groups, they can help to amplify or repress particular voices and interests in the political environment. Because their operations will strengthen or weaken particular constituencies, managers can lend aid and comfort to particular outside groups, or deny it. And, in implementing policies, they can choose to exaggerate, accommodate, or resist the claims made by different outside groups.

In making such choices, managers expose themselves to moral risks, for each of the political forces surrounding them can reasonably make a claim to be heard and accommodated. Therefore, a manager willfully supporting or ignoring one claim at the expense of another is making an important decision not only about what is publicly valuable but about to whom they are democratically accountable.

[. . .]

In general, in a democracy, it is probably a greater virtue to keep lines of communication and accountability open to many people with interests and views in what should be done. That remains true until such openness allows too many "special interests" to creep in and makes it impossible for managers to respond to new political or technical possibilities.

Obligations to one's subordinates

Other times the tough moral question facing managers will be how deeply to challenge their own organizations. The moral dilemma arises here because, over time, most public sector organizations (and the particular purposes they embody and the particular skills they depend on) have become at least a home, sometimes even a temple, to those who work there. If managers commit to a strategy that makes a wrenching change in their organizations' purposes and, with that, their architectural arrangements and most important tasks, many employees will be discomforted. They will lose their utility and value. Even worse, they will lose their faith. They will feel betrayed by their managers and leaders, whom they had trusted to protect them. They will press that view on the managers whose decisions forced the unwelcome changes on them. For their part, the managers will feel their employees' pain and wonder if they did the right thing. That is an important moral question as well as an operational one.

[. . .]

Because such people have served well in the past, they may have the right to expect decent treatment and support from their incoming managers. It is not their fault that the world has changed. They may be entitled either to the opportunity to make the case for their way of doing things or to enough time and retraining to see if they can make the necessary changes.

The limitations of traditional answers

One of the things that make the moral questions raised by the adoption of a particular organizational strategy so interesting and compelling is that the commonly given answers to the troubling moral questions are almost certainly wrong. For example, a common answer to the question of how much risk a manager should impose on society is "none"; public managers shouldn't gamble with the public's money! But that cannot be the right answer, for managers always impose risks on society. [. . . S]tanding pat in changing circumstances is often far more hazardous to managers, to organizations, and to the public than groping in a direction that seems suited to the new politically expressed values or the new technical or administrative possibilities.

But there ought to be some relationship between the degree of risk imposed and the amount and neutrality of the consultation managers rely on for authorization.

[. . .]

Similarly, with respect to the issue of what political claims managers should accommodate, it is almost certainly incorrect to say either that they should respond to all claims or that they should answer only claims made by elected chief executives. The first is wrong because there are many political claims that should be rejected since they reflect too particular an interest or too idiosyncratic a conception of public value. The second is wrong because the claims of other elected overseers in legislatures, and the claims of past political agreements expressed in laws, also demand allegiance from public managers. Thus, managers often have no choice but to exercise their own discriminating judgment about which claims from their political authorizing environments should be accommodated and to what degree.

Finally, with respect to the important question of how much managers owe their employees and the past traditions of the organization, it is certainly wrong to say that their duty is to protect their employees or guarantee the continuity of their organizations. Often organizations need to be challenged to rethink their purposes or methods. Other times ways must be found to reduce their claims on the public purse, not because their cause is not important but simply because other enterprises now seem more important. In such circumstances, public managers may have an affirmative duty to expose rather than insulate their organizations to these harsh realities.

Yet it is also clear that they owe their employees, and their organizations' tradition, some respect. These should not be written off casually, for there are both moral claims and practical wisdom in what employees and organizations have done in the past.

The duties of public executives as explorers

Perhaps the best that can be said, then, about the moral obligations of public executives is that they owe a conscientious, publicly accountable, effort to search for public value. In that search they are duty bound to have and articulate a vision. But that vision has to accommodate the aspirations of those in their authorizing environments, as well as what they know or think is important based on their professional or administrative expertise, or what techniques of policy analysis and program evaluation can tell them. They are also responsible for accurate reporting on what they are doing and what is being produced. The articulation of their purposes and the reporting of activities and accomplishments become the crucial signposts that allow them to be held accountable to – and, through their accountability, learn from – their overseers.

Sometimes, the feedback and pressures they receive from the political forces in their authorizing environment will carry them forward in their search and away from past practices. In those circumstances they must bear the moral burden of deciding how deeply they should challenge their organizations and the employees who have come to attach meaning to the organization as it operated in the past.

Psychological challenges of public leadership

Living up to the moral challenges of leading public sector organizations helps to clarify why being a public sector executive is psychologically as well as ethically challenging. Because public executives work for all of us, because we all have different ideas about what would be valuable for them to do, and because we all feel entitled to express those views, an enormous amount of pressure accumulates within their offices. Precisely because they channel public aspirations, they become lightning rods for social conflict. Hardly ever can they act to universal applause. At best, their actions are greeted by a grudging tolerance. Their critics' voices always seem louder and more public than their supporters'. Indeed, because character assassination has become such an important tool of policy advocacy, they often become the focus of unfair or damaging attacks on their personal values and conduct as well as on their professional performance.

The false search for refuge

Under such intense pressure, public managers naturally seek psychological refuge. They typically find it in one or both of two common forms: deep convictions about the rightness of their cause; and consistent encouragement from a small circle of close associates who either share their public purposes or care for them personally. Sometimes that small group of supporters is drawn from those in the political environment who share their views. Other times it comes from within the organizations they lead – the people with whom they have long worked.

But if the managers are to live up to their stern moral obligations to seek visions of public value that are politically inclusive and (sometimes) challenging to the organizations they lead, then they must distance themselves from these common sources of comfort. They must be skeptical of their convictions about their purposes because they have to hold open the possibility that their view of public value is wrong, or idiosyncratic, or not suitable to the times. They must hold at arm's length the comfort of close allies because they are duty bound to hear and respond to the views of others who disagree with their supporters. They must resist the comfort of their subordinates because they may have to challenge them to perform in new ways.

"Walking the razor's edge"

The job of the public manager is psychologically demanding, then, because public sector executives must strike a complex balance between two commonly opposed psychological orientations. First, they must have strong enough convictions about what is worth doing that they are willing to work hard for them and to stake their reputations on the values that they pursue. Yet their convictions cannot be so strong that they are impervious to doubt and the opportunity for continued learning. Their views, the ones for which they labor so mightily and with which they are closely identified, must be held *contingently*. Second, they must be willing to act with determination and commitment while retaining a taste and a capacity for thought and reflection.

Moreover, these difficult balances between conviction and doubt, action and reflection, must be struck not once but every day, in the way that managers approach their jobs – sometimes insisting on their views and taking actions that commit their organizations to a particular course of action; other times leaving themselves open to the views of others and changing the direction of their organizations.

My colleague Ronald Heifetz characterizes such challenges as learning to "walk on the razor's edge." He points out that a high degree of balance and poise is necessary to avoid two different kinds of failure common to leaders of groups and organizations.

One kind comes from lacking the courage to challenge current understandings and arrangements in the political and organizational realm. This kind of failure sacrifices the responsibility that leaders have to identify and pursue opportunities to produce value. This failure allows the current balance of political forces, organizational tradition, and past practices to determine what is worth doing. While allowing this may be appropriate on many occasions, it is wrong to assume in advance that this is always true. Indeed, given the enormous pressures to preserve the status quo, one might even treat one's first considered judgment that such a course is appropriate as suspect.

A second kind of failure comes from challenging current arrangements so deeply, and at such an accelerated pace, that managers are metaphorically "assassinated" either by their political overseers, or their subordinates, or both, because these groups cannot stand, or do not agree with, the direction in which their leaders are trying to take them. This kind of failure sacrifices managers' continued capacities to be useful.

The crucial role of partners

In Heifetz's view, the only way to walk the razor's edge confidently is to reach for the balancing poles that come from both feedback and reflection. Managers must step forward again and again. But to keep their balance, they have to absorb the reactions from those affected by their actions, including clients, overseers, and staff. Managers cannot hear only from those who are applauding, because supporters might be leading managers down a path that gets narrower and narrower and finally disappears.

[. . .]

Managers must have partners to help keep them upright. Without partners, it is impossible for managers to succeed, or to be sure that they are on the right course, or to have the psychological confidence and energy required to carry on. But our cases also suggest that managers must draw their partners from the ranks of their opponents and rivals as well as from their supporters, for the opponents are almost certainly telling managers or leaders something important. They are opposed, and powerfully opposed, because some important value is being sacrificed. It is not just that they are corrupt or evil. Public managers in a democracy must acknowledge and respond to their concerns. Thus, as part of learning how to doubt, managers must learn how to take their opponent's views seriously.

[. . .]

Index

Note: Page numbers in italics indicates illustrations.